D0660853

Dear Steve,

I hope you will find comfort and guidance with this Guideposts devotional for each day in your new journey working in Chicago.

With all
my love,

Amy

Daily Guideposts

2014

Guideposts
New York

Daily Guideposts 2014

ISBN-10: 0-8249-3429-6
ISBN-13: 978-0-8249-3429-3

Published by Guideposts
16 East 34th Street
New York, New York 10016
Guideposts.org

Copyright © 2013 by Guideposts. All rights reserved.

This book, or parts thereof, may not be reproduced, stored in a retrieval system, or transmitted in any form or by any means, electronic, mechanical, photocopying, recording or otherwise, without the written permission of the publisher.

Distributed by Ideals Publications, a Guideposts company
2630 Elm Hill Pike, Suite 100
Nashville, Tennessee 37214

Guideposts, Ideals and *Daily Guideposts* are registered trademarks of Guideposts.

Acknowledgments

Every attempt has been made to credit the sources of copyrighted material used in this book. If any such acknowledgment has been inadvertently omitted or miscredited, receipt of such information would be appreciated.

Scripture quotations marked (AMP) are from the *Amplified Bible*. Copyright © 1954, 1958, 1962, 1964, 1965, 1987 by the Lockman Foundation.

Scripture quotations marked (CEB) are taken from the *Common English Bible.* Copyright © 2011 by Common English Bible.

Scripture quotations marked (CEV) are taken from *Holy Bible: Contemporary English Version.* Copyright © 1995 American Bible Society.

Scripture quotations marked (CJB) are taken from *Complete Jewish Bible.* Copyright © 1998 by David H. Stern. All rights reserved.

Scripture quotations marked (ESV) are taken from the *Holy Bible, English Standard Version,* Copyright © 2001 by Crossway Bibles, a division of Good News Publishers. Used by permission. All rights reserved.

Scripture quotations marked (GNB) are taken from the *Good News Bible Today's English Version.* Copyright © 1992 by the American Bible Society.

Scripture quotations marked (KJV) are taken from *The King James Version of the Bible.*

Scripture quotations marked (MSG) are taken from *The Message.* Copyright © 1993, 1994, 1995, 1996, 2000, 2001, 2002 by Eugene H. Peterson.

Scripture quotations marked (NAS) are taken from the *New American Standard Bible,* Copyright © 1960, 1962, 1963, 1968, 1971, 1972, 1973, 1975, 1977, 1995 by the Lockman Foundation. Used by permission.

Scripture quotations marked (NIV) are taken from *The Holy Bible, New International Version.* Copyright © 1973, 1978, 1984, 2011 by Biblica, Inc. Used by permission of Zondervan. All rights reserved worldwide. www.zondervan.com

Scripture quotations marked (NKJV) are taken from *The Holy Bible, New King James Version.* Copyright © 1982 by Thomas Nelson, Inc.

Scripture quotations marked (NLT) are from the *Holy Bible, New Living Translation.* Copyright © 1996, 2004, 2007 by Tyndale House Foundation. Used by permission of Tyndale House Publishers Inc., Carol Stream, Illinois 60188. All rights reserved.

Scripture quotations marked (NRSV) are taken from the *New Revised Standard Version Bible.* Copyright © 1989 by the Division of Christian Education of the National Council of the Churches of Christ in the United States of America. Used by permission. All rights reserved.

Scripture quotations marked (RSV) are taken from the *Revised Standard Version of the Bible.* Copyright © 1946, 1952, 1971 by Division of Christian Education of the National Council of Churches of Christ in the United States of America. Used by permission.

Scripture quotations marked (TIB) are taken from *The Inclusive Bible: The First Egalitarian Translation.* Copyright © 2007 by Priests for Equality. All rights reserved.

Scripture quotations marked (TLB) are taken from *The Living Bible.* Copyright © 1971 by Tyndale House Publishers, Wheaton, Illinois 60187. All rights reserved.

Scripture quotations marked (TNIV) are taken from *Holy Bible, Today's New International Version.* Copyright © 2001, 2005 by Biblica. All rights reserved worldwide.

Andrew Attaway photo by Doug Snyder; Evelyn Bence photo by David Singer; Brian Doyle photo by Jerry Hart; Edward Grinnan photo by Jane Wexler; Rick Hamlin photo by Nina Subin; Roberta Messner photo by Jan D. Witter/Camelot Photography; Elizabeth Sherrill photo by LifeTouch.

Cover and monthly page opening design by Müllerhaus
Cover photo by Corbis
Interior design by Lorie Pagnozzi

Monthly page opener photos by Shutterstock
Indexed by Patricia Woodruff
Typeset by Aptara

Printed and bound in the United States of America
10 9 8 7 6 5 4 3 2 1

INTRODUCTION

Imagine the year ahead filled with God's love and goodness each waking dawn, all day long, and at peaceful rest at dusk. Three hundred sixty-five days of living await you, and each one is perfect. In *Daily Guideposts 2014*, forty-eight writer-companions will help you to welcome a fresh, clean morning of compassion, renewal, and blessings to come from an all-loving, ever-present God Whose mercies have no end (Psalm 103).

These contributors will greet you, share their good news, and walk hand in hand with you through the year. Their collective offerings reflect our theme "New Mercies." "The steadfast love of the Lord never ceases; his mercies never come to an end; they are new every morning; great is your faithfulness. 'The Lord is my portion,' says my soul, 'therefore I will hope in him'" (Lamentations 3:22–24, ESV).

These writers will help you watch for the daily compassion-gifts from God. Meet longtime *Daily Guideposts* authors Julia and Andrew Attaway, Carol Knapp, Scott Walker, Carol Kuykendall, Edward Grinnan, and many others. Embrace the younger folks like Ashley Kappel and Sam Adriance. And welcome our newcomers Bill Giovannetti, Natalie Perkins, and Katie Ganshert, who writes about "The Path to Adoption." Each person offers his or her new-mercy discoveries: An upset child is comforted by an adult's kind words on an airplane ride; an owner's dog gets a longed-for playful companion in a child; and a father's busy day is happily interrupted by his grown son's international phone call.

At Eastertime, walk with Mark Collins and remember the great sacrifice at the Cross, and what it means today, in the series "Remain in Me." During Advent and Christmas, Patty Kirk shares intimate sorrows and joys in the series "Gifts of Mercy," and Marion Bond West writes about "The True Gifts of Christmas." Discover how the holy season of giving can open your hearts to one another and draw you closer to God. Throughout the year in "Life Lessons from Those I've Met," Elizabeth Sherrill shares unforgettable subjects—famous and everyday—about whom she has written over her decades as a celebrated author. Marci Alborghetti talks about "A New Way to Serve," and Brigitte Weeks offers "Hope in Hospice."

So imagine again each new morning bringing you mercies, and your receiving them with thanks and praise. Throughout *Daily Guideposts 2014,* you'll come to know God's presence and power—that secure, unbroken connection—Whose mercies are forming you anew in the year ahead.

CONNECT WITH US ONLINE

We love hearing from our readers!

Whether you tweet, use Facebook, or still enjoy sending handwritten letters, we want to connect with you.

Find us at DailyGuideposts.org and Facebook.com/dailyguideposts. Or follow us on Twitter@DailyGuideposts.

Write us at DailyGPEditors@guideposts.org or *Daily Guideposts* Editor, Guideposts Books, 16 East 34th Street, New York, New York 10016.

DAILY GUIDEPOSTS IN YOUR IN-BOX

Now you can enjoy the faith-building inspiration of *Daily Guideposts* wherever you are! Receive each day's devotion on your computer, tablet, or smartphone. This is a valuable benefit that Guideposts offers only to members of the *Daily Guideposts* family. Visit DailyGuideposts .org/DGP2014 and enter this code: mercy.

JANUARY

Know therefore that the Lord thy God, he is God, the faithful God, which keepeth covenant and mercy with them that love him and keep his commandments to a thousand generations.

—DEUTERONOMY 7:9 (KJV)

Wed 1

Use hospitality one to another.... —I PETER 4:9 (KJV)

In the South, we are somewhat famous for hospitality. But in reality this is not an exclusive Southern trait. In the Bible, from Leviticus to Hebrews, hospitality is all the rage. And no matter where you go in this big world, there's always someone ready to dish out a warm welcome or a liberal dose of neighborliness.

When I was a child, people often stopped by our house unannounced. "We've got *companeeee*!" I'd call out as I headed for the door. You'd never know who might be standing on the porch: a relative, a neighbor, or a long-lost friend. Whoever it was, they were invited in and royally entertained. If my mother didn't have a fresh-baked cake on hand, a big smile would spread across my daddy's face. "Come on in and make yourselves at home," he'd say. "I'll be back in a jiffy." And off he'd go to Toddle House, a nearby restaurant that was part of a chain famous for its pie. In no time he'd be back with a delectable pie, rich and chocolaty, "to die for," we might say today.

It seems that we've lost a bit of that spontaneity, and people don't just drop in anymore. But a few years ago, I happened on a recipe that, with a bit of tweaking, replicates that old-time pie. And while I can't bring back those days when people felt free to visit unannounced, I can recall the delight by whipping up one of those pies.

I've read recently that there's been some effort to build on the flavor of more neighborly times by designing a new wave of front porch subdivisions. I hope it works. In the meantime, maybe each of us can create our own brand of hospitality and work to make our homes and neighborhoods into places where no one is a stranger. With a new year ahead and a good recipe for pie or vegetable soup or fresh baked muffins, take that first step and invite a neighbor in!

Father, show me how I can welcome the visitor You send to my door.

—PAM KIDD

Digging Deeper: LK 14:12–14; ROM 12:13; HEB 13:2

Thu 2

This is the day which the Lord hath made; we will rejoice and be glad in it. —PSALM 118:24 (KJV)

I've created a habit of trying to categorize every day of my life, ranking moments from good to best. My parents took my brother and me to Disney World when we were little; waking up on that morning was the happiest day of my life. Or perhaps it was waking up super-early every Christmas, bursting to see what Santa Claus had left for me under the tree. Surely those were the happiest days of my life. Or was it the day I was offered my first cruise contract as a professional singer? Or even better, my first national tour! The. Happiest. Day. Ever. Or maybe it was just one year ago when I received my admissions acceptance letter from Union Theological Seminary. Best day of my life. Well . . . so far, at least.

I struggle with allowing each day to stand as its own experience and gift from God. So I'm making a conscious effort to let it happen. I start every morning saying out loud, "This is the day that the Lord has made. I will rejoice and be glad in it!"

It felt strange in the beginning, but now I can't help but do it. Sometimes it brings a huge smile to my face and sometimes laughter. Sometimes it simply encourages me on a day that will be particularly difficult (or as my mother would call it, "a character-building day"). And sometimes it simply helps wake me up on a day when nothing of importance seems to be on the schedule and I've hit Snooze for the third time.

I remind myself that today is a day that was given to me as a gift, not as a promise. I will treat it thusly, and rejoice!

Heavenly Father, thank You for the many blessings You bestow upon me, including the ones I overlook. Help me remember that even the small ones are a privilege.

—NATALIE PERKINS

Digging Deeper: 1 THES 5:16–18; JAS 1:17

January

Fri 3

Let us not lose heart in doing good, for in due time we will reap if we do not grow weary. —GALATIANS 6:9 (NAS)

As I grow older, staying in good physical condition becomes more difficult. My schedule is demanding and my best intentions to exercise are often interrupted by a student who needs to talk, an impromptu meeting, an urgent errand, or fatigue that creeps over me at the end of the day. Many dynamics can interfere with strong resolve and wreak havoc on the best-planned schedule. So I have developed a philosophy of "minimum results."

On days that I cannot ride my bike, go to the gym, or my back aches and I cannot run, I have resolved to walk a minimum of one mile. One mile is not a challenging distance nor will it prepare me for a marathon, but it keeps me consistently active and in a better state of mind.

Last night I came home at ten o'clock, fed our golden retrievers, Bear and Buddy, and moved toward my lazy chair. Bear suddenly barked, and Buddy moved toward the front door. This is how they say, "Let's go for a walk!"

For a moment I groaned; I just wanted to rest. Then I thought, *It's only one mile, a brisk twenty minutes.* Suddenly, a smile crossed my face as their excitement exploded and my thoughts of a soft summer night beckoned. One mile is better than no miles, and minimum results beat no results any day.

Lord, help me not to be deterred by maximum results and rigid schedules. Give me the joy of a minimum goal achieved consistently. Amen.

—SCOTT WALKER

Digging Deeper: 2 CHR 15:7; PRV 24:27; 2 THES 3:5

HOPE IN HOSPICE

Sat 4 *Be joyful in hope, patient in affliction, faithful in prayer. Share with the Lord's people who are in need. . . .*
—Romans 12:12–13 (NIV)

FAITHFUL IN PRAYER

When I first began to visit patients in hospice, I felt shy and anxious that I would say the wrong thing or say too much or too little. Sometimes a patient was nonresponsive or may have just been sleeping. How would I know? But I knew that being a quiet presence was an important part of the work of a volunteer. So I found a chair and sat down with Adrian. His eyes were closed and his breathing labored. I couldn't help wondering if he might die while I was sitting with him. I knew what to do, but the idea seemed scary in the presence of reality.

Then, without warning and without opening his eyes, Adrian said clearly, "A prayer, please." My mind went blank. I was unprepared. *What kind of prayer would be right for the dying?* I felt as if I had failed.

Suddenly, a complete prayer came into my mind; I'd known it my whole life. "Our Father, Who art in heaven, hallowed be Thy name," I began. I got to the words *Thy will be done,* when another voice joined in. Adrian was praying the familiar words with me. Together, we made it through to *Amen.*

Prayer is the common language we all share as we stand before God, and as a hospice volunteer I have learned to speak it a little more fluently.

Dear God, may I learn from experience and always have faith in the power of prayer.
—Brigitte Weeks

Digging Deeper: Mt 6:9–15, 21:22

Sun 5

For by grace you have been saved through faith, and that not of yourselves; it is the gift of God. —Ephesians 2:8 (NKJV)

When I was nine years old, I accepted Christ as my Savior and requested membership in the Seventh Avenue Baptist Church. Halfway down the aisle, my legs wouldn't carry me and that's when the pastor's wife, Anna Lee, met me and walked the remaining distance by my side.

Fast-forward four and a half decades; Anna Lee was dying of pancreatic cancer at the local hospice. I went to visit and pray with her. "You walked with me all those years ago," I told her, "so I'm here to help you make your heavenly journey."

When they had Anna Lee's estate sale, I purchased her Victorian cameo, so I would have something to remember her. But on the day I took the brooch to the jeweler to have it made into a slide, it dropped into the heater vent of my car. The cost to retrieve it was prohibitive. "Now I don't have anything to remember my friend by," I told the jeweler. I was inconsolable.

"We sell lots of pretty things here," the jeweler told me, "but I always tell people, it's the memories, not the mementos, that are the real treasures."

Thank You, Lord, for friendship in all its blessed forms.
—Roberta Messner

Digging Deeper: Prv 27:9; Eccl 4:9–12

Mon 6

When I consider thy heavens, the work of thy fingers, the moon and the stars, which thou hast ordained; What is man, that thou art mindful of him? and the son of man, that thou visitest him? —Psalm 8:3–4 (KJV)

I'll always remember the first time that I was home alone for several hours with my son Joseph. I was a little nervous, a young father. Joe was only seven months old.

We had a good time playing with his toys. I read him some books, and we watched *Barney* on television. After a while, Joe was snoring on the living room floor on top of his baby blanket. He was so cute; he looked like he'd fallen asleep midcrawl.

I sat there staring at my boy for a good half hour, just contemplating how beautiful he was—this creation of God.

When it was close to Joe's bedtime, I placed his blanket on my shoulder, preparing to carry him off to bed. Just then, as I picked him up from his slumbering, he raised his head, opened his eyes, looked at me . . . and threw up. That shocked me; the beautiful moment was suddenly gone.

But even now, at seventeen years old, I look at my son and wonder how it is that God made Joe, and gave him to me, and what a blessing it is.

I am thankful today, God, for all that You have given me.
—Jon Sweeney

Digging Deeper: Pss 127:3–5, 139:13–16

Tue 7

For in this hope we were saved. But hope that is seen is no hope at all. Who hopes for what they already have? But if we hope for what we do not yet have, we wait for it patiently.
—Romans 8:24–25 (NIV)

I know I'm in trouble when I start changing the font on my computer. Usually I resort to this tactic when I am procrastinating on a project or having trouble getting started. I'll decide that the real problem is I'm bored with the typeface I've been using, and it's well nigh time for a change. Or I'll convince myself that the current font is totally inappropriate for the subject I'm addressing and then kill an hour or so finding just the right font that will inspire me.

Of course I know that this is a game I'm playing with myself, that sooner or later I have to stop messing around and get down to the business at hand. It's something I tend to do in my prayer life as well.

I have trouble getting started sometimes, trying to figure out how to formulate what I want to pray for rather than just saying it, as if God will judge me on my prayer font rather than what's in my heart. I'll put off what I really need to share with Him because I'm afraid to commit to the prayer, as if completely revealing my desires and feelings means letting go of things I don't want to let go of, giving them to God when I really want to hang on for dear life. So I fool around with my spiritual typeface rather than getting down to business.

But God is infinitely patient. He knows what's in my heart, even when I don't or when I'm not ready to face it. He is infinitely tolerant of my prayerful procrastinations and will wait until I am finally ready to get honest, get real.

Lord, even after all these years, I still sometimes have trouble getting started with You. Silly, right? But when I am finally willing to hand You my burdens, Your arms are always outstretched.
—Edward Grinnan

Digging Deeper: Ps 86:15; Lk 11:9–13; Rom 8:26

Wed 8

Not only so, but we also glory in our sufferings, because we know that suffering produces perseverance; perseverance, character; and character, hope. —Romans 5:3–4 (NIV)

Brandon ran up to a small group of boys pretending to be superheroes. My son loves superheroes and has a drawer full of costumes in his room, his favorites being Spider-Man and Superman. I could see the excitement in his face when he asked, "Can I play with you?"

One of the boys yelled right into his face, "No!"

Brandon looked over at me but didn't come running for consolation. He just sadly walked away.

I felt my son's pain so deeply that all I wanted to do was throw on a cape and come to his rescue. First, I'd capture the villains and throw them in time-out jail. Then I'd rally up the coolest superheroes in town to play with Brandon. I wouldn't stop until that beautiful smile returned to his sad little face.

But instead, I just stood there, broken by the thought of all the inevitable hurt, rejection, pain, and sadness he'd have to face in his future. I stood there because as much as I'd love to protect and shelter Brandon from every negative experience, he'll need to learn how to get through most of them by himself.

My son moped around for a bit but eventually found another group of kids to play with. As he ran around with reddened cheeks and a breathless smile, my heart lightened. *He'll make it through the rough times,* I thought—something we all must learn to do.

This world can often be a sad and scary place. Thank You, Lord, for helping me and those I love to persevere.
—Karen Valentin

Digging Deeper: Rom 5:2–5, 8:37–39

Thu 9

I urge, then, first of all, that petitions, prayers, intercession and thanksgiving be made for all people. —1 TIMOTHY 2:1 (NIV)

At a dinner party, I finally had a chance to speak to my hostess's grandson who was briefly in town after returning from his second deployment to Afghanistan. Unbeknownst to the young soldier, I had been praying for him for over three years on my daily prayer walk at a certain spot where there's a small maple tree. I called it his tree. In the fall, when the leaves turned vivid yellow, I carried one home and pressed it in my Bible. In the hot summer, when the leaves brought refreshing shade, I thought about the young soldier serving in a hot, rugged land.

As seasons passed, I prayed through the many seasons of a soldier's life: when his unit was in a terrible battle and one of his close buddies was killed in action; when he met a young woman at his stateside base, fell in love, and got married; when he deployed again and had to leave his new wife and their adorable baby.

I approached the young man, thinking, *Because I've been praying for him, I feel closely connected to him. But he doesn't even know my name. Do the prayers of strangers really matter?* I introduced myself and mentioned that I had been praying for him every day.

"That really means a lot," he replied. "One day when I was deployed and feeling down, I Googled my name and found out that a woman I didn't even know in Alabama had posted online that she was praying for me! I couldn't believe that people I didn't know cared."

I gave the soldier a hug, thankful that there's no such thing as strangers when it comes to those for whom you pray.

Dear Father, help me to faithfully serve You and Your big wide world by praying for at least one person I don't know. Amen.

—KAREN BARBER

Digging Deeper: MK 11:24; LK 11:1–11

Fri 10

Place these words on your hearts. Get them deep inside you....
—DEUTERONOMY 11:18 (MSG)

Last night I had trouble sleeping, which is a rarity for a woman who has been nicknamed "the log" by her husband. For as long as I've known Perry, he has lived by two surefire rules for remedying occasional insomnia: First, stay in bed. "Even if you aren't sleeping, your body can rest." Second, while you lie there not-sleeping, recite Bible verses until your body gives way.

For the past week, I've been reading a handful of psalms. And when I say "reading," I mean over and over again, until I'd allowed those divine words to read me. So as I lay there not-sleeping, I decided to give Perry's methods a shot. I folded my hands across my chest, let my heavy eyelids fall shut, exhaled my frustrations over my wakefulness, and began to whisper the poetic fragments God had graciously been writing on my heart:

For you created my inmost being; you knit me together in my mother's womb. I praise you because I am fearfully and wonderfully made.

Blessed is the man who does not walk in the counsel of the wicked or stand in the way of sinners or sit in the seat of mockers... he is like a tree planted by streams of water.

Even in darkness, light dawns for the upright, for the gracious, compassionate, righteous man.

Within minutes of murmuring those passages, I had drifted off to sleep. Truth is the most comfortable of pillows for the body, the mind, the soul.

Father, thank You for the unparalleled restfulness I find in Your timelessly tranquil Word.
—ASHLEY WIERSMA

Digging Deeper: Pss 1, 61:1, 62:1–2

Sat 11

And the streets of the city shall be full of boys and girls playing in the streets thereof. —Zechariah 8:5 (KJV)

Just for fun, my wife and I climbed into the car and headed north, with no plan except to drive through Amish country and observe these dedicated people whose faith is expressed in simplicity. It was beautiful, like taking a time machine back to another century.

"Look at the children playing softball," Sharon said, pointing to a meadow beside a one-room schoolhouse. "Aren't they adorable?"

Girls were running bases in long dresses and bonnets and boys in suspenders and black hats—all playing happily together in different parts of the meadow. There were no ambitious parents hovering about, shouting advice to their kids. No coaches with clipboards full of tricky plays. No costly uniforms, umpires, bleachers, fences, or scoreboards. Just children, playing for fun with a wooden bat and a big, fat softball.

"It reminds me of sports when I was a kid," I said to Sharon, "when we played kickball in the streets, with no supervision."

The Amish have long been an example to me of how to work hard, but today they showed me something about how to play. Maybe I don't need an expensive membership in that exercise club. After all, I can ride my bike in the park for free or play in the church softball league. Some of my happiest memories are of playing catch with my dad on the front lawn and playing hockey on a frozen creek.

Father, help me not to make life more elaborate
and costly than it needs to be.
—Daniel Schantz

Digging Deeper: Mt 6:19–21, 18:2–3

Sun 12

The Lord has done it this very day; let us rejoice today and be glad. —PSALM 118:24 (NIV)

Longtime members of my small church joke that on Sunday mornings we celebrate holy Eucharist followed by holy coffee hour. After the dismissal, "Let us go forth into the world, rejoicing in the power of the Spirit," most of us file downstairs for snacks and conversation.

When I'm welcoming newcomers, I talk about the church and stay focused on the positive.

When I'm giving a personal update to friends who know the cyclical feast-or-famine nature of my self-employment, or inquire about my informal neighborhood mentoring, or maybe just ask, "What's new?" I've traditionally veered toward the negative.

Then a month ago, I noted a quotation from Ingmar Bergman's classic *Fanny and Alexander*. At the climax of the film, a curmudgeon uncharacteristically pronounces, "Let us be happy when we are happy." Sounding so biblical, being so straightforward, the "Let us" proclamation settled into my mind.

At the next coffee hour, chatting with my friends Julia and Jane, I swung into my usual mode: some version of "I'm all right but . . . " Hearing myself in a new light, I corrected my course. "No," I said, "I'm not going to add the *but*. I have plenty of work. I've had a pleasant weekend. This morning's worship encouraged me." I quoted the line "Let us be happy when we are happy," and our conversation opened up. Jane reported that her unemployed daughter had landed an interview. Julia, who is painstakingly downsizing, had worked through a closet. Slow and—not *but*—sure progress.

Since then, we intentionally encourage one another when leaving church to rejoice in the day, in the Lord, in the power of the Spirit.

Lord, help me claim the happy moments that come my way this week.
—EVELYN BENCE

Digging Deeper: PHIL 4:4–9

Mon 13

He is before all things, and in him all things hold together.
—Colossians 1:17 (NIV)

We'd rushed my son Christopher to the emergency room with a serious back injury. They took him in quickly for X-rays. I was directed to a crowded area where other families anxiously sat, waiting for news from the doctors. There was not an empty seat in the room.

An elderly lady with the word *Volunteer* embroidered on her white lab coat motioned me over. "Honey, there's a place in the back that I can offer you to sit if you'd like."

"Yes, thanks," I said. I followed her to a tiny room and sat down in a chair. I leaned my head back against the wall and closed my eyes.

I reached for the tiny silver cross hanging on a thin chain around my neck. "Please take care of Christopher," I prayed, "and, Lord, could You take care of me too? Because right now I feel like I'm falling apart."

Just then the volunteer came back into the room. "Doing okay?" she asked.

"Better now," I said, still touching my cross. I looked down at it. "This is what's holding me together right now."

She smiled and sat down next to me. "Have you ever heard of laminin?" she asked.

I shook my head.

"My husband is a retired doctor," she explained, "and it's something that he still marvels at. Laminin is a molecule that helps our cells stick together. Without these molecules, we would literally fall apart."

She pointed at my cross and continued: "Interesting, isn't it? When looked at under a microscope, the laminin molecule is shaped just like a cross."

Lord, Your immense and elaborate design
holds me together physically and spiritually.
—Melody Bonnette Swang

Digging Deeper: Prv 16:1–4, 9; Phil 1:6; Col 1:15–20

Tue 14

I instruct you in the way of wisdom and lead you along straight paths. —Proverbs 4:11 (NIV)

I'm not giving up!" I told myself as I crawled around on our bathroom floor, shining a flashlight over every square inch, looking for my contact lens. I've worn hard contact lenses since I was a teenager and almost always find lost ones, which are expensive to replace. Usually I can see them easily because they are tinted light blue. Not this time.

With mounting determination, I stood up and reenacted my early-morning routine. I'd popped the contacts into my eyes over the sink. I then began putting on some mascara and realized one lens was not in my eye. The sink stopper was in place and the lens wasn't there. Next I examined my clothes, an open drawer near the sink, and then I hit the floor . . . again.

Soon the minutes ticked into an hour. Already I'd missed my exercise class and now I needed to get to work. But I couldn't quit! My refusal to do so is a habit that goes all the way back to some childhood messages: You can do anything you want to do, if you just try hard enough. Never ever, ever give up. With God, all things are possible.

Possible, I've learned, but that's not a promise that all things will happen, regardless of how hard I try. Sometimes it takes more determination to know when to quit. Like now.

With that I stood up and went to the phone to order a new contact lens.

Lord, when it's time to quit, may I trust You.
—Carol Kuykendall

Digging Deeper: Pss 9:10, 20:7

January

Wed 15

"For I know the plans that I have for you," declares the Lord, "plans . . . to give you a future and a hope."
—Jeremiah 29:11 (NAS)

I can't help it. The second or third bitter week of January I start searching for signs of spring. Five o'clock on a weeknight, I look out my office window. Not the deep dark of night anymore, is it? There was a hint of blue, wasn't there? I'm at a party and I hear someone say, "It's staying light a little bit longer now."

"Have you noticed that?" I say, glad to hear someone else acknowledge what I secretly pine for: more light. The winter solstice has passed. We hardly saw it back then because we were so busy singing Christmas carols, doing last-minute shopping, baking cookies, and sending out cards.

But now around Martin Luther King Jr. weekend a glance at the morning sky makes me think, *The sun is rising a little earlier now, isn't it?* Soon I won't have to wake up in the dark. Soon I'll be able to do my morning jog in sunlight. Soon I'll leave the office in full glorious daylight. I gaze at a thick crust of ice in the garden and say to myself, *You know, we should be seeing those crocuses in another few weeks.* Here the kids are coming back from sledding, dusting the snow off their boots, and I'm planning for spring.

I know there are spiritual advantages to living in the present, appreciating all the beauties of the day we've been given, but I can't help yearning for what's ahead—a week, two weeks, a month, two months—down the pike. The world spins on its axis and I spin ahead in hope. More light, more sun, more life.

Faith is built on hope. The hope of the Resurrection, the promise of God's kingdom coming. I dig my fists into my parka, wrap the scarf tighter around my neck, pull down the wool hat and walk on, filled with thoughts of spring.

Give me hope, Lord, on the darkest days. —Rick Hamlin

Digging Deeper: Rom 8:24–25; 2 Cor 4:16–18

THE PATH TO ADOPTION

Thu 16 *Take delight in the Lord, and he will give you the desires of your heart.* —Psalm 37:4 (NIV)

ALIGNING OUR DESIRES

Another negative pregnancy test. That made twelve. Twelve months of one line on the test stick, when I longed and prayed for two. I didn't understand it. I had gotten pregnant before without any problems, so why wasn't it happening this second time around?

"I want to have another child," I told my husband.

"We will," Ryan said.

I didn't understand how he could sound so confident, so sure, especially when all I felt was confusion. My doctor recommended fertility drugs, but I didn't want to go on them, not when my body was doing everything it was supposed to do on its own. And all the while, well-intentioned neighbors and acquaintances would say, "When are you going to give that boy of yours a little brother or sister?"

I'd smile and shrug, but inside I hurt. Every morning, I got down on my knees and I surrendered my desire to God. Despite the ache, I chose to trust in His goodness. Slowly, something amazing started to happen. God didn't take away my desire; He simply refined it.

Perhaps I didn't need to get pregnant to have another child. Maybe those twelve negative pregnancy tests wasn't God saying *no*. Maybe it was just a prelude to a higher *yes*, the revealing of a different path—a path that would open our eyes to His mercy and compassion in a way they'd never been opened before.

Thank You, Lord, that You don't say no to the desires of our hearts; instead, You align them to match Your own.

—Katie Ganshert

Digging Deeper: Ps 37; Prv 2:3–5; Mt 5:6

Fri 17

And let us not grow weary in well-doing....
—GALATIANS 6:9 (RSV)

While on line at the coffee shop one morning, I watched as the shabbily dressed, skinny woman at the front of the line carefully counted out change for a cup of hot tea.

"Have a buttered roll with that," the teenage counter girl told her. The woman hesitated, and the girl said, "My treat. It's my birthday today. God bless you." The older woman gratefully took the roll and, eyeing it hungrily, left the store.

When it was my turn, I said, "That was very nice of you to treat her on your birthday. Happy birthday!"

She blushed, and the young man at the next register laughed. "Oh, it's always her birthday when that homeless lady comes in."

My jaw dropped. "You mean..."

"I just feel bad that she doesn't have enough to eat," the girl mumbled.

I took my coffee and waved away the change. "That's for you," I told her. "God bless you."

"But it's too much—"

"That's okay," I said, smiling. "It's my birthday."

Lord, let me give a little extra today to someone who can use it.
Thank You for always giving a little extra to me.
—LINDA NEUKRUG

Digging Deeper: MT 6:25–26; HEB 10:24

Sat 18

Giving thanks always for all things. . . .
—Ephesians 5:20 (KJV)

I met the D. family when I arrived at their home to tutor the third- and fourth-grade boys in reading and math. Resettled from a refugee camp in Bhutan where the parents had lived for seventeen years, the boys had learned English only a year earlier. About halfway through the first session, the mother inquired, "Teacher? Nepali tea?" The beaming woman silently prepared and served me the sweet, milky drink fragrant with cardamom and cinnamon, and each time we parted, she bowed slightly, palms pressed together in traditional greeting: "*Namaste.*"

During our months together, whenever I brought an armload of library books, they thanked me and excitedly paged through them at once. When I gave out notebooks, pencils, and flash cards from the dollar store, they thanked me as if they'd been handed World Series tickets.

Near the end of the semester, Mother began setting platters of rice, steamed vegetables, and lamb on the table. I rushed to pack up loose papers. "No!" she scolded me, then spoke rapidly in Nepali to her son.

"She wants you to eat with us," he explained. So I did.

As we parted, Mother forgot "*Namaste.*" Instead, she spoke deliberately in her new language: "You teaching . . . very good . . . my sons . . . Very, very thank you." Such simple words for a rich benediction.

Father of all, You give me unlikely tutors to teach me true gratitude. May I learn their lessons well.
—Gail Thorell Schilling

Digging Deeper: Col 2:6–7; Jas 1:17

January

Sun 19

Moses was . . . more humble than anyone else on the face of the earth. —NUMBERS 12:3 (NIV)

I felt lost the first Sunday without John, our pastor of eighteen years, but I hope we don't try to replace him as quickly as I replaced our dog Liz.

Liz was one of two pups my wife and I adopted after we moved into the home I built in an isolated area south of town. Liz and Crystal became vigilant guard dogs, barking madly whenever anyone came to our house, and they protected us from all perceived intruders for the next nine years. The morning after Liz died, I went outside to feed both dogs. I filled Crystal's bowl and wept at the sight of Liz's empty bowl. Crystal seemed lost without Liz; I was lost without her too! That afternoon I adopted a new pup. Jordan protected us for the next twelve years.

We at our church are trying to turn to God for leadership. A pastor's longevity at a church is a mixed blessing; the congregation can grow lazy in terms of leadership. The first Sunday without John was sad, but it was also exhilarating. We sang. We prayed. We worshipped. We are a family missing a brother who moved away, but God has not left us.

Dear God, thank You so much for being the real leader of our church.
—TIM WILLIAMS

Digging Deeper: PRV 11:14; MK 10:45

Mon 20

The Lord gives sight to the blind. . . .
—Psalm 146:8 (NIV)

On a Monday in January, I wasn't looking forward to another week at the high school where I taught math. I didn't feel invested in what I was doing and I often wanted the day to end, to retreat to my home, where I could contemplate the things I cared about.

This Monday, I got my wish. When I pulled into the driveway, I didn't see the crowd of teenagers I expected, and the parking lot was vacant except for rows of empty school buses. It was Martin Luther King Jr. Day, and I'd forgotten.

Back at my apartment, I still didn't take much time to think about the significance of MLK Day until I came to a very moving online post. A blogger I love linked to a profile his grandfather had written about Dr. King just days before his assassination. In the article, Dr. King described the two times in his life he had been scared: when he marched through Chicago and had a crowd of people throwing rocks at him; and when he gave a speech in the wake of the murders of three civil rights workers—with the suspected murderer standing right behind him!

Dr. King described himself as thinking, "Well, it came time to pray and I sure did not want to close my eyes! Ralph [Abernathy, his colleague] said he prayed with his eyes open!" This—praying with your eyes open—was what Dr. King had always done: being contemplative and asking for God's help, but always with his eyes on the people in front of him. In retreating as I did, I'd closed my eyes to the vitality and needs of the students I taught every day; it had left me unsatisfied and mediocre at my job.

When I went to school the next day, I thought of Dr. King and kept my eyes open. I had wonderful students whose success mattered to me, and as I saw that I realized I loved my job.

Thank You, Lord, for the chance to see You more clearly.
—Sam Adriance

Digging Deeper: Jas 1:22; 1 Jn 4:4

January

Tue 21

"For I am the Lord your God who takes hold of your right hand and says to you, Do not fear; I will help you."
—ISAIAH 41:13 (NIV)

I'll let you in on a little secret that I think most working moms would agree with: The work part is easier than the mom part.

Don't get me wrong; I love being a mom. I love nature walks through our garden, reading stories, baking chocolate chip cookies, and watching my three young kids pull every single carefully folded blanket out of my linen closet to create an elaborate fort.

But when push comes to shove (and, admittedly, there is sometimes a lot of pushing and shoving at our house), it feels downright relaxing to sit and pull out my laptop and work. I look forward to those hours when my kids are napping or with a babysitter and I can escape to a world where I can stop for a coffee break. A world where my thoughts aren't interrupted with questions about whether Rainbow Brite can go with Luke Skywalker on the Millennium Falcon. A world where I actually get paid for my efforts.

Guilt seeps in as I wonder why I would choose a laptop over my own children, why I'd choose to speak into other people's lives instead of into the lives of the kids that God has so generously blessed me with. But God has provided me opportunities to use the gifts He has given me as a mom and as a writer, and I need to pursue both paths with passion and grace.

Father God, You are my rock. Help me to find balance as I juggle a career and a family so that I can be the best for my work and the best for my kids.
—ERIN MACPHERSON

Digging Deeper: 1 SM 2:2; MT 6:33, 25:14–30

Wed 22

Always try to do good to each other and to everyone else.
—1 THESSALONIANS 5:15 (TLB)

When a friend's sister asked me to be her personal chauffeur when she came to Florida to visit her mother in a nursing home, I accepted the job gladly, thinking, *This will be an easy way to earn some extra money.*

I picked up Sondra at the airport, drove her twenty miles to her mother's nursing home, then returned later that evening to pick her up and take her to another relative's house. I made two trips back and forth each day, plus took her shopping a couple of times. I'd come home each night dead tired and somewhat crabby from all the driving.

She paid me on the last day, but because I have an old gas-guzzler, it took half the money just to pay for the fuel I'd used. The rest netted me less than three dollars an hour for my time, not to mention the wear and tear on my car.

When she asked me to do it again a few months later, I hesitated. But then I thought about my time with Sondra: I'd enjoyed our conversations in the car; she shared interesting stories about her family and friends; I'd learned about driving in new neighborhoods.

I certainly wasn't volunteering the way many of my friends do at church, but I was giving my time to a woman in need. The best part is that my friendship with Sondra grew each time she returned to visit her mother. The miles I put on my old car with Sondra are definitely some of the happiest ever.

Father, help me to be a helper for the sake of helping
and not because of financial gain.
—PATRICIA LORENZ

Digging Deeper: LK 12:32–34

January

Thu 23

Do your best to improve your faith. You can do this by adding goodness, understanding, self-control, patience, devotion to God, concern for others, and love.
—2 PETER 1:5–7 (CEV)

I was in my doctor's office for the third visit in one week. My symptoms were shortness of breath, tightness in the chest, constant coughing, and fever. While waiting, I thought of grilling him with thousands of questions: "Doc, do you really care about helping me feel better? Have you lost your passion for your vocation? Why can't you figure out what is wrong with me? Aren't you a *doctor*?"

I didn't. Despite my frustration, I knew he was working hard to find out what was happening to me.

He walked into the room, and I said, "Doc, I'm feeling terrible. I want to know what is going on with me."

He looked at me compassionately and responded, "I plan to do several things to better understand what is happening to you so that I can help you."

I wasn't feeling physically better, but his demeanor and plan of action assured me that he was on top of the situation. "Thank you," I said.

"Don't thank me yet. Not until we get this resolved," he responded.

His graciousness got me thinking about how every time he sees me, I'm not feeling well. Yet he's consistently kind and helpful. I was thankful for not letting my emotions get the best of me.

Lord, help me to manage my emotions and deepen my faith, especially when things are not going my way.
—PABLO DIAZ

Digging Deeper: ECCL 7:9; ROM 12:12; JAS 1:19

Fri 24

"Therefore a man shall leave his father and mother and hold fast to his wife, and the two shall become one flesh." This mystery is profound.... —EPHESIANS 5:31–32 (ESV)

For our golden wedding anniversary, my husband, Don, gave me a card with a picture of a cat hugging a dog. The caption read: "Weird, but it works." That phrase summarized our day.

First, the vacuum cleaner broke. Then the pressure switch on the water system got stuck. My phone died and took all my contact information with it. So we spent the day solving problems. We ate our anniversary dinner in the car; hamburgers and french fries at our favorite fast-food place—and enjoyed it!

As I thought about the "celebration," I realized Don's card also summed up the years of our marriage. We like different things, and we disagree on issues such as money and politics. I love mysteries, and he reads only nonfiction. My idea of a great vacation is Disney World; he prefers fishing. He roots for Oklahoma State's basketball team while I'm a true Kansas Jayhawker. Our personalities are different, too, but we make a good team. I appreciate Don's calmness and the way it balances my tendency to panic. He's even-tempered and always has a positive attitude—attributes I'm still working to develop.

We're still happily together because we love each other and God. We've learned to rely on His amazing grace to handle not only our differences but the many times when everything goes wrong.

It's weird, but it works.

Thank You, Lord, for joining us together in
this profound mystery called marriage.
—PENNEY SCHWAB

Digging Deeper: PRV 18:22; EPH 5:33

Sat 25

God setteth the solitary in families. . . . —PSALM 68:6 (KJV)

When I was a toddler, the people who filled our dining room, wearing pointy hats and singing "Happy Birthday," included an interesting collection of folks who might have otherwise spent the day alone: widows, widowers, or never-been-marrieds. As I grew older, I remember enviously attending friends' celebrations and laying it on thick: "Aw, Mom, Jimmy had Madame Fee-fee, the gypsy magician, at his birthday!"

But my mom always had the perfect rebuttal: "Yes, Brock, but when you share your special day with people who love you as much as 'the old people' do, you get a present that lasts forever and it's better than anything money can buy."

Now, as my fortieth birthday approaches, I find myself thinking of those long-ago parties and those dear 'old people,' most of whom have died. I think about greeting Mae Davis at the door as my father folded up her walker and helped her to the couch. I remember Louise, Kathleen, Walter, and Gordon sitting around the table, cheering as I blew out the candles. And, of course, there was always Kate; never married and without a family of her own, she was adopted into our family early on.

All these years later, the present my mother alluded to is a very real part of who I am. It might have been a challenging lesson for a ten-year-old boy, but it is a powerfully pertinent one to a soon-to-be-forty-year-old man.

So on the morning of my fortieth, I made a phone call. "Hey, Mom, how about meeting me over at the nursing home for a minicelebration before my birthday dinner? I can't imagine celebrating my special day without a visit with Kate."

Father, keep me mindful to open my home and my heart
to Your lonely children. —BROCK KIDD

Digging Deeper: LK 14:12–14; 1 PT 4:8–11

Sun 26

"Six days you shall labor and do all your work, but the seventh day is a sabbath to the Lord your God. On it you shall not do any work...." —DEUTERONOMY 5:13 (NIV)

Henry spread a soft blanket across the living room floor. I thought he was going to lie down and read a book, but then when I looked up from my newspaper, he was on all fours spreading out another blanket beside the first one.

"What are you doing, Hen?" I asked.

"I'm making a soft world," he said.

I went back to reading my article and pushed away thoughts that I should go upstairs to my home office and get a jump start on the week ahead by checking e-mail and diving into my projects.

I heard Henry go upstairs and then I heard *thump, thump, thump* as he came down, his arms overflowing with blankets from his bed.

His brother Solomon rested in his favorite reading spot with his nose in a book. His father worked on the Sunday crossword, and I went back to the paper. I kept one eye watching Henry cover the living room floor with blankets, pillows, and a bunch of his stuffed animals. When everything was just so, every pillow exactly where he wanted, he rolled around on his favorite blue blanket, grinning from ear to ear.

"Like it? This is my soft world." He hugged his favorite stuffed dinosaur.

I'm so glad I stayed downstairs with my family. Had I gone off to do work, I would have missed the soft world.

Dear God, thank You for the day of rest—
just what I need to relax and feel blessed.
—SABRA CIANCANELLI

Digging Deeper: GN 2:3; LK 6:1–11

A NEW WAY TO SERVE

Mon 27 *"You are the salt of the earth. . . ."*
—Matthew 5:13 (NRSV)

FRIENDSHIP THROUGH BOOKS

I met Bill years earlier when he'd joined the St. James Literary Society, a book and discussion group at New London, Connecticut's homeless shelter. Bill was what we used to call a "rag man," one who collected bottles and other castoffs to sell or give away. He always had a shopping cart crammed with stuff. Initially, he fought my friendship with the tenacity that only a street person possesses; to survive, Bill believed he could love no one and allow no one to love him.

I lured him and other shelter residents with their love of books. I'd learned from volunteering that many homeless people enjoy reading; books provided an escape.

Bill was a voracious reader. We found nearly one thousand tattered books in his apartment after he died, most purchased for a few cents. Although he preferred books to people, eventually he began talking. *But are our meetings making any difference in his life*, I wondered. Then, one night, we were discussing childhood memories, and Bill told us he'd been a Boy Scout, had earned a service badge for collecting eyeglasses. I teased, "Too bad I have to drag these things out of you."

He didn't laugh. Instead, he met my eyes directly—a rare occurrence—and said, "Until this group, I wouldn't have told anyone these things."

And then I was the wordless one.

Lord, I praise You for giving me the opportunity to love and be loved.
—Marci Alborghetti

Digging Deeper: Mt 5:1–20

Tue 28

Finally, all of you, have unity of mind, sympathy, brotherly love, a tender heart, and a humble mind.
—1 Peter 3:8 (ESV)

When I was a teenager, a thousand years ago when the world was young and I think Abraham Lincoln was president, I wanted, more than anything, to be cool.

My twenties were more of the same; like many men, my twenties were a second try at the teenage years, this time with better cars and clothes. In my thirties, however, I grew up a little and realized that the world was not actually my oyster and that my job was to harness and hone what gifts I had been given, however minuscule they seemed to be, and bring them to bear against darkness and despair. Also, a woman married me then. My forties were more hard work at my craft, learning how to catch and share stories so as to elevate and electrify and entertain my fellow travelers. Also, three children arrived from the stars then.

And now I am in my fifties, and I think about when I was a teenager, a thousand years ago when the world was young, and I think how far the road is from what I wanted then and what I want now. I am not cool. I will never be cool. I don't care a fig for cool.

I want to be tender and compassionate and kind. I want to make people laugh and weep and hold hands. I want to sing stories of grace and guts beyond the imagination of murderers. I want to sing the holy, everywhere evident and profligate, if we could only claw the selfish blinders off our eyes. I want to do my small part to shove the universe forward two inches toward the extraordinary day when war is a joke and violence is a memory. That's what I want, now that I am older than dirt.

What do *you* want?

Dear Lord, aw, thanks for making it so easy for me to be a fool. It makes the country of almost-maturity a rich and humble place to live. You are a subtle One, yes, You are.

—Brian Doyle

Digging Deeper: Eph 2:8–9; Col 3:17

Wed 29

Dear friends, let us love one another, for love comes from God. Everyone who loves has been born of God and knows God. —1 JOHN 4:7 (NIV)

I've always been something of a loner. In middle school, I preferred a good fantasy novel to time on the playground, and in college, I often chose to do homework or watch a movie rather than spend time with friends. Even at church, I chose to sit in pews toward the back, where I could pray alone. Sometimes my desire to be on my own was so strong that I would snap at people just to get them to leave me alone.

I'd like to say all that changed when I met Emily; that her warmth and beauty opened my heart so wide I couldn't hold it in any longer. But it didn't; at least not at first. It took weeks of hanging out together before I worked up the courage to ask her out, and even when we started dating, I still found myself drawing away.

After a night where I raised my voice at Emily for simply asking if we could have dinner together, I knew I had to change. Not only was I endangering the most important relationship in my life, but I wasn't living by Christ's precept to love and care for one another.

I didn't become a new person overnight. It took months of work and prayer to stop pushing Emily away. Ultimately, I had to accept that I wanted to watch her laugh as much as anything on earth—and I would change, in any way necessary, to protect and keep her in my life with God's help. My relationship with Emily—and my family and friends—is ongoing....

Thank You, Lord, for always leaving Your heart open for me, thereby teaching me to open my heart to others.

—SAM ADRIANCE

Digging Deeper: 2 COR 5:17; GAL 2:20

Thu 30

And let us not be weary in well doing. . . .
—Galatians 6:9 (KJV)

It's impossible!" I wailed, annoyance flaring to the boiling point. "This is stupid. It's just a feed truck! Why do we need a turn signal anyway?"

For a half hour I had stood on a five-gallon bucket, fumbling blindly in the contorted space behind the light housing. The twelfth time my cramped hand slipped off the wrench and bloodied my knuckles I was ready to throw the tools to the ground and quit.

My temples throbbed and actual tears of frustration were building at the obvious defeat to which I was about to succumb. I was losing control.

Do it as if for Me. The voice came out of nowhere, so softly I barely heard it. I'd read recently that to be successful in life, do all things as if you were doing them directly for God.

I stared at the old truck. What if this were God's? What if He had asked me to fix the light? Would I be on the verge of a wrench-flinging screaming fit? No. I'd be thrilled to do something for Him.

My shoulders relaxed. My breathing slowed. Calmly, unhurried, I worked the wrench. My hand didn't slip when my grip wasn't so fierce. I unscrewed the backing of the light and replaced the shattered signal within minutes. But even better than that, I'd discovered the key to success.

Lord, please inspire me to be my best. What utter joy I find when everything I do is for You.
—Erika Bentsen

Digging Deeper: Phil 2:14–15; Col 3:23–24

Fri 31

"It laughs at fear, afraid of nothing; it does not shy away from the sword." —Job 39:22 (NIV)

Colby, my golden retriever, pounded through the woods, enjoying his first visit to Blue Ridge, Georgia. We turned down a gravel lane that looped by several houses perched high above the water when, suddenly, Colby froze.

In front of my eyes, my sweet, loving golden tucked his tail and stood completely still; the high-pitched whine emanating from the back of his throat was his only giveaway. My eyes followed to where his gaze locked: our neighbor's life-size, two-dimensional metal cutout of a bear.

From where we stood, the bear looked to be crossing a stream a few yards away from us. Had Colby noticed the bear a few feet earlier or later, he would've seen what I knew to be true: This harmless, flat, rusted bear was only a lawn ornament. Instead, Colby cowered and whimpered until I carried him far enough along the path so that he could recognize the bear was only metal.

I often wonder how many times God has had to pull me past certain trials that I don't notice until I'm knee-deep in them and cowering. If I'd seen them coming or had the patience to wait until the fear subsided, I might've been better prepared to call out to God in prayer. Instead, I collapsed in a pile of woe and wailing, panicked at the situation I faced.

Now, when I comfort Colby when he encounters something scary, I remember that God does the same with me. I may not be able to see the leash, but if I pay attention, I can feel the tug on my heart to follow Him.

Lord, remind me that diving into my fear only allows it to bloom.
Remind me to follow You out of the darkness and into the light.
—Ashley Kappel

Digging Deeper: Ps 23:4; Is 41:10; 1 Jn 4:18

DAILY MERCIES

1 ______________________________

2 ______________________________

3 ______________________________

4 ______________________________

5 ______________________________

6 ______________________________

7 ______________________________

8 ______________________________

9 ______________________________

10 ______________________________

11 ______________________________

12 ______________________________

13 ______________________________

14 ______________________________

15 ______________________________

January

16 ____________________

17 ____________________

18 ____________________

19 ____________________

20 ____________________

21 ____________________

22 ____________________

23 ____________________

24 ____________________

25 ____________________

26 ____________________

27 ____________________

28 ____________________

29 ____________________

30 ____________________

31 ____________________

February

But I will sing of thy power; yea, I will sing aloud of thy mercy in the morning: for thou hast been my defence and refuge in the day of my trouble.

—Psalm 59:16 (KJV)

Sat 1

Moreover, He said to me, "Son of man, take into your heart all My words which I will speak to you and listen closely."
—Ezekiel 3:10 (NAS)

I do the dishes at our house, and, to help the time pass, I plug a pair of earbuds into an iPod and listen to podcasts or lectures or music. But the combination of the earbuds and the running water (not to mention my aging ears) prevents me from hearing much else. So a not-infrequent exchange goes something like this: Wife or child comes into kitchen and moves lips.

Andrew (turning head to kitchen doorway, removing right earbud): "Huh?"

Wife or child (turning away and exiting kitchen): "Never mind."

It's not just conversations that die aborning in a fog of husbandly or fatherly inattention. Doorbells and phones go unanswered, and disagreements among siblings (okay, fights) go unmediated while Daddy zones out on a discussion of some arcane subject.

Lately my prayer life has been a lot like dishwashing time.

Andrew: "Dear Lord, I really need Your help with this. My earbuds are cutting me off from the family... *What was it I was listening to last night? I have about half of that discussion left to listen to... Don't I have a book about that somewhere? I ought to download this week's episode of...*

God:

Andrew: *What was it I was supposed to do about John's prescriptions? What did I do with my keys?*

God:

The chatter in my head works a lot like my iPod. It insulates me from what I ought to be hearing. How can the Lord talk to me if I'm not listening?

Dear Lord, help me to open my ears and my heart to You and to the world around me. —Andrew Attaway

Digging Deeper: Dt 15:5; Pss 50:1, 119:18; Prv 2:1–5; Rv 3:20

Sun 2

The Lord is good to all: and his tender mercies are over all his works. —Psalm 145:9 (KJV)

The gray clouds hung below the mountain peaks, smothering the sun. A cold breeze brushed across my cheeks as I tossed hay in the feeder for the horses and mules. I glanced at the brown grass in the pasture rimmed by the skeletal trees. Not a sprig of life showed anywhere. The gloomies seeped into my soul. How I longed for signs of life! *Lord, I need You to brighten my day.*

I heard a low bellow from the neighbors' pasture a few hundred yards away. *Uh-oh, it sounds like a cow's having problems giving birth.* The neighbors lived miles away and wouldn't be back to check on the cows for a couple more hours. "C'mon, Sunrise," I called to my golden retriever, "let's go check it out."

As we neared the pasture, I noticed a lone black cow standing with her head down. Keeping my distance, I stood on tiptoes, craning my neck. A brand-new wet calf lay on the ground. "Isn't this exciting? What a cute baby!" Sunrise's nose wiggled as she caught the scent of the baby.

For the next hour I sat in the pasture, watching the newborn struggle to stand on its stiltlike legs. I giggled as the calf sucked on its mom's knees and elbows before it found the udder and slurped.

Lord, when my days are glum, remind me to ask You to brighten them.
—Rebecca Ondov

Digging Deeper: Pss 8, 84:11

February

Mon 3

Therefore we are always confident and know that as long as we are at home in the body we are away from the Lord. For we live by faith, not by sight. —2 Corinthians 5:6–7 (NIV)

I was clicking though my usual Monday morning e-mail glut when I noticed in the reflection of the monitor that I'd missed a spot shaving. Now I was beating myself up about being so careless and felt like the Wolfman himself, transmogrifying from human to beast. I recalled that somewhere deep in the recesses of one of my drawers was a razor. A second later I was ransacking my desk in search of it. That's when Carlos walked in, a gentleman who shows up once a week with his watering can to check on our office foliage. "What are you looking for?" he asked.

"Nothing, really," I muttered.

"You are looking awfully hard for nothing," he said. His watering can gurgled as he attended to one of my philodendrons.

"I'm trying to find a razor. I missed a spot shaving this morning."

"Stubble is fashionable on men these days," he said.

"I look like the Wolfman."

"Maybe people will appreciate what a good job you did on the rest of your face."

I turned from my rummaging and shot Carlos a look. He was laughing, his face crinkled up with mirth. All of a sudden I was laughing too.

"Don't take yourself so seriously, Mr. Edward. It's only Monday. You have the whole week ahead of you!" Then Carlos and his watering can were off to the next office.

He was right: A whole week lay ahead—a good week, if I wanted it to be.

Lord, it's me again, Mr. Edward. Thank You for Carlos and beard stubble and gurgling watering cans and thirsty philodendrons and all the other stray blessings You bestow upon this too often insecure soul.

—Edward Grinnan

Digging Deeper: Ps 118:24; Mt 6:11

Tue 4

The Lord my God lightens my darkness.
—Psalm 18:28 (RSV)

Nursing a grouchy mood, it was with leaden feet I trudged up the hill that morning to check the newborn calves on our family ranch. I determined that nothing could cheer me up, but in an instant my sour grapes were forgotten. I couldn't believe my eyes when I first saw the calf with her mother standing over her proudly. Normally our calves are around seventy to ninety pounds. We weighed Mini, just to be sure. Full term and full of life . . . and only twenty pounds.

As a precaution, Mini is spending the first few weeks of her life living in an insulated, heated room in the barn, breathing warm air and where her mother won't accidentally squish her. Twice a day we carry her out to nurse the cow. She can just reach if she stands on her toes. Plus, we bottle-feed her periodically throughout the day and night. We took pictures of Mini next to the cats, and they're the same size!

I told a friend that I don't know why Mini is that size; all of the cow's other calves were normal. "Every now and then," she replied, "God sends us a present that will always make us smile."

She's right. No matter what misery I'm dwelling on, whenever I see Mini, it all goes away and I can't help but grin.

There are times when I get caught up in negativity, Lord. Please don't let me forget Your big blessings in however small a package.
—Erika Bentsen

Digging Deeper: Ps 21:6; Eph 3:20–21

Wed 5

Your heavenly Father knoweth that ye have need of all these things. —Matthew 6:32 (KJV)

"How am I going to keep doing this, God?" I shot the prayer up under my breath. The stock market had been frenetic, and the global economy was stoking the fire. As an investment adviser, my job was to manage my clients' savings as well as their expectations. While I love what I do, sometimes the stress of it all becomes overwhelming. As the closing bell rang, I decided to call it a day.

At home, I was eager to spend a little time with our six-month-old baby girl. "Daddy's got you, Mary Katherine!" I swooped my daughter up in the air and smiled as I looked into her bright hazel eyes. She cooed back at me with a big, toothless grin. I could feel my stress melt away as she giggled and squealed. Before long, her happy cheer turned into a fussy whine. I knew this meant "Daddy, I'm sleepy." It was nap time. I fed her a bottle and gently patted her back until she burped. Then I rocked her for a bit, and soon she was sound asleep.

"There are few things as peaceful as a sleeping baby," I said to my wife, Corinne, as I walked into the kitchen.

"So how was work?" she asked, sensing my weariness.

"Stressful."

She smiled and rolled her eyes. "Brock, you just spent an hour taking great care of Mary Katherine. God has been taking care of you for forty years! Do you think He is going to stop now?"

Suddenly, my burden felt a bit lighter. *Daddy's got you, Mary Katherine,* I thought to myself, *and my Father in heaven has me too.*

Father, sometimes even a grown-up needs a daddy. Thanks for being mine.

—Brock Kidd

Digging Deeper: Phil 4:19; 1 Jn 3:1

Thu 6 *"I will change my expression, and smile."*—Job 9:27 (NIV)

When I was arranging a meeting with a woman I'd never met to talk about my nonprofit organization, I sent her a link that had a thumbnail picture of me smiling big. I typed, "I'll smile, so you'll recognize me!"

On our meeting day, I arrived at the restaurant/bakery fifteen minutes early. I sat down in a seat facing the door. As the door swung open, I tried to gauge the likelihood that the person coming in was the woman I was meeting. This person seemed too old. This one was dressed like she'd just come from the gym. After a while the second-guessing became exhausting, so I gave up and smiled at every stranger who glanced in my direction. They, in turn, smiled back at me. The more I smiled in those fifteen minutes, the more I became aware once again that we're all God's beloved children, deserving of a smile from a stranger.

At long last someone asked, "Are you Karen?" I nodded in relief.

My fifteen-minute experiment in smiling showed me that it takes more energy to mentally separate people into categories of potential friend versus stranger than it does to briefly acknowledge everyone—all deserving—with a welcoming smile.

Dear heavenly Father, may my deliberate act of smiling renew my awareness that we're all beloved children of Yours. Amen.

—Karen Barber

Digging Deeper: 2 Cor 6:17–18

Fri 7

"I will not let you go, unless you bless me."
—Genesis 32:26 (RSV)

I was racing around like crazy because my husband, Keith, was in the hospital. I rushed home to feed the animals and let our dog out. Once Anjin was back inside, I thought I'd done everything I needed to and was ready to go back to the hospital. I grabbed my purse and fished for my cell phone. It wasn't there.

Under normal circumstances, losing my cell phone would be nothing more than a bother, but these weren't normal circumstances. All the phone numbers I needed were programmed into that phone, and it was the number the hospital would use to reach me. I dialed the cell number from our landline, but I couldn't hear ringing anywhere in the house. I searched my car and the garage.

It had been a long time since I'd yelled at God, but I did. I planted my feet in the middle of the living room and shouted, "I don't want to keep bugging You, God, but I will, because I need my cell phone and I need those numbers! I can't find them myself, so I need help!"

I searched the house again but found nothing. Then, for the second time, I searched the car. Under the passenger seat, my groping hand encountered a smooth metal lump, which turned out to be my phone.

Sometimes I hesitate to call for Your attention, God, but when I really need You, I'm grateful that You hear me. Thank You.

—Rhoda Blecker

Digging Deeper: 1 Chr 5:20; Pss 34:4, 54:2

Sat 8

And He will be the stability of your times....
—Isaiah 33:6 (NAS)

I'm not a fan of flying. It doesn't seem natural to be suspended miles in the sky. I fly because I have to. When you have family in Alaska, it's a bit of a drive from Minnesota. The night before I flew out to visit them, I prayed for peace, remembering how Jesus told His disciples: "Peace I leave with you" (John 14:27).

Everything went fine until I had to travel on a small commuter plane from Anchorage to Homer, situated on the Kenai Peninsula coastline. That day a blizzard hit. The plane was delayed but flying.

When we boarded on the snowy runway, the young pilot stood by the steps to greet us. Someone asked how the weather was in Homer and if we'd be able to make a landing. Unbelievably he replied, "Well, it's good enough to *try*!"

I have to get there, I thought, as I found my seat. Again I asked Jesus for His peace. At takeoff, the pilot informed us, "If we can't land in Homer, we're flying to Kodiak." *Kodiak Island!* I knew no one there. Besides this, we were told that several bags had been randomly removed to "make weight" and would arrive later.

We had a smooth flight above thick clouds. Homer had cleared, offering a breathless view of Katchemak Bay with its glistening mountains. A familiar green and black bag even popped up on the conveyor belt.

I fly because I have to... because there are times when if I didn't need to ask God, I might never experience His perfect peace like I did on that trip.

Lord of earth and sky, it's when I feel small that I know I have a big God.
—Carol Knapp

Digging Deeper: Ps 119:165; Is 26:3; Jn 14:27

February

Sun 9

Mercy and truth are met together; righteousness and peace have kissed each other. —Psalm 85:10 (KJV)

When my husband, David, made the heart-wrenching decision to leave his post as senior minister at Hillsboro Presbyterian Church, the church was strong, thriving, and ripe for new leadership. But leaving was complicated.

No one has ever loved a congregation more than David, and the congregation responded in kind. So it was infinitely sad when an influential person began working to erase David's legacy. We had looked forward to returning to Hillsboro after the proper transition period, but now amid the confusion, the outlook was cloudy. Would it work for David to come back? Would we lose our church family forever?

Finally, a new minister was chosen. For me, I wasn't sure how I would feel until I met Chris. My reaction was immediate. I have a pastor! *But what about David?* I would never go back to Hillsboro without him.

Well, it seems God had planned ahead. Chris sent out a letter to the congregation, addressing the misperception that "it's not possible to love the new pastor if you still love the previous pastor." He dispelled that notion with five simple words: "It's okay to love both." Chris went on to describe his meetings with David and to announce that he had invited him to come back to Hillsboro where the two of them "share a love for the church and its people."

And so it was finished. We had a church home once again, where we could come and worship with our family and friends, a place where there's enough love for everyone, and a new minister wise enough to know that's true.

Father, I pray for the day when all of us grasp the unlimited reservoir of Your love and can finally see its regenerating power.

—Pam Kidd

Digging Deeper: Ps 132:7; Eph 4:15–16; Col 3:14–17

LIFE LESSONS FROM THOSE I'VE MET

Mon 10 *So foolish was I; and ignorant. . . .* —Psalm 73:22 (KJV)

LORNE GREENE, ACTOR

I was a very new, very inexperienced writer, just arrived in California on my first *Guideposts* assignment. I was checking into my hotel when my editor phoned with another story lead: "I've got you an interview with Lorne Greene!"

Lorne Greene? I'd never heard of him, but from the excitement in the editor's voice, I knew it must be someone famous. And rather than expose my ignorance, I said, "Great!"

"He'll meet you on the *Bonanza* set." He gave me a TV studio address.

We didn't yet own a TV, but I'd read about the new quiz shows offering big prizes. *Bonanza*, I decided, must be one of those. I'd interview Mr. Greene about competitiveness! I spent two hours writing out a long list of questions.

The next day I stood in the wings of the soundstage, staring at a log cabin, a covered wagon, a backdrop of Ponderosa pines . . . I crumpled my sheet of questions.

We sat at a table while I fumbled for a question. Beneath his broad-brimmed hat, smiling brown eyes met mine. He must have perceived immediately that a novice writer had asked a busy man for his time and then arrived unprepared. He took pity on my floundering efforts. "I was a radio interviewer in Canada before I got into acting," he said. "I think I have a story you'll like."

No thanks to me, I flew home with a wonderful piece. And a new petition for my daily prayers:

Father, grant me the grace to say, "I don't know."
—Elizabeth Sherrill

Digging Deeper: Prv 22:4; Jas 4:6

Tue 11

"For my thoughts are not your thoughts, neither are your ways my ways," declares the Lord. —ISAIAH 55:8 (NIV)

Our plans were set to visit friends in Boston over the weekend. My wife, Elba, and I were excited; we'd known Hilda and Frankie for over thirty years.

However, on my way home from work to begin the weekend, I got a call from Hilda. "Pablo, we need to postpone your visit. We have a stomach bug and don't want you to catch it."

When I got home, the first thing out of my mouth was, "Honey, you are not going to believe it, but our trip was canceled."

"What happened?" asked Elba.

"I am so disappointed. I was really looking forward to going away," I responded, not listening to my wife's question.

"Why was it canceled?" she asked.

But I didn't answer, so focused on my own concerns was I. "We had this trip planned for weeks! You know how much I enjoy spending time with Frankie. I'm so frustrated."

When I finally got around to telling Elba the reason, she responded in her usual way: "God knows everything." This is how she looks at unexpected circumstances in life: postponed trips, getting stuck in traffic. It doesn't matter what it is, Elba sees life through the lens that shows God is in control, God has a reason, God has our best interest.

Lord, help me to trust that Your plans and ways
are filled with Your goodness.

—PABLO DIAZ

Digging Deeper: Ps 135:6; Prv 16:9

Wed 12

This service that you perform is not only supplying the needs of the Lord's people but is also overflowing in many expressions of thanks to God.
—2 Corinthians 9:12 (NIV)

One Sunday afternoon, early in November, I felt I just had to get out of the house. After calling ahead, I drove to visit friends, old enough to be my parents. Anne and I chatted warmly while Dick, suffering the effects of a stroke, smiled, nodded agreements, and haltingly tried to contribute. Before leaving, as if asking for a prayer, I admitted that I'd been depressed.

Anne and Dick gave me more than a prayer. Midweek Anne called. "Would you like to join us for Thanksgiving?"

Among three generations of their family, I sat down to a feast: turkey, stuffing, mashed potatoes, apple pie. Taking the empty dessert plates into their kitchen, I whispered in disbelief, "Anne, are you throwing away that carcass?"

"You want it? Please take it."

I went home with more than a festive memory. That weekend I made a mess of soup, a quart of which I delivered to Anne and Dick. I slid a few more cups of deboned turkey into the freezer for a later time.

Which happens to be today. Dick has had another stroke and is dying. My response to the news? I chopped onions and celery and am simmering soup to take to Anne.

An hour ago, when a maintenance man came by to fix my kitchen radiator, he exclaimed, "It smells like Thanksgiving in here."

Wrong month, wrong day of the week, and I hadn't thought of it in those terms. But, yes, this tureen is indeed about more than turkey soup.

Lord, show me ways to give tangible thanks
to those who have been kind to me.
—Evelyn Bence

Digging Deeper: Lk 6:38; Col 3:17

February

Thu 13

"Don't recite the same prayer over and over as the heathen do, who think prayers are answered only by repeating them again and again. Remember, your Father knows exactly what you need even before you ask him!"
—Matthew 6:7–8 (TLB)

Back in the 1980s when I lived in Wisconsin, I admitted to my friend Betsy that I had never balanced my checkbook. She was aghast and insisted on showing me how to do it.

I pretended to pay attention to her step-by-step instructions but, truth be told, I still haven't done it. I subtract the checks that I write, but every month the statement says I have more money in there than I think I do, which means I also don't know how to subtract correctly. Or maybe I don't add in the deposits correctly.

It's the same with my prayer life. I often don't say enough prayers for those I've promised to pray for. I give it a halfhearted try, adding and subtracting people from my prayer list willy-nilly. I'm sure there are people I forget to include in my prayers and others I forget to take off when prayers for them have been answered in one way or another. I guess it's best to err on the side of too many people on my prayer list than not enough.

Over the years I have come to trust God to keep it all squared away, just like I trust the bank to keep my checking account in good shape.

Father, help me to add the needy to my prayer list, subtract the ones whose prayers have been answered, divide the sorrows, and multiply the joys of all around me. And thanks for keeping it all straight.
—Patricia Lorenz

Digging Deeper: Mk 11:24; Lk 18:1; 1 Thes 5:17

Fri 14

Be completely humble and gentle; be patient, bearing with one another in love. —EPHESIANS 4:2 (NIV)

I checked the mail one more time, but there was still no package. Emily, my girlfriend, called from the car: "You ready?"

I hesitated, looking on the front stoop just to make sure. "Yeah, let me just get my bags." I kissed her lightly and tried to smile.

"What's wrong?" she said.

I shook my head. "Nothing."

We were about to drive to Maine for a long weekend, and what I thought was the most important part of our getaway—a diamond ring for Emily—hadn't come in time. Still, we spent the next day and a half relaxing together, taking walks on the beach, and reading books to each other. It was blissful.

As we got ready to go out to dinner, I decided to do what I'd planned to, even without the ring. I touched Emily's face and said, "These last two years with you have been the best of my life. I never believed I could love someone as much as I love you." I got down on one knee and continued: "Emily, will you marry me?"

She said yes, and we kissed. But I had to explain: "I bought a ring, but it had to be resized and—"

"It doesn't matter," she said, and kissed me again.

I guess I was wrong. The missing ring hadn't been the most important thing at all.

Thank You, God, for always showing me what's most important.
—SAM ADRIANCE

Digging Deeper: PRV 18:22, 19:14; 1 COR 13:4–8

February

Sat 15

Trust in the Lord with all your heart, and do not lean on your own understanding. In all your ways acknowledge Him, and He will make straight your paths. —Proverbs 3:5–6 (ESV)

When I was twenty, I fretted over graduate school. In my thirties, I became an overly concerned young father. During my forties, I was consumed with my profession. Turning fifty, I was sure that I would never get three children through college without robbing a bank. And now in my sixties, I am anxious about preparation for retirement. Does worry ever go away?

Well, no, it doesn't. The primal state of human beings is anxiety. We are hardwired to anticipate the future and to prepare for all contingencies. The hallmark of a human being is not so much a smile but a furrowed brow.

Yesterday, I visited my ninety-year-old mother who is the most serene person I know. Driving home, I pictured myself at her stage of life and grew anxious. Lost in thought, I was not aware that I was humming. Slowly, I recognized the tune and began to sing the words of the children's hymn my mother taught me years ago: "*Trust and obey, for there's no other way, to be happy in Jesus, but to trust and obey.*"

The key to happiness is to obey God in the present and to trust God for the future. This was Jesus' recipe for living, and it needs to be mine too.

Dear Lord, may I remember Jesus' final words: "Father, into Thy hands I commit my spirit." Amen.

—Scott Walker

Digging Deeper: Ps 55:22; 1 Pt 5:6–7

Sun 16

In this vision he saw an angel of God coming toward him.... —ACTS 10:3 (TLB)

Susan Days are always good days," my granddaughter Olivia said when I dropped her off at school. Olivia has some lingering memory problems caused by a traumatic brain injury and needs extra help with algebra. My friend Susan's willingness to tutor twice a week is the answer to prayer, and Olivia looks forward to it.

The next week, in Sunday school, our conversation turned to angels. "God sent angels to earth back in Bible times," someone said, "but I don't think that happens today." Some people agreed, but others had experienced angelic visitors or instances of help coming in inexplicable and mysterious ways.

The church bell ended the discussion, but as we prayed, I thought of Susan and other earthly angels who'd blessed my family. There was Orville who lent me his pickup when a rock shattered my windshield. He also arranged to have the windshield replaced. When I was on vacation, a hiker warned me not to try a trail that looked easy. "The middle two miles are a steep grade," she said. I'm not a climber and would have been in trouble without her advice. A young friend, Wes, helped us clear snow from our long drive, so we could get to a doctor's appointment.

I'd love to be visited by a heavenly angel, although I would probably be afraid! At the same time, I am truly thankful for the earthly angels who brighten my world almost every day.

Dear Jesus, help me make today a "Susan Day."
—PENNEY SCHWAB

Digging Deeper: PS 91:11; HEB 1:14

Mon 17

"I truly understand that God shows no partiality, but in every nation anyone who fears him and does what is right is acceptable to him." —ACTS 10:34–35 (NRSV)

We stared at the school handout. "That's pouring it on pretty thick," Kate said.

I nodded. "Was it like this when we were in school?" I asked.

Presidents' Day was approaching, and Frances's school was hosting a patriotic assembly. The kids had a packet of songs and poems to memorize. Some of them seemed over the top in their worship of the United States.

Don't get me wrong. I love America. I studied abroad in college and returned home profoundly grateful for my sprawling, boisterous, beautiful, dynamic country. But no country is perfect, and the United States is not the kingdom of God.

Was it right to fill impressionable kids' minds with such unvarnished patriotic worship? Aren't we supposed to see the world through God's eyes, thankful for our religious freedom, but calling out greed and injustice when we see it?

"Maybe I learned some of these songs in school," Kate said. "I can't remember."

"Well, then probably Frances won't remember either," I said. "She'll form her own ideas as she grows up." And, suddenly, I realized *that* was the point of patriotism. Frances could form her own ideas. She was free to think and believe what seemed right to her. She was free to grow up and disagree with Kate and me completely. That was the glory of America.

Lord, help me to see the world through Your eyes.

—JIM HINCH

Digging Deeper: Ps 22:28; Is 30:21

Tue 18

"Love your enemies! Do good to them. Lend to them without expecting to be repaid. Then your reward from heaven will be very great, and you will truly be acting as children of the Most High, for he is kind to those who are unthankful and wicked."
—LUKE 6:35 (NLT)

The late-night call to the hospital twisted my stomach into a hard knot. Danny, a strong, passionate college student studying for ministry, had been in an accident. He lay in a medically induced coma, survival uncertain.

I was one of his teachers. I rushed to the hospital and joined his friends. Danny's parents had not yet arrived; they faced an agonizing four-hour drive. As we waited, we pieced together the tragic story.

Danny had seen a homeless man begging on the side of the road. He sensed God's whisper to feed him; the fast-food gift certificates he had in his pocket would be perfect. While turning his car around, he was T-boned by a pickup truck. His girlfriend suffered minor injuries; the other driver wasn't hurt, but Danny now fought for his life.

We waited and prayed and tried to comfort his parents when they arrived. The waiting stretched into days. Danny's father, however, was not content with waiting. He had a mission. The day after the accident, he drove to the fast-food joint, loaded up with food, drove to that fateful place, and finished the task his son had begun. While his son lay in a coma, Danny's father fed that same homeless man who would never fathom the cost of his meal; God's boundless compassion, disguised as fast food.

Danny's recovery was slow but strong. I saw him recently, working on campus. He waved. He'd just gotten married. Danny, by his life and through his family, has become my teacher.

Heavenly Father, grant me grace to press through my heartaches to a place of total forgiveness, supernatural love, and abundant life.
—BILL GIOVANNETTI

Digging Deeper: JN 15:4; EPH 4:32; JAS 2:8

THE PATH TO ADOPTION

Wed 19

"For if you remain silent at this time, relief and deliverance for the Jews will arise from another place . . . ."
—Esther 4:14 (NIV)

SAYING YES

Names, children, jobs—basic introductory stuff. It was our first meeting as a new small group. Halfway around the circle, we met Kristin. She and her husband had adopted a son from South Korea and would be traveling to China to pick up their daughter.

My husband, Ryan, and I exchanged a look. It seemed everywhere we turned—videos, news stories, friends, acquaintances—we kept running into adoption. It made us uncomfortable. As much as we liked the idea, the reality was too much.

The next day, I found myself reading the book of Esther, and this profound truth jumped off the page: God was going to save the Jews, with or without Esther's help. But He invited Esther to be a part of His plan. She said yes, and because of that, she experienced God's power and grace in a way she never would have if she'd said no.

As I sat in my room with my Bible, I could hear God whispering: *I have something great planned. Are you going to say yes?*

I won't lie; I was terrified. Adoption is scary and uncertain and often messy. I could play it safe and say no. Or I could say yes and experience something profound, something breathtaking, something bigger than myself. That night, Ryan came home from work. "I really think we should adopt," I said.

He looked at me and smiled. "Yeah, me too."

Thank You, Lord, for inviting us to be a part of Your amazing plans. You don't need us, but You choose to use us. That is truly amazing!
—Katie Ganshert

Digging Deeper: Ps 32:8; Prv 16:9; Phil 2:13

Thu 20

Behold, this is the joy of his way, and out of the earth shall others grow. —JOB 8:19 (KJV)

I often tell people that sometimes life is like Roller Derby: We may be skating along at the back of the pack, until God grabs our hands and whips us to the front to score.

But sitting on a plane departing Atlanta for Kansas City, I was discouraged. I had been hard at work on a project that I thought would take six months to complete. Six months stretched to two years and then five. The more I worked, the further behind I was.

The flight attendant interrupted my thoughts: "We will be taking off as soon as our last few passengers arrive." When a young woman slid into the seat beside me, I glanced at her and the other interesting-looking last-minute boarders. Two words popped into my brain: Roller Derby!

"Hi," I said to my seatmate. "Are you all some sort of team?"

She nodded. "We play for the Kansas City Roller Warriors."

I giggled as I recalled Roller Derby matches I'd watched on TV as a child. I rejoiced thinking that I sat in the presence of roller-skating angels, living reenactors of the metaphor I used to encourage others. I chuckled. Life *is* like Roller Derby. I am never so behind that God cannot reach down His mighty hand and whip me forward.

God, thank You for making me smile. When I feel frustrated or too far behind, help me to remember Your Roller Derby angels.

—SHARON FOSTER

Digging Deeper: PRV 17:22; PHIL 4:4

February

Fri 21

Be ye kind one to another, tenderhearted. . . .
—Ephesians 4:32 (ASV)

Jamie, our oldest daughter, spent the night with us. She had one request: to watch her favorite show, a popular TV dating program. I've caught a few snippets but I've never watched an entire show. Such silliness!

I made homemade lasagna, one of Jamie's favorites, and picked up some chocolate ice cream, but I planned to finagle a way out of watching the program with her. After supper, she helped me clear the table and load the dishwasher. Then her show started. Her daddy stretched out in his recliner, and Jamie sat on the sofa near him.

"I'm going to take my bath, ya'll," I announced. "Be back in a little while." I knew I'd bailed on her, but was it really that important?

Sinking into my warm bubbles, I overheard Jamie and her dad discussing which one special woman might be chosen for a date with "the prince." Rick wasn't poking fun at the far-fetched island drama. I knew he'd rather be watching sports, but he made interesting comments and listened to Jamie's observations—to his daughter's heart, really.

Something I'd ignored.

After my bath, I put on my pajamas and crept back into the den. Only the last few minutes of the show remained. As I sat beside Jamie, a lump rose in my throat. "Sorry I didn't watch the whole thing with you. I should have."

"It's no big deal, Mom."

"Yes it is. This program's important to you. Let's do dinner again next week and we'll watch it together. I promise."

Lord, little things matter so much. Help me listen with my heart and be kind—just like You.

—Julie Garmon

Digging Deeper: Prv 31:26; Phil 2:4; 1 Pt 3:8

Sat 22

Lord my God, I called to you for help and you healed me.
—Psalm 30:2 (NIV)

Dressed for yard work, I went outside and fetched the wheelbarrow. Yesterday was the anniversary of my sister's death, and I needed to be outside to think things through.

As I walked through our yard, I picked up sticks that had fallen during the harsh months of the winter. A favorite of mine, a gnarled old apple tree in the far corner of our field, lost a heavy limb. The maples and ash trees lost small twigs. I picked up the sticks and looked closely at the small buds of new growth.

Last winter was tough. Harsh winds and an early, heavy, wet snow did a lot of damage. I thought about yesterday. My family had gathered at the cemetery. We flew kites in memory of my sister. My son played a hymn on his trumpet while we sang. As the music filled the air, I felt better. It seemed the weight of our loss had lightened, shifted to grace and gratitude of the memories we have of her.

I walked the perimeter of our yard, picking up sticks. The first year of Maria's death, I wondered if I'd ever feel normal again. For months, I was plagued with a terrible feeling that another tragedy was looming.

Some say time heals all wounds, but I think it's faith. I looked down at my full wheelbarrow of dead wood. The storms of life spiritually prune me, tearing away doubt and fear.

Dear Lord, help me to break free of the deadwood
that blocks me from Your presence.
—Sabra Ciancanelli

Digging Deeper: Ps 30:5; Jn 15:1–17

Sun 23

We do not know what we ought to pray for, but the Spirit himself intercedes for us through wordless groans.
—Romans 8:26 (NIV)

C'mon guys, it's time to leave!" I call. The younger kids head toward the door.

"No!" John bellows so loudly that Stephen clasps his ears. I take a deep breath. It's my fifteen-year-old's Sunday-morning anxiety attack, which manifests itself as belligerence. I have Andrew go on ahead with the other kids. It's better to handle this without an audience.

I talk to John for a bit. It is the usual problem: He is afraid God is angry and will not forgive him for some of the things he's done in the past. We talk about grace, mercy, and love. We discuss the irrationality of thinking you're the only unforgivable person in the world. I pray for him silently, because he won't let me pray out loud.

Then I have to decide: Is he safe and capable of calming down on his own? Should I stay home to make sure he's okay? I head out the door, hoping John will join us at church in a little while.

A deep ache grows in my heart as I walk the two blocks to church, the grief of a mother whose teenager's troubles stretch far beyond her ability to solve. I try to articulate my feelings in prayer but cannot. Not knowing what else to do, I shove the groan in my soul God-ward, as if to say, "Here. This is what I mean. You know." And God does.

Holy Spirit, speak the words I cannot utter.
—Julia Attaway

Digging Deeper: Rom 8:26–28; 1 Thes 5:17

Mon 24

Be still before the Lord and wait patiently for him....
—Psalm 37:7 (NIV)

Here are two of my favorite things: salads and multitasking. So combining them is like a cosmic explosion of awesomeness—until this happened.

I was sitting at one of the neighborhood restaurants, eating a bowlful of spinach, grilled chicken, raw beets, toasted Parmesan, and spicy lime dressing.

Meanwhile, my brain was working on overdrive, running through to-do lists for the rest of the day and thinking of witty observations to post on Twitter. My fingers were pecking at my phone, checking e-mail. I was getting things done; I was happy.

And then it hit me: I couldn't taste my salad. Or rather, I hadn't tasted it for several minutes. I hadn't noticed the crunchy umami flavor of the toasted Parmesan. I hadn't sensed the tangy spice of the dressing on my tongue. I was not experiencing one iota of pleasure from this salad.

I've heard about slowing down and living in the moment, but I had always assumed this sort of advice came from inefficient people, the nonmultitaskers of the world. Sitting there, eating my salad, I realized, though, that if I didn't notice the gifts God was offering me in that moment, I was not merely opening myself up to stress and being overwhelmed, I was forgoing the pleasures that moment had to offer.

So I turned off my phone and, as best I could, my brain as well, looked at my colorful salad, and thanked God for its delicious explosion of flavor.

God, help me to slow down and to appreciate what this moment—
each moment—has to offer.
—Joshua Sundquist

Digging Deeper: Eccl 5:18; Jn 1:16; Phil 2:13

February

Tue 25

I urge, then, first of all, that petitions, prayers, intercession and thanksgiving be made for all people.
—I TIMOTHY 2:1 (NIV)

In the middle of a busy morning at the office, I'd just finished a long e-mail to a colleague when the phone rang. I didn't recognize the number but answered. A faint voice said, "I'm Bernadette."

"I'm Rick Hamlin," I replied, trying to remember if there was a Bernadette in any story I was working on. "May I help you?"

"I need someone to pray for me," she said. "My friend Mary is very sick from cancer. They've just put her on hospice care. I don't know what to do . . . " Her voice broke.

"You need to speak to someone at OurPrayer . . . ," I started to say. OurPrayer is our ministry here at Guideposts with dedicated, trained staff members and volunteers who pray for people on the Web and on the phone. But if I transferred the call, Bernadette might hang up, lose her nerve. I couldn't put her on hold. "Tell me about your friend," I said.

They knew each other from childhood. They talked on the phone every day. The cancer had come very quickly. Bernadette was in shock. Each time she visited her friend, she was afraid of dissolving in tears. "If I could just pray with someone," she said.

I found myself asking, "Want me to pray with you right now?"

"Yes, please," she said.

I closed my eyes and lowered my voice, hoping none of my colleagues would interrupt. I'm not sure what I said, but I trusted that the right words would come. "Be with Mary and Bernadette," I ended. "Amen."

"Amen," Bernadette said. "Thank you, sir. That was nice of you."

She hung up, and I returned to work. Maybe Bernadette was supposed to get my number. Perhaps praying for her was the most important thing I would do all day.

Dear Lord, let me know how to say yes when You call. —RICK HAMLIN

Digging Deeper: EPH 6:18; COL 4:2

Wed 26

Love one another . . . as members of one family. . . .
—Romans 12:10 (AMP)

I sometimes brood about my mothering days when my children were young. Observing other mothers with their children now, I realize how simple it would have been to have bent over to their level more, hugged more, and said to each of them more often, "I love you."

Now I was certain it was too late.

Recently, my daughter Julie was going through a difficult day. As she left my house, we stood at the back door, saying good-bye. Suddenly, she threw her arms around me, and I grabbed her tight. "I love you, Mother."

"I love you too, Julie."

"It's so good to hear you say it, Mother."

"I thought you were too old." I tightened my grip.

Julie shed her tears openly.

Mine got stuck somewhere down inside of me.

"You didn't say it much when we were little," she whispered so softly, I could have missed the words.

"Oh, I'm so sorry, Julie. Can you forgive me?" She nodded, unable to speak. "Thank you, Julie Babe."

"I want to hear them, Mother. I always did." Still holding my daughter, I spoke the words again. So did she. The powerful words went straight to my heart and rested there like a contented kitten.

Now, each time we end a telephone conversation or say good-bye in person, we add "I love you," simultaneously.

Oh, my Father, I've neglected to speak the words to You too. Thank You that it's never too late to change. I love You. I love You.
—Marion Bond West

Digging Deeper: Lk 6:31; Eph 4:32, 6:4

Thu 27

Love never fails.... —1 CORINTHIANS 13:8 (NKJV)

Believe it or not, when my wife hands me a list of "honey-do" chores, I do them immediately.

It wasn't always that way. Early in our marriage she had to trick me into doing these jobs by pretending to be helpless. I caught her trying to fix a wooden recipe box, using her high-heeled shoe as a hammer. Both the box and the shoe showed signs of severe trauma. "Here, let me do that. A high-heeled shoe is not a hammer!"

Then there was the big, heavy framed picture that hung over the living room couch. It had pulled loose from its anchor. "Danny, you need to fix that picture or it will fall on one of our guests and hurt someone."

"Yeah, okay," I said, but I dallied a few days.

One day I came home to find the house dark and Sharon nowhere in sight. I finally found her in the living room, sprawled out on the floor, with the heavy picture lying on her head. I was actually fooled for a while, until she started giggling. I rehung the picture right away.

In midmarriage, it occurred to me that these undone chores were a source of great angst to her that she would stoop to such tricks. I don't like to see Sharon suffer. She has enough problems with her bad knees and terrible eyesight. So I changed my motivation from grudging duty to an expression of love for her, and that made all the difference.

I'm no hero, just slow to mature. We both win when Sharon is happy; plus I get a lot of good exercise doing those tasks.

I have since discovered that most of my duties in life can be made easier with love.

Help me, Lord, to do my work with a spirit of affection, not dread.
—DANIEL SCHANTZ

Digging Deeper: EPH 5:25; COL 3:23

Fri 28

Our Father which art in heaven, Hallowed be thy name. Thy kingdom come.... —MATTHEW 6:9–10 (KJV)

Who was it who said that we learn most of life's lessons in elementary school? The older I get, the more often this seems to be true.

When I was a kid growing up in suburban Chicago, we loved when it snowed. The more, the better! My friends and I would sled down the middle of abandoned streets, pick playful snowball fights with one another, and romp around late into the evening.

One night when I was ten, a blizzard hit Chicago in late February. My brother and I, and two other friends, went outside to enjoy weather that most of our neighbors had trouble appreciating. It is good to be a kid! After a short while, we came upon a motorist stuck in a snowbank. We stopped and helped him unbury his car. As it turned out, that, too, was fun!

So we ran home, grabbed our shovels, and went back out into the night, looking for other people in need. Over the course of the next three hours, we found eleven other cars in trouble, tires spinning, drivers stranded, including one van that was full of senior citizens. Digging those people out was both enjoyable and a good deed.

The experience taught me much about the moments I'm given, which I have too easily forgotten in adulthood.

Father, continue to help me to remember good deeds can be fun.
May my life contribute to Your kingdom today.
—JON SWEENEY

Digging Deeper: MT 6:33; LK 10:30–37

February

DAILY MERCIES

1 __________

2 __________

3 __________

4 __________

5 __________

6 __________

7 __________

8 __________

9 __________

10 __________

11 __________

12 __________

13 __________

14 __________

15

16

17

18

19

20

21

22

23

24

25

26

27

28

March

Blessed are the merciful:
for they shall obtain mercy.

—Matthew 5:7 (KJV)

Sat 1

Rejoice always, pray continually, give thanks in all circumstances; for this is God's will for you in Christ Jesus.
—1 THESSALONIANS 5:16–18 (NIV)

I thought the exhortation to "give thanks in all circumstances" was hyperbole, in the same genre as someone saying that the line at the grocery store "took forever."

I realize now that I may have missed the point. I decided to take the verse literally, figuring that if giving thanks in every situation was really part of God's will for me, then I could do worse than summon the focus to give it a whirl for a week. Unfortunately, it wasn't a very good week. Monday brought with it a mountain of deadlines I feared I'd never scale. Tuesday, I received an e-mail proving to me the friendship I feared was fractured in fact was. Wednesday, my husband learned his biggest sales deal had fallen through. Thursday, a friend called to say she was pregnant, which only reminded me I'm not. Friday brought a stomach flu that leveled us for the next six days.

I stared at that verse from 1 Thessalonians. *I'm supposed to thank God for a week like this?* But then a tiny preposition caught my eye. The verse says "in" all circumstances, not "for."

I don't thank You for this mountain of deadlines, Father, but I thank You *in* my distress.

I don't thank You for this friendship fracture, but I thank You *in* the disillusionment and pain.

I don't thank You for Perry's deal falling through, but I thank You even *in* the disappointment.

I don't thank You for my presently empty womb, but I thank You *in* the waiting.

I don't thank You for stomach flu, but I thank You in this state of disease.

In all things, Lord, I choose to give thanks. —ASHLEY WIERSMA

Digging Deeper: 1 THES 5

Sun 2

If any man among you seem to be religious, and bridleth not his tongue, but deceiveth his own heart, this man's religion is vain.
—James 1:26 (KJV)

When I was in my twenties, I started going to the opera. An enthusiastic novice, I'd walk joyfully to the lobby for intermission, only to hear the dismissive remarks of the jaded veterans. A fine performance by Pavarotti? "He has no *squillo.* You really should have heard Corelli in that part." An incredible high note from Joan Sutherland? "Too bad you couldn't have heard her twenty years ago." I'd go back to my seat for the second act, regretting that I wasn't twenty years older rather than enjoying the singing that night.

I've tried, with diminishing success as I've grown older, to be less of a curmudgeon. But the place I've failed utterly has been church. Walking home on Sunday mornings, I've recited a litany of complaints. "The music here is terrible. Do you remember the choir at St. So-and-So's?"

"There was no meat in that sermon. Father X was so much more thoughtful."

"Did you see the sneakers the altar server was wearing? We'd never have let that pass at St. Thingummy's."

Finally, my wife, Julia, had enough. "What are you doing for Lent?" she asked.

"Giving up peanut butter, like always," I answered.

"How about giving up all that negativity?"

So I tried. Sometimes I'd just keep quiet. Sometimes I'd catch myself mid-complaint. Sometimes I'd even say something positive! And you know what? I found myself praying rather than looking for things I didn't like. After all, I was there for God's sake, not my own. You know what else? This Lent I'm going to find something good to say every Sunday.

Lord, keep my attention where it really belongs—on You.
—Andrew Attaway

Digging Deeper: Jl 2:12–13; 1 Pt 5:6

Mon 3

. . . Who through faith . . . whose weakness was turned to strength . . . . —HEBREWS 11:33–34 (NIV)

I probably shouldn't have checked my computer one last time after a very tiring day. One click and I was staring in disbelief at an e-mail from our church prayer planning committee leader with more than one hundred prayer requests attached! The petitions had been gathered at our Ash Wednesday service, and no one thought about who was going to pray for them once they were placed on the altar. Although we weren't an intercessory prayer group (we plan prayer events), our committee was elected! I was even more overwhelmed when I glanced at the list: chemotherapy, job losses, marriages falling apart, the death of young adults, anger issues, serious child behavior problems . . .

I felt absolutely unable—and unwilling—to tackle the job. So instead of praying, I escaped to the laundry room to take the clothes out of the dryer. As I vigorously shook out a shirt, this thought came to mind: *Here you are thinking it's impossible to pray for one hundred requests. God not only hears billions of requests an hour, He also follows through and acts on them.*

I printed out the requests and put them by the chair where I do my morning prayers, and each morning I prayed for ten of them until I finally finished all of them.

Dear Creator of the universe, help me to say yes *to the spiritual tasks You assign me even when I feel unequal to the task. Amen.*

—KAREN BARBER

Digging Deeper: MK 10:45; 1 PT 4:10–11

Tue 4

But as for me, it is good to be near God....
—Psalm 73:28 (NIV)

My friend Brent lives next door and was known throughout our neighborhood as a mild-mannered, quiet, thoughtful person. This all came to an abrupt end one morning when he watched his only daughter suffer a terrible tragedy. I don't even want to reveal what that tragedy was, but suffice it to say that Brent's daughter was hurt more than any teenager should ever be—and Brent was furious with God.

It was shocking to see. Sitting in his living room, Brent explained bitterly, "The deal is over. God is supposed to love us, and I don't see any love left." He was mad, but his anger masked a very deep sadness and sense of loss.

What does someone say in this sort of situation? I had no idea, even though I had read the books and articles and heard the sermons that explained how God is love and is ready and waiting to love us, even, and especially, when awful things happen.

But what do you say to your friend who already knows all of that? I just listened... and listened for the better part of a year. At the end of that year, I began to see Brent's daughter heal. And just when I was about to suggest to Brent what I'd wanted to suggest earlier—that God is good and wants all that is good for us even though this world often offers up what is painful—he beat me to it.

Today, Brent and his daughter and God are all back on the same page. Of course, they always were.

I praise You, God, for Your enduring presence, even when
I am angry or frustrated with You.
—Jon Sweeney

Digging Deeper: Ps 107; Rom 8:28; 2 Pt 3:9

Wed 5

Let us draw near with a true heart in full assurance of faith, having our hearts sprinkled from an evil conscience, and our bodies washed with pure water. —HEBREWS 10:22 (KJV)

Surely, this is one of the loveliest verses in all the Bible, which inspired the hymn "Blessed Assurance" by Fanny Crosby (1820–1915). "Jesus is mine! / O what a foretaste of glory divine!" the hymn sings, and that is what this day—special to many of us—is all about.

Ash Wednesday is when we begin our Lenten disciplines—in imitation of Jesus Who went into the wilderness to be tempted for forty days—and we start to focus on our need for discipline, prayer, and concentration in our spiritual lives.

Crosby knew about discipline and prayer from a unique perspective: She was blind from childhood. Some doctors believed that a treatment of her eyes, when she was a baby, damaged them and rendered her blind. Others have imagined that her blindness was congenital and simply went unnoticed by her parents in the first months. Either way, this remarkable girl began life in a special kind of darkness.

At fourteen, her mother enrolled Fanny in a school for the blind, and there she learned to play the organ, piano, harp, and guitar. Her mother also encouraged her to memorize the Bible, which Fanny did after hearing it read out loud, and by the time she was a teenager she knew the Gospels by heart.

I would never wish to be blind, but I wish to focus in prayer these next forty days like I've never focused before. You see, Crosby once remarked, "If perfect earthly sight were offered me tomorrow, I would not accept it. I might not have sung hymns to the praise of God if I had been distracted by the beautiful and interesting things about me."

I want to bring my life into Your focus these next forty days, Lord.
—JON SWEENEY

Digging Deeper: ROM 8:5; COL 3:2; HEB 10:19–25

Thu 6

Therefore, if anyone is in Christ, the new creation has come: The old has gone, the new is here!
—2 Corinthians 5:17 (NIV)

It's amazing what a few gallons of butter-yellow paint can do for your soul. As I stepped out of a difficult year that included financial hardship and a painful divorce, I wanted my home to reflect not only my survival, but also my hope and renewed joy.

I got rid of every painting and hung up blank white canvases waiting for colors and inspiration. Old photos were taken down and new ones were framed. My dingy linoleum floors were covered by bright laminate wood, and the dining room chairs were newly dressed in dark, childproof upholstery.

As my home was undergoing its slow rebirth, I asked advice from carpenters who had come to my church on a missions trip from North Carolina. "I'm thinking of building a loft bed for my boys," I said. I wanted them to have space for all their toys. "Is it safe to use my old bed frame to build it?"

"Why don't you wait till we get back to New York City next month?" they responded.

I waited and painted my sons' walls the color of sunny skies, and when the team finally returned they had a surprise waiting for me: the loft bed! I was overwhelmed by their generosity and love. As they installed the bed, I could feel God's hand in it. He'd done so much to transform me on the inside and now He was helping me transform everything else.

Lord, thank You for the gift of renewal.
—Karen Valentin

Digging Deeper: Rom 12:2; 1 Pt 1:13

Fri 7

"Stop judging by mere appearances, but instead judge correctly."
—John 7:24 (NIV)

Driving home from work, I glanced into my rearview mirror to see a beautiful pink sky. It looked like another great sunset.

I turned onto my street and noticed three young teenage boys hanging out two doors down from where I live. *Too bad they won't notice this great sunset*, I thought.

I pulled into my driveway and walked inside. My husband, Johnny, called out from the backyard, "Beautiful sunset tonight! Come on out!"

The sky had turned a bright crimson red with streaks of leftover pink etched through it. I glanced to where the boys were still talking. "Those boys have no clue that there is a magnificent sunset happening right before their eyes! Too bad," I said, shaking my head.

At that moment, I heard one of them call out, "Hey, guys, check it out! The sky's all red! It looks awesome!"

"Wow!" the others exclaimed in unison. "Cool!"

"Oh my," I said, dismayed, "I sure jumped to a mighty quick conclusion."

Later that evening, I read an inspirational quote that comes daily to my in-box: "When you're forming your opinions, do it carefully—go slow; hasty judgments oft are followed by regretting—that I know. —Anon."

After work the next day, I saw the boys again. I pulled the car over and rolled down the window. "Hey, guys," I called out, "great sunset last night, huh?"

"Yes, ma'am!" they all replied. One of the boys held up his cell phone. "I got a really good picture of it on my phone. Want to see?"

"Sure," I said with a big smile. "I'd love to."

Forgive me, Lord, for I truly want to see the best in everyone—
right from the start.
—Melody Bonnette Swang

Digging Deeper: Prv 12:18, 31:26

Sat 8

Gracious words are like a honeycomb, sweetness to the soul. . . .
—Proverbs 16:24 (ESV)

The bustling Grand Bazaar in Istanbul, Turkey, enticed us with acres of unique souvenirs and gifts. After several hours of shopping, I had found perfect gifts, including both rose and pistachio *lokum* (Turkish delight), a sweet jellied candy. Our last stop was a textiles stall to buy a scarf for my son. I chose variegated gray cotton and handed the young clerk ten lira. Simultaneously, my host offered to include the scarf in his purchase. I thanked him but declined. The clerk whisked himself away to make change and bag our choices.

When he returned, he offered change to my host but not to me. "You took your money back," he insisted. I distinctly remembered seeing the bill in his hand, so I pursued the matter until the proprietor approached.

"This is a busy place with every day much confusion, so we have a video camera." He pointed overhead. "Please to come upstairs. We will watch the video, then we will have agreement." I knew I was right and chafed at the wasted time.

My host duly viewed the video and returned with the scarf seller who spoke first: "You must be very tired." That was all.

My host whispered, "You took your money back. I saw it." I burned in embarrassment, too stunned to offer an apology to this gracious young man who took no offense at my mistake but instead offered empathy.

Back home, the Turkish delight was a big hit. However, the sweetness of the kind scarf seller will stay with me for a long time.

*Father, forgive us our trespasses as we forgive our trespassers—
with sweetness.*
—Gail Thorell Schilling

Digging Deeper: Jn 15:12; 1 Pt 3:8

Sun 9

"As long as the earth endures, seedtime and harvest, cold and heat, summer and winter, day and night will never cease."
—Genesis 8:22 (NIV)

As I walked to my mom's house next door, I looked at the silhouettes of birds in the trees with the sun setting behind them. The road was still warm beneath my bare feet, and my leg muscles were tired from hours spent doing yard work and clearing the garden for winter (or "putting it to bed" as my husband calls it).

Blackbirds rested on the stark branches, watching me until I was just beneath them, and then they flew away in a rush of energy. Today was warm. The sun bright. Most of our trees have lost their leaves, but our maple by the barn was holding on, wearing its marvelous colors like an ornate cloak.

"Sabra, put shoes on!" the neighbor shouted from her doorway. "It's nearly winter, don't you know?"

This is our joke. Every season she notices my feet and my tendency to be barefoot as long as possible. In March she calls out, "It must be spring! You don't have shoes on!" And then when the snow falls, she yells, "Oh no, look at those boots! We must be in for a long winter."

With each step, I feel the warm tarry road beneath my feet. In a week or two, I'll be wearing big thick socks and warm shoes. For now, I take in the beauty of a sunny path and hold it as a gift to help me through the long winter ahead.

Dear Lord, may I always be mindful of the beauty in every season You have placed beneath my feet.
—Sabra Ciancanelli

Digging Deeper: Ps 19:1; Eccl 3:1–4

LIFE LESSONS FROM THOSE I'VE MET

Mon 10

O that today you would hearken to his voice!
—Psalm 95:7 (RSV)

MARIA, INSPIRATION BEHIND HOLY ANGELS HOME

Maria was nine in 1965 when I first wrote about her, a bright, little girl with an impish smile. Born hydrocephalic, without legs, a "vegetable" who could not survive, she'd dumbfounded experts and become the inspiration behind a home for infants with multiple handicaps. Now I was back at Holy Angels in North Carolina to celebrate Maria's fiftieth birthday.

I had to trot to keep up with Maria's motorized wheelchair through a maze of new buildings, home now for adults as well as infants. At each stop, Maria introduced me to staff and volunteers who simply exuded joy.

And yet the people they were caring for had such cruel limitations! How could everyone seem so happy, I asked, working day after day with people who'll never speak, never hold a spoon, never sit up alone?

"None of us would be happy," Maria said, "if we looked way off into the future like that." Here, she explained, they looked for what God was doing in each life, just that one day. "That's where God is for all of us, you know. Just in what's happening right now."

How intently one would learn to look, I thought, *to spot the little victories.* In my life too.... What if I memorized just the first stanza of Millay's "Renascence"? What if I understood just one more function on my iPhone? What if just one morning I didn't comment about my husband's snoring?

"Thank you, Maria," I said as we hugged good-bye, "for showing me the God of the little victories."

Through what small victory, Father, will You show me Yourself today?
—Elizabeth Sherrill

Digging Deeper: Ps 118:24; Mt 6:34

Tue 11

"For the mouth speaks what the heart is full of."
—Luke 6:45 (NIV)

One morning before a church meeting, I made the sign of the cross over my mouth as a quick prayer to keep me from saying negative or critical things. All went well until the end, when we discussed trying a new form of worship. Suddenly, a quick criticism fell right out of my mouth: "The powers that be won't like it, and they'll probably veto it." I immediately felt a twinge of guilt, but I pretended nothing was wrong.

After the meeting I knew it was time to visit the prayer chapel. As I knelt, I recalled that last Sunday in class we'd seen a video where the speaker had two glasses filled to the brim with beads. When he knocked them together, several beads popped out of both of them because of the impact. The speaker explained that we can't blame other people for bringing out the worst in us because nothing can come out of us that's not already in there to begin with. I left the chapel knowing I had been forgiven, but I still felt I'd let down God and myself.

Driving home, I hit road-construction traffic and turned off on a street I rarely take. As I was passing a church, my eye caught a message board sign out front. "Jesus still loves you" was all it said. I let out a deep cleansing breath, thankful that not only are God's mercies new every morning but so is His unchanging love.

Dear Jesus, show me the hidden places inside of me where I need Your mercies every morning, so I can live better days for You. Amen.

—Karen Barber

Digging Deeper: Jl 2:12–13; Heb 4:16

Wed 12

Be ye strong therefore, and let not your hands be weak: for your work shall be rewarded.
—2 CHRONICLES 15:7 (KJV)

Five below and snowing hard. The alarm clock shatters my dreams. It's nights like this that make me want to run away from our family ranch and work at a resort in Hawaii. I shrug into my coat as I stagger out every half hour throughout the night to check on the newborn calves.

This is our version of March Madness: calving in abysmal spring weather that more closely resembles winter. We aren't completely insane; it must happen now to line up with the grass and the markets. We have to watch the herd closely. While we try not to intervene with the cattle's abilities to care for their young, we won't abandon them to nature.

Although I sometimes dream of leaving, I stay. We are each given unique talents with which we can serve the Lord. Some are called to teach. Some prophecy. I was placed here to tend the animals God created. It's a high honor. And, honestly, I wouldn't trade it for anything—not even a beach in Hawaii.

Lord, give me strength when I falter in the course You set for me.
Help me rise to the challenges in my path and do my utmost
for You and the life You have chosen for me.
—ERIKA BENTSEN

Digging Deeper: 1 CHR 16:11; PHIL 4:11–13

Thu 13

Blessed are they which do hunger and thirst after righteousness: for they shall be filled.
—MATTHEW 5:6 (KJV)

Hey, old man." It was my sister Keri on the line. "I can't believe you are about to turn forty."

Hearing those words rang hard in my head. How could I be forty? It was time for a reality check. I was passionate about my career. My son Harrison was a wellspring of joy, and six-month-old Mary Katherine had forever changed Corinne's and my life for the better.

Yet, I couldn't help but think about my shortcomings. Did I reach out to others or was I too self-centered? Was I giving back in proportion to what had been given to me? Was I mindful enough of the teachings of Jesus? Was I His defender? I tortured myself remembering that Dietrich Bonhoeffer and Dr. Martin Luther King Jr. achieved greatness before age forty. How could my life ever measure up to theirs?

My big day started with birthday calls, but by lunch I was feeling disappointed. How anticlimactic it seemed. In the afternoon, Corinne suggested we take a drive to a friend's farm. She led me to a converted barn and swung open the door.

"Surprise!" The room was filled with family and friends.

Toasts followed. One friend spoke of our work in Africa; another thanked me for helping his parents through a hard financial time; another mentioned my work in the inner city. *Small steps*, I thought. *Tiny acts far from greatness.*

But wait! Why am I treating forty as a deadline? What better age to begin again to make the world right, to reach out, to give, to defend God's rightness? Everything old turned new in that moment, and I was on my way.

Father, I want to do more than long for a better world. Come with me. Help me make it happen. —BROCK KIDD

Digging Deeper: GAL 6:9; EPH 2:10

Fri 14

Since God chose you . . . you must clothe yourselves with tenderhearted mercy. . . . —Colossians 3:12 (NLT)

Unrelenting screams drifted down the Jetway and through the plane as I searched for my seat. Scooting next to the window, I stuffed my long legs in place and looked up to see a mother wrestling a three-year-old boy—the source of the screams—into the seat next to mine. I closed my eyes. *God, this must be a mistake.*

In spite of the mother's trying to comfort her son, the screams escalated when the plane lurched back from the gate and rumbled down the runway. My ears throbbed. Staring out the window, I whined, *God, please shut him up.* Yet in my spirit I heard, "Help him." *But, God, I don't have anything to offer.* "Show him My mercy."

I groaned. A white jet stream zigzagged across the sky. I looked at the boy. "Can you see that cloud?" Tears streamed down his face. I continued. "That's a jet." The boy's brow furrowed. I asked, "Do you ever watch jets fly overhead?" He sniffled and nodded. I managed a smile. "Did you know that there are little boys watching us fly over? Let's wave at them."

His face brightened as he peered out the window, waved, and said, "Hi, little boys."

The rest of the trip he waved while his mother and I chatted. When we deplaned his mother said, "I sure am glad that you sat next to us."

I grinned. "Me too."

Lord, thank You for showing me the answer: Your mercy.
—Rebecca Ondov

Digging Deeper: Ps 86:5; Heb 4:16

Sat 15

Satisfy us in the morning with your unfailing love, that we may sing for joy and be glad.... —PSALM 90:14 (NIV)

A dear friend of mine is dying.

First he lost weight, and then hair, and then energy, and now it's sentences. He has a million words in his head, but now they are coming out on their own rather than in deft, wry, coherent sentences like over the last fifty years. He'll start a story and then it just sort of wanders off on its own. You have to laugh or else you would just cry all day.

He laughs, for which you have to give him major credit. Thank God for that. I think laughter will be the last thing to go because it was the first thing to arrive. His mom says he laughed all the time when he was a baby. His wife says she gets in bed and holds him a lot, and sometimes now he laughs so quietly you can't hear him laugh but you can *feel* him laugh if you are holding him in bed. What else can you do? You might as well laugh. That's how we started and that's how we will end, I guess. You could do a lot worse, she says.

Me, personally, I reply, more and more I think laughter is prayer. It's humble and appreciative and there's no ego in it. You can't be greedy and violent and arrogant when you are laughing, right? So I think we pray best when we laugh, honest and clean, and from the bottom of our bellies. My dear friend could curl up and weep here in his last days, but he doesn't. He laughs really quietly, with his wife holding him in the bed and laughing too, and I think that's brave and holy and sweet and holy.

Dear Lord, hold my friend in Your hand, okay? Please? Because I love that guy. I have loved that guy for fifty years. He grew warmer and gentler and funnier by the year, and You made him, and I miss him, and tell me quietly I'll see him again, okay? Please?

—BRIAN DOYLE

Digging Deeper: PHIL 3:20–21; RV 21:4

Sun 16

Moses built an altar and named it The Lord is My Banner.
—Exodus 17:15 (NAS)

When a younger friend wanted to have a mentoring Bible study with me, we selected a book on the names of God revealed throughout Scripture. Together, we discovered how God has made Himself known in names: *Creator, God Who Sees, God Most High, All-Sufficient One, the Lord Will Provide, the Lord Is Peace*, and many more. The one I especially like is *the Lord Is My Banner—Jehovah-nissi.* We learned that a banner in the days of the Israelite exodus from Egypt was not the flag we think of today, but a bare pole topped with a shiny ornament that glittered in the desert sun.

Early in their journey the Israelites refused to enter the land God had promised when scouts reported the inhabitants were "too strong" and "men of great size" (Numbers 13). But after Moses informed them that their lack of trust was going to cost them forty years of desert wandering, they rethought it.

The problem was, they decided on a course of action that did not include God. *Jehovah-nissi* was not out in front leading the way. The incident was disastrous for them, and they endured forty years of wilderness for failure to follow God.

There is a place where God shows His banner. If I am hesitant to follow—or off chasing something else—I could likely end up where I don't want to be. Going my own way once nearly cost me my family. God's *Jehovah-nissi* name is really about protection. God's way leads to the "path of life" (Psalm 16:11). In following, I am protected.

Lord, turn my eyes to where You are shining, and
I will have found my way.
—Carol Knapp

Digging Deeper: Mt 16:24; Jn 8:12

Mon 17

Let the nations be glad and sing for joy. . . .
—PSALM 67:4 (KJV)

My wife was poring over a map of Europe. "Look, Danny. My homeland is a tiny little country. I had no idea it was so small."

"I know, you could put maybe half a dozen Irelands inside the state of Texas."

It may be small, but Ireland has made a huge impression on the world. More than a dozen US presidents and some thirty-four million Americans trace their roots to Ireland, including my own auburn bride. Officially, Saint Patrick's Day honors the missionary who came to Ireland about 1,600 years ago. There he started hundreds of churches and baptized thousands, thus raising the moral profile of Ireland. But most of his life is a mystery and forgotten.

Unofficially, Saint Patrick's Day is everybody's opportunity to be Irish for a day, regardless of religion or nationality. By the simple act of wearing green, I can be lucky or bonny or practice a bit of blarney. In short, I can be happy for a day.

There are many ways to celebrate the day. Some daring types dye their hair green or wear shamrock tattoos. Others march in parades or attend Irish festivals, where they dance an Irish jig or enjoy an Irish stew. More serious types demonstrate for green causes or go to spiritual retreats, where they pray for missionaries.

Yes, I will wear green today, so I don't get pinched. And I will listen to some fine Irish music, starting with my favorite, "Danny Boy." I will also pray for some of my former students who are currently missionaries in Ireland. Most of all, I will try to be happy for the day. That's what it's really all about, isn't it? And if I can be happy for one day, why not every day?

There is much to be happy about, God. Help me find a reason to sing with joy every day. —DANIEL SCHANTZ

Digging Deeper: Ps 16:9; Is 55:12

March

Tue 18

"You're blessed when you're at the end of your rope. With less of you there is more of God and his rule."
—Matthew 5:3 (MSG)

"What is God doing in your life right now?" the e-mail asked in the Subject line. "Share your answer at our women's ministry meeting tonight."

Normally that kind of question energizes me, but this morning it frustrated me because I had no answer. Besides, I didn't want to go to the meeting. I'd been in a funk lately and not dealing well with the ongoing adjustments to my husband's brain cancer issues. I didn't want to talk to anyone about it and felt way too needy to be a productive member of a group tonight.

I turned off my computer and headed for the door. Going for a walk often helped me sort through my feelings, so off I headed, down the street and onto a well-worn path across a field. Soon God's words started echoing through my head. "I am the way" through hard places and adjustments in life. "I am the way" through frustration when you have your head in the freezer, trying to figure out what's wrong with the ice maker.

Shortly after I got home, the phone rang. It was my daughter Lindsay, who was going to the meeting. "Can I pick you up tonight?" she asked.

"I'd like that," I answered without hesitating. I wasn't sure why I changed my mind, but I really wanted to go now.

That night, I had an answer when it came my turn. "What is God doing in my life right now? Reminding me that patience or kindness or hope doesn't come out of my own strength, but out of walking and talking with Him."

Lord, spending time with You changes me.
—Carol Kuykendall

Digging Deeper: Jn 14:6, 15:1–11

Wed 19

"It will produce branches and bear fruit and become a splendid cedar. . . ." —Ezekiel 17:23 (NIV)

I e-mailed my siblings: "Prayers appreciated for a talk I'm giving on Thursday afternoon." Several responded, relaying the sentiment "God is with you, and so are we."

At the appointed hour, I encouraged participants to compare their prayers to trees. I displayed photographs and artists' renderings of gnarly olive trees, weeping willows, deserted palms, orange-laden orchards. . . .

I handed out colored pencils and suggested they draw a tree that represented their recent prayers. "Imagine Jesus as the trunk—the core 'vine'—and your prayers as the branches. Then consider the big picture: Whom is your prayer tree shading or protecting? Where is it in the seasonal cycles—producing hopeful spring blossoms or mature fruit? Do your prayer-branches reach for the sky in praise or bend close to the ground with requests? Is your tree in a solitary setting, or do you prefer praying when you're surrounded by peers, as in a grove?"

Eventually I asked them to explain their pictures. A husband had sketched two leafy trees side by side, representing his prayers with his wife. A mother had envisioned a passel of umbrella-shaped twigs, symbolizing parental prayers of protection.

When I was packing up, a woman who'd held back earlier showed me a nearly hidden detail of her flourishing tree. At the base of the trunk, underneath grassy cover, she'd outlined deep roots. "They represent the grounding of my family, my upbringing."

"Oh my!" I smiled. "You introduced a whole new dimension."

I drove home with a revitalized prayer—like limbs stretching upward with thanksgiving—for my natal family and many others who have enriched my relationship with God.

Lord, thank You for the grounding of my faith through my family and the family of God. —Evelyn Bence

Digging Deeper: Ps 103:17–18; Prv 22:6

Thu 20

"And remember, I am with you always. . . ."
—Matthew 28:20 (NRSV)

Like many five-year-olds, Frances is afraid of the dark. She wants her blinds left open, her door ajar, and a light on. Even so, she dreads going to bed. "I don't want to close my eyes, Daddy." She crawled into bed and clutched her blanket. Her lip quivered.

I groped for something to say. What I wanted to communicate to Frances was that with God watching over her there was nothing to fear. But that was such an abstract idea.

Suddenly, I thought of the fun time we'd had after dinner, listening to some music. At one point I'd looked over at the kitchen table and watched Frances bent industriously over her coloring book. She looked up at me and smiled. "I love this song, Daddy," she said. "It makes me happy."

Sitting on the edge of her bed, I reached over and stroked her hair. "Remember when we were in the kitchen and Mom and I were doing the dishes while you and Benji played?" I asked. She nodded. "That was fun, right?" She nodded again. "Well, that was God's love we were all feeling. And that love is right here in this room with you now. It never goes away."

Frances made her concentrating face. She didn't say anything, but I could tell my words were connecting. "You think you can close your eyes and try to sleep now?" She nodded. I bent down and kissed her forehead. She closed her eyes. "God is with you," I whispered as I stood to go. This time I knew she understood.

God, help me to see You in all things.
—Jim Hinch

Digging Deeper: Dt 31:6; Ps 23

Fri 21

He heals the brokenhearted and binds up their wounds.
—Psalm 147:3 (NIV)

It had been more than a year since our son Paul was in a car accident, an accident so brutal it severely injured all involved—and killed a passenger in the other car. Paul's physical recovery was amazing, given the extent of his neck injuries. Within three months, he was back at the office, driving two hours round-trip to work, and working out in the gym. However, Elba and I wondered how he was doing emotionally. We were constantly praying, "Lord, help our son express his emotions from the accident. Heal him on the inside as well."

One evening, I inquired how the civil case was going. "Paul, did you call the lawyer?" "No," he replied. I pressed on: "You know, it is important that you call him and stay up to date on this matter." I sensed his lack of interest in the topic. I persisted: "Paul, you need to be responsible and reach out to him." The look in his eyes told me that I had crossed the line.

Standing tall with tears in his eyes and anger in his voice, he said, "I just want this thing to be over with."

His mom quickly responded, "Paul, we know that you are struggling and want to put all of this behind you. How can we help you?" There was a long pause. He finally answered, sharing his feelings for the first time since the accident, grieving for everyone affected—particularly the deceased.

Our prayers were answered: We now knew how much Paul had been hurting. This was the beginning of his emotional healing.

Lord, heal my hurts, especially those deep within me,
unknown to those around me.
—Pablo Diaz

Digging Deeper: Ps 103:2–4; Jer 17:14

Sat 22

O Lord, you have freed me from my bonds and I will serve you forever. —Psalm 116:16 (TLB)

When I volunteered to be an usher at the Largo Cultural Center, our local venue for concerts, plays, and musicals, I was excited that I'd get to see professional entertainment for free.

I arrived at my first gig, quickly found out where the ushers were to sit for the performance, and was happy I'd be able to see it without any problem.

When the show began, I noticed an old woman with her walker, sitting in front of me. Midway through the lively concert, the woman turned and whispered, "Do you know where the restroom is?"

I thought about the two big double-doors leading out of the theater, the wide lobby, and the two doors into the ladies room and knew she couldn't navigate all that herself. "Would you like me to take you?" I asked, feeling a little miffed that I'd miss some of the show.

"Oh yes, thank you."

Inside the restroom, I made lively conversation, handed her dry paper towels, and opened the doors as she scooted out. "How long have you been ushering?" she asked.

"Tonight is my very first night."

"Well, I guess I picked the right usher to ask where the bathroom is," she said, giggling.

Suddenly, my angst about missing some of the concert evaporated. At that moment, I learned that my job wasn't to find the best seat in the usher section but to make sure that all of the patrons were comfortable, seated, and I could be counted on should anyone need anything.

Father, thank You for giving me the opportunity to be a servant to others, for it truly does come back to me a hundredfold.

—Patricia Lorenz

Digging Deeper: Mt 20:16; Mk 9:33–35

Sun 23

. . . Forgetting those things which are behind and reaching forward to those things which are ahead.
—PHILIPPIANS 3:13 (NKJV)

Chuck Lawrence is the minister at Christ Temple Church in Huntington, West Virginia. He's also an accomplished musician and songwriter. In the 1980s, he wrote "He Grew the Tree," which won a variety of accolades, including several Dove Awards. Barbara Mandrell recorded the sacred song about Calvary, which spoke of God nurturing the very tree that would become the old rugged cross.

But today in his sermon Chuck had a different take on his accomplishment. He referred to Philippians 3:13, which says we are to forget those things that are behind us. "I believe that means even the good things. In 1982 I wrote 'He Grew the Tree,' but it's not supposed to be my pinnacle. God wants us to look forward with anticipation to each new day."

Chuck's words gave me pause. The 1980s were banner years for me too. I wrote for ten home-decorating magazines, where my byline was featured. Now, given the many changes in the publishing industry, I'm hard-pressed to find even one of my own articles. Chuck was urging me to look forward—not to yesterday, but to now, glorious today.

Today's a brand-new era, Lord. Help me
to really look forward to it. Amen.
—ROBERTA MESSNER

Digging Deeper: JER 29:11; PHIL 3

Mon 24

"I was hungry and you gave me food. . . ."
—MATTHEW 25:35 (RSV)

I sat through lunch at the usual eatery, hoping the woman would be gone when I walked back to the office. The sight of her was just too upsetting: a disheveled-looking mom at the top of the subway steps, begging with her two young children in tow.

"If she's gone when I go back, I won't have to do anything," I told myself. I'd be off the hook. But just the image of her had kept me on the hook. Why weren't her children in school? Where did they live?

"I shouldn't give her anything because she's probably an addict," I rationalized. People who know more about these things than I do tell me beggars will take whatever money you give them and use it for drugs or alcohol. But what about her kids? They weren't addicts. They were wearing clean T-shirts, jeans, their hair braided with beads. "I'll pray for them," I told myself. But to leave it at that seemed like a cop-out.

Maybe they're there because God wants you do something, Rick. Not just for them but also for you. The poor and hungry should not just be ignored.

I swallowed the rest of my sandwich and went to the counter to buy some more food. Not for myself this time.

I carried my bag and rounded the corner. She was still there. "What's your name?" I asked the woman.

"Dolores," she said.

"Dolores, this is for you." I gave her the food and promised to pray for her.

Back at the office I put her name on a note with the names of the other people I pray for. I've never been good about praying for big concepts like hunger or the poor, but now I had these three faces and one name.

Harden not my heart, Lord, from the pain in the world.
Let me know how I can relieve it.
—RICK HAMLIN

Digging Deeper: MT 25:31–46; 2 COR 1:3–4

Tue 25

Joy cometh in the morning. —PSALM 30:5 (KJV)

It is early morning as I make my way through the unlit house, moving toward the smell of fresh brewing coffee. I have always liked the quiet dark before daybreak.

In the kitchen, the air is chilly, telling me that I missed closing the window the night before. Now, through the opened window, I hear a lone bird singing: "*Purdy . . . purdy . . . purdy . . .*" It fills the kitchen, so I sit down at the table and listen. And then a second sound: "*What-cheer . . . what-cheer . . . what-cheer . . .*" And a third: "*Chewick . . . chewick . . . .*" Soon there's a symphony of birdsong greeting the dawn!

Later, as I go full throttle into the day, I think of the bird who led the way, how he sang because he could, how the other birds followed. Stopping by the shoe shop, I dash in to pick up my favorite clogs. I notice the smell of leather and polish and the sound of a sewing machine whirring. Somehow, the shop seems beautiful. I call out to the repairman, "I want you to know how much I appreciate your work! These are the most comfortable shoes imaginable . . . and you've given them new life."

A smile spreads across his face. And as I leave the shop, I hear a second customer adding, "You know, she's right. You do a mighty good job."

That night, I was careful to leave the window opened to whatever possibilities a new day might offer. If one lone bird can claim the moment with his optimistic song, then whatever comes tomorrow, surely I can find a way to do the same.

Father, I don't want to skim over the days You give me. Help me to listen, to live deeply, and to give with great joy.

—PAM KIDD

Digging Deeper: ROM 15:13; GAL 5:22

Wed 26

He gives food to every creature. His love endures forever.
—Psalm 136:25 (NIV)

It was an impossible choice: Adopt a rescue dog or pick out a puppy? At first, the answer had been clear. Brian and I finally had a fenced-in backyard, and we could give a home to a dog in need. We monitored the rescue Web sites, waiting to find our perfect pup.

Finally, tired of waiting for direction or guidance, we headed to north Georgia, where one litter of puppies was ready to leave their mom. As we looked for the rural address, we got a call—a miracle, really—in an area with little cell reception. It was the adoption agency telling us they had an eighteen-month-old golden retriever named Colby who was perfectly healthy, homeless, and ready to be loved. I told her we'd think about it as we pulled into the driveway of the puppies' house.

Brian and I spent the next hour surrounded by impossibly furry bundles of energy whose teeth were so small we couldn't even feel them gnawing on our shoes. We held them, snuggled them, then looked at each other and knew: These pups weren't for us.

We hopped in the car and headed for Atlanta, where we found Colby waiting for us. When we walked in the room, he came over and sat down between us, as if he'd known he was ours all along.

As I often do, I tried to rush God's plan, forcing a litter of puppies to fit into the hole in our family made just right for Colby. God allowed me to follow my own path but then gently nudged me back.

As we packed Colby into the car and headed home, he crawled into my lap and I knew that this decision—God's decision—had been right all along.

Lord, thank You for the love animals bring into our lives. We are blessed!
—Ashley Kappel

Digging Deeper: Gn 1:21; Ps 145:9

Thu 27

All my longings lie open before you, Lord; my sighing is not hidden from you. —Psalm 38:9 (NIV)

It was a rough start to the day. Spiritually, I was feeling flat. There were a few things that I really wanted for my family and my career. My prayers had turned repetitive. I felt like a broken record as I laid them before the Lord once again. And just like every other morning, I came up against a deafening silence that made me want to scream.

Not only that, but my son woke up at 5:30 AM—much too early. It didn't take long for my sweet little boy to turn into a monster, the kind that whines and cries and throws temper tantrums and makes messes everywhere he goes. The kid was tired.

With expiring patience, I carried him to his room and made him lie down while he screamed and cried and did everything humanly possible to get out of that bed. I sat outside his room, resting my head against the wall, and heard every single one of his heartbreaking cries for Mama. He wanted to get up, go to the park, play. But that's not what was best for him. He needed sleep.

After a thirty-minute battle, he finally gave in. The house was quiet. As I sat there in the silence, I couldn't help but think how similar I was to my son, crying out to my *Abba*, mistaking His silence for absence, unable to see that He was right there. God knows what's best and He knows what He's doing.

Thank You, Lord, for the promise that You hear every single one of our sighs, for being a God Who says no for the sake of a better yes.

—Katie Ganshert

Digging Deeper: Is 55:8–9; Mt 6:25–34

March

Fri 28

"Therefore do not worry about tomorrow, for tomorrow will worry about itself. Each day has enough trouble of its own."
—MATTHEW 6:34 (NIV)

Each summer I have the opportunity to give a keynote speech at a big conference. It's a lot of fun and significant to my career.

Pretty much from the second I walk offstage, I start brainstorming about what I will say in my speech the following year and continue to do so until the next summer rolls around. It's exciting to look forward to that speech! And I'm not worrying, after all. Worry is anticipating negative events; the conference is a positive.

A few days ago I was blindsided by the news that I was not invited to speak there this summer. After the initial wave of disappointment, the first thing I thought of was how much I had been consumed by the conference all year. Taken together, it must have been many hours, if not days—time I could have been thoughtfully engaged in that day's activities.

Worry is, at best, a waste of time and, at worst, a destructive downward spiral of negative thinking because the things we worry about often don't happen. This experience with the conference is teaching me that planning and fantasy—what we might call "positive worry"—isn't much better. The things I am looking forward to sometimes don't happen either, and if I fritter away hours in endless fantasy, I am misplacing my attention, missing out on what God has given me today, and not trusting Him to provide for me tomorrow.

Lord, please let me trust You with all of my hopes and fears.
—JOSHUA SUNDQUIST

Digging Deeper: MT 6:27; PHIL 4:6

Sat 29

My strength and power are made perfect—fulfilled and completed and show themselves most effective—in [your] weakness. . . . —2 CORINTHIANS 12:9 (AMP)

Opening my eyes, I knew immediately it would be another day without energy. My autoimmune diseases can render me almost helpless sometimes.

I made it to the recliner in the living room and stared out the window. The grass had turned bright green, seemingly overnight. Bluebirds and robins were excited. Thor, our yellow Labrador, slept in a spot of morning sun on the porch. Three red tulips bloomed by the birdbath. Tiny, brave buds dotted branches of dogwood trees, and the sky was a cloudless blue.

I wanted to wash the sheets and hang them out in the sun; throw the ball with an eager Thor; let my thirteen-year-old cat Girlfriend venture outside with me. Nothing major, just stuff most people could complete quickly without a second thought.

I don't think I can stand being a shut-in again, I complained to myself.

Wait until you are endued with power from on high (Luke 24:49).

God, is that You speaking to me about my mundane desires?

Wait until you are endued with power from on high, Marion.

Oh, Lord, please endue (I love that word) me with Your power from on high.

A short time later, I tugged the king-size sheets off our bed, washed, and hung them on the banister of the back porch. Girlfriend came outside and chewed on the new, green grass. An excited Thor trotted over to me with a ball in his mouth.

As I tossed it, the warm sun brushed my face like a gentle touch. A breeze stirred up the sweet aroma of a tea olive tree, and anticipation found me.

Oh, Father, forgive me for not calling on You more quickly.
—MARION BOND WEST

Digging Deeper: Pss 46:1–2, 121:1–3

Sun 30

Great are the works of the Lord; they are pondered by all who delight in them. —Psalm 111:2 (NIV)

The church I attend recently celebrated its 150th anniversary. It's been a festive year, replete with special dinners, panel discussions, and a book on the church's history.

But what amazed me even more were all the little stories that formed the big story—those quiet, individual witnesses of faith who, taken together, made up this grand sweep of 150 years. One woman has been a member for nearly half the church's life. Fifty-two Sundays times seven decades is how many church services? "You've heard thousands of sermons!" I said. "What do you remember about the best ones?"

She smiled. "The best sermons are the ones I think about all week. Because then I know God is working in me."

That simple lesson of faith was the start of a new practice for me. When I hear a phrase or sentence in a sermon that especially strikes me, I'll write it down on the bulletin or on whatever I have handy. (Once it was the palm of my hand!) Then I pin that phrase to the bulletin board behind my computer. This week's was: *May God give me the grace to understand that the world is too small for anything but Love.* I see it every day, reminding me to ponder how I might live that message.

Like my friend at church, I've been able to see in a new way how God is working in my life—all week long.

Guide my life, God, by Your Words; that in hearing them,
I may live according to Your wishes.
—Jeff Japinga

Digging Deeper: Pss 105, 111, 119:18; 1 Pt 2:2

Mon 31

He leadeth me beside the still waters. He restoreth my soul. . . . —PSALM 23:2–3 (KJV)

I grew up on a farm, doing chores after school and helping with garden or livestock during the summer. I worked hard as a farm wife and mother, and later held a demanding job with a church social service agency. Although I'm now retired, I'm still most comfortable with a never-ending to-do list.

That's why I said *no* when my husband, Don, asked me to attend a business conference with him. "There wouldn't be anything for me to do," I explained. "The resort brochure lists golf as the main draw, and I don't play." Don didn't give up, so I reluctantly packed my suitcase and off we went.

The hotel was surrounded by the golf course. There were four swimming pools, but the daytime temperatures were in the low sixties. For the first time in years I had nothing to do. No schedule, no phone calls, no meetings.

To my great surprise, I enjoyed it! I read the entire newspaper and worked both crossword puzzles. I ate lunch outdoors amid an improbable but stunning landscape of palm trees and pines, grape hyacinths, honeysuckle, and a dozen types of cacti. Afternoons, I walked the easier trails, sat in the sunshine, and watched ducks paddle around a pond. Since there was nothing productive I could do, I didn't feel guilty about not doing it.

The best part, though, was the lesson I took home: God speaks most clearly when I don't *do*; I simply *be*.

Heavenly Father, thank You for teaching me to still my soul.
—PENNEY SCHWAB

Digging Deeper: Ps 46:10

March

DAILY MERCIES

1 ____________________

2 ____________________

3 ____________________

4 ____________________

5 ____________________

6 ____________________

7 ____________________

8 ____________________

9 ____________________

10 ____________________

11 ____________________

12 ____________________

13 ____________________

14 ____________________

15 ____________________

16 ________

17 ________

18 ________

19 ________

20 ________

21 ________

22 ________

23 ________

24 ________

25 ________

26 ________

27 ________

28 ________

29 ________

30 ________

31 ________

APRIL

Praised be the Abba God of our Savior Jesus Christ, who with great mercy gave us new birth: a birth into hope, which draws its life from the resurrection of Jesus Christ from the dead.

—1 PETER 1:3 (TIB)

LIFE LESSONS FROM THOSE I'VE MET

Tue 1 *In your light we see light.* —PSALM 36:9 (NIV)

ELENA ZELAYETA, BLIND CHEF

Without warning at age thirty-six, Elena Zelayeta, pregnant with her second child, totally lost her sight.

She had been the chef at a popular restaurant she and her husband owned. A sixty-seven-year-old widow now, she continued to prepare her famous Mexican dishes, marketing them with the help of her two sons, the younger of whom she'd never seen.

Typical of San Francisco, it was raining when I arrived at her home. The door was opened by a very short, very broad woman with a smile like the sun. Well under five feet tall, "and wide as I am high," she said, she led me on a fast-paced tour of the sizable house, ending in the kitchen, where pots bubbled and a frying pan sizzled.

Was it possible that this woman who moved so swiftly and surely, who was now so unhesitatingly dishing up the meal she'd prepared for the two of us, really blind? She *must* see, dimly at least, the outlines of things.

At the door to the dining room, Elena paused, half a dozen dishes balanced on her arms. "Is the light on?" she asked.

No, she confirmed, not the faintest glimmer of light had she seen in thirty years. But she smiled as she said it. "I hear the rain," she went on as she expertly carved the herb-crusted chicken, "and I'm sure it's a gray day for the sighted. But for us blind folk, when we walk with God, the sun is always shining."

Let me walk in Your light, Lord, whatever the weather of the world.
—ELIZABETH SHERRILL

Digging Deeper: Ps 97:11; 1 Jn 1:5

Wed 2

Remember now your Creator in the days of your youth, before the difficult days come, and the years draw near when you say, "I have no pleasure in them."
—ECCLESIASTES 12:1 (NKJV)

I was making rounds at the veterans hospital where I work, when an elderly gentleman in a wheelchair pointed his cane to a sign on a bulletin board. "Look, hon," he said to his wife, "they're having an old-fashioned Easter egg hunt on Saturday. It says here that the kids can compete in a bunny-hop sack race for prizes." He barely came up for air. "Remember when we used to have those Easter egg hunts on our farm? The kids would color eggs at our kitchen table and get dye all over everything."

Just then, his wife noticed the smell of popcorn in the air. Volunteers sell it for a bargain price—fifty cents a sack. The veteran didn't miss a beat. "Remember when we used to have movie night and you would pop corn? We've got to start doing that again, hon. I love popcorn. Movies too."

As I took in this amazingly joyful man, I thought of things I used to be able to do before neurofibromatosis took over my body. It was nothing to run a couple of miles; I walked everywhere.

Instead of rejoicing in the past, I too often complain about my restrictions. Rather than marvel how I always used to walk downtown, shopping, I complain about having to use a handicap placard on my car so I can park close to the mall, which I complain about as well.

But today, with all my heart, I want to be like that veteran and remember my yesterdays with joy.

Help me, dear Lord, to recall the past with pleasure.
—ROBERTA MESSNER

Digging Deeper: EPH 4:29; PHIL 2:14

A NEW WAY TO SERVE

Thu 3 *The Lord bless you and keep you; the Lord make his face to shine upon you, and be gracious to you.*
—Numbers 6:24–25 (NRSV)

BEARING THE BURDEN OF LOVE

I'm not what you'd call a natural volunteer. I'm just not social enough. I'm too quiet. Given the choice between feeding the hungry and clothing the needy by dropping off canned goods and clothes at a charity or serving meals and passing out socks at a soup kitchen, I'd choose the drop-off.

However, challenged by Christ's teachings, I started volunteering at St. James Shelter to try to do some good. But as the song says, something happened along the way. The people I met—from Judy and Celida to my Scrabble partner Ben and those in my book group—have lodged in my heart. I didn't intend for this to happen. It's no fun wondering if someone you love is being beaten after returning to her abusive husband. Or if the foster parents of the eighteen-year-old who loves books will let him come home now that the state has stopped paying them. Or if the man you talked into entering his eighth recovery program will make it this time.

I love these people. I'm still not sure I wanted that to happen. But I'm pretty sure God did.

Lord, give me the strength to bear the burden of love.
—Marci Alborghetti

Digging Deeper: Col 3:14; 1 Pt 4:8; 1 Jn 4:7

Fri 4

"God has dealt graciously with me and . . . I have plenty."
—Genesis 33:11 (NAS)

I have to be out of town," my rabbi said, "and we got this request from the Congregational Church for someone to speak about Shabbat (the Jewish Sabbath) for their adult ed series during Lent."

My best friend, Bonnie, agonized over what to give up for Lent and I'm not sure what our Shabbat had to do with it, but I was game for interfaith work and agreed to speak. The pastor said there would be breakout groups who would need something to take away and reflect on, something meaningful for their Lenten preparation.

I could say something about the Torah origins of Shabbat; I could give some indication of the hundreds of years of arguments about the rules governing the weekly observance; I could explain the ritual objects involved in our home celebration. But what was there for the church members to meditate on that could enrich them during Lent? What kind of new perspective could I suggest?

"There's one rule for Shabbat that's very hard for me to follow," I told them at my presentation. "We're not supposed to say prayers of petition or ask for anything for ourselves on the Sabbath. On Shabbat, we're supposed to remember that God provides everything we need, no matter what we think we lack or what we've lost or given up."

The congregation seemed to really respond to that, and they were eager to workshop about it. And I would pray on that as well.

Teach me to remember, God, that You will give me the words to say, just as You give me everything else.
—Rhoda Blecker

Digging Deeper: Dt 8:3; Ps 37:25

Sat 5

But everything comes from God.
—1 Corinthians 11:12 (NIV)

My children have outgrown the neighborhood Easter egg hunt. Unable to slip in unnoticed between the five-year-olds, Maggie took on a one-hour slot as a face painter and Stephen was an official egg hider. I had to rush off to work backstage at Mary's ballet performances, so I dropped off the kids and headed to the grocery store to pick up a halftime snack for Maggie's afternoon soccer game, which I was not attending. I brought home the clementines and bananas, pausing to write out a list of what to take (asthma inhaler, water bottle, shin guards) and a note detailing who was picking up Maggie.

While hurrying to the subway, it occurred to me that this schedule was insane. Before I knew it, I was backstage, fixing costumes and hooking bodices in the wings. During the break between performances, I went out for coffee and laughed with some of the other parents. And then I had fifteen minutes with nothing to do and nowhere to be.

I walked along West 60th Street, enjoying the cool air . . . alone. My heart lifted, and I murmured, "Thank You, God. Thank You for egg hunts, face paint, soccer, pointe shoes, coffee, and all the good things in today that aren't necessary for salvation." And then it hit me: Almost everything I ever say thank you for isn't necessary for salvation, which is an interesting measure of God's goodness.

Jesus, thank You for all You give me—over and above grace—
that I neither earn nor deserve.
—Julia Attaway

Digging Deeper: Jn 1:16; Jas 1:17

Sun 6

. . . That God will open up to us a door for the word, so that we may speak forth the mystery of Christ. . . .
—Colossians 4:3 (NAS)

Because of a staffing snag, our church's teen class on Sundays had dwindled to practically no one. I offered to step in as teacher. So began a string of Sunday morning "sit-ins." Many times I waited alone.

But there was the day a boy dropped by with two cousins in tow. The sisters' troubled home situation in another state had them temporarily residing with their aunt. We discussed the story of the Bible's "cutter"—a wild man living among the tombs who cut himself with stones—and how Jesus healed him. The girls absorbed every word of this account of things gone wrong made right. They needed such hope.

Another morning there was one girl. We each created a "word portrait" of ourselves and then explored the Bible's portrait of Jesus. For an hour we talked animatedly about ourselves and Jesus. Where we were like Him (in joy and caring and love for nature and children) and where we had work to do (in areas of trust and self-control). She liked that Jesus was outside the mainstream of His day. She, too, felt different from others and was encouraged in her authenticity.

The weeks of showing up every Sunday "just in case" had a reason. God wanted to open doors in these young lives . . . and made me a doorkeeper.

Father, what I do for You matters . . . even if it's to be a doorkeeper, waiting "just in case."
—Carol Knapp

Digging Deeper: Ps 84:10; Mt 19:14; Jas 3:18

Mon 7

"Be strong and courageous. Do not be afraid; do not be discouraged, for the Lord your God will be with you wherever you go." —Joshua 1:9 (NIV)

Tomorrow I'm going in for one of my regular cancer tests, and today I'm fighting my "What if" fears.

What if my cancer comes back?

I'm nearly seven years out from being diagnosed with stage IV ovarian cancer when I was given a two-year life expectancy. I've beaten all odds. But a couple of doctors told me that "stage IV ovarian cancer always comes back." So far, I've proven them wrong, but every time I make an appointment for a checkup, the "What if" fears start creeping in.

What if my test is not good?

"Don't go there," a friend advises me. But I have to go there. My way of dealing with my fears is to look the worst-case possibilities square in the face. I've even created my own scenario for this fear-facing exercise. I imagine my fears stuffed into an imaginary room. It's a scary but sacred place, because I know that nothing in that room surprises God—and He invites me to "go there" because Jesus is there too. He walks alongside me as I explore each fear, imagining what my life would be like if that worst possibility became a reality.

What if my cancer comes back?

I picture Jesus answering, "If your cancer comes back, I will still be with you. I will still give you what you need, one day at a time. I will still love you with an everlasting love. And I will still give you a future with hope."

Soon, I know that even if my worst fears become reality, Jesus' promises are still true. That gives me courage as I go off to my cancer test once again.

Lord, Your promises sustain me. Always.
—Carol Kuykendall

Digging Deeper: Prv 1:33; Phil 4:19; 2 Pt 1:1–11

THE PATH TO ADOPTION

Tue 8 *Trust in the Lord with all your heart and lean not on your own understanding.* —Proverbs 3:5 (NIV)

LEARNING TO TRUST

I clicked my pen against the couch cushion and stared at my husband, waiting for him to respond. So far, the notebook on my lap was empty.

"I don't know," Ryan finally said.

I sighed. Earlier that day, we had officially decided to send out support letters for our adoption. We were sitting in our living room, attempting to make a list of people to whom we should send them. We weren't sure if many of our aunts and uncles and cousins would understand our heart for the orphan.

We had already run into our fair share of interesting reactions when we announced our intention to adopt. Family members didn't understand why we would take this emotional and financial risk to travel to a war-torn country, just so we could bring some kid we don't know into our home. Some of them looked at us like we were crazy.

Our worries reached their peak, so we put down the notebook and did what we should have done in the beginning. We prayed. And afterward, when we said our amens, Ryan looked at me. "God can work in any heart—even the ones we think are unlikely."

That afternoon, we sent out the letters to everyone.

Forgive me, Lord, for all the times I've let my fear and doubt limit Your power. Help me to be faithful with what I can control and trust You with the rest.

—Katie Ganshert

Digging Deeper: Jo 1:9; Ps 56:3–4; 2 Tm 1:7

Wed 9

Christ is . . . in all. —Colossians 3:11 (KJV)

We were whizzing down the interstate when I noticed a man trudging down the side of the road.

Oh my, I thought, *poor thing. He must have lost his mind. He could be dangerous.*

Abby, our granddaughter, had a far different response. "Big Dad," she yelled to my husband, "did you see that? I think we just passed Jesus!"

Well, maybe. The man was wearing a white robe and had a beard, and he did have a big wooden cross hoisted over his shoulder and was dragging it. "Probably it's a person on a mission," I said to Abby. "Since Easter's next week, maybe he's traveling to a certain spot or trying to remind people that Easter's coming."

"I think it was Jesus," she answered. "Let's go back and see."

David looked wary; I felt perplexed. What could we do but circle back? We retraced our route, but the man was nowhere to be seen.

"Oh well," Abby said, "someone must have given him a ride. That cross looked really heavy." Already, she was settling back into the book she'd been reading. I, on the other hand, was in the front seat, struggling with my response to the "freeway Jesus." How easily I had dismissed him as a crazy person to avoid dealing with him. I'd even noted that his beard was unkempt . . . Jesus would never look scraggly!

I was beginning to see a truth in myself I didn't like. Didn't Jesus say that when we do something for the lowliest person, we are doing the same for Him? How many times had I found excuses to avoid reaching out to those Jesus talked about, labeling them crazy, dangerous, scraggly?

Abby was right; that cross did look heavy. But if that man on the side of the road—and everyone else I chanced to meet—was Jesus, the burden was beginning to look pretty light.

Father, let me see a chance to serve You in every person who comes my way.

—Pam Kidd

Digging Deeper: Mt 25:31–40

Thu 10

I lay down My life for the sheep. —John 10:15 (NAS)

Just before Easter, I made special efforts setting the dining room table. I'd purchased a pastel tablecloth with cute rabbits and decorated eggs on it. My ancient, flowered dishes, which had been my mother's, blended in perfectly. For a centerpiece, I decided on a lavender, velveteen rabbit and purple irises from our yard.

Still, I wasn't quite satisfied with my handiwork. Something seemed to be missing. The back door opened and I heard, "Mom." My son Jeremy had stopped by after getting off from work. We sat down in the living room.

"Anything happen at the restaurant today?"

"Yeah, it did. Today I served a fellow. We made small talk. He was alone. When I went to clear off his table, he handed me a bill. I almost just stuck it in my pocket. I don't usually look at tips. But I did this time."

"And?"

"A twenty!"

"Wow."

"I ran after him, almost to his car. 'Sir, you gave me a twenty by mistake.' He turned to me, smiled, and said, 'No mistake. I wanted you to have it.' 'But it's way too much. You don't have to do this.'

"Looking right into my eyes, he said, 'Jesus didn't have to go to the Cross either.'"

After my son left, I found a small wooden cross and stood it by the purple irises on the dining room table.

Jesus, keep me near the Cross—daily.
—Marion Bond West

Digging Deeper: 1 Cor 1:18; Gal 6:14; Col 2:14

Fri 11 *The Lord is my rock. . . .* —PSALM 18:2 (KJV)

Even though my father retired as minister of the church where my sister, Keri, and I grew up, we were committed to staying and raising our own families there. Neither of us anticipated just how difficult this was going to be.

All those years my father faithfully led the congregation, he had a knack for bringing peace to the most stressful situations. When an interim minister was hired, we watched helplessly as the church became divided. Keri and I often met for lunch, just to comfort each other. One day a realization suddenly appeared: "This isn't about where we are with the church. It's about where we are with God." While it was a painful time of change, our hearts needed to be aligned with God. The same God Who had been with us every moment of our lives was still here, and His house was still our true home.

Finally the Sunday came when my family joined Keri's to hear our new pastor's first sermon. He exuded a peaceful presence, and his message was strong and confident. Already he embraced our beloved church and its congregation as if he had known us forever.

"God is surely the rock of this church," he was saying. I caught Keri's eyes and smiled. Pastor Chris was saying what we already knew, but we certainly didn't mind hearing it again.

Father, let us look past every difficulty and see You ever as our rock.

—BROCK KIDD

Digging Deeper: Ps 18; Is 44:8

Sat 12

"For I am the Lord your God who takes hold of your right hand and says to you, Do not fear; I will help you."
—Isaiah 41:13 (NIV)

One day I was standing in line at the store, when a woman tapped me on the arm. "Remember me?" she asked.

It was Margo, a girl I'd gone to middle school with. We did the usual those-were-the-days banter and then she said, "A while back I picked your mom up one night on Lahser Road."

My mother was fighting the onset of Alzheimer's, and she used to get up in the middle of the night, don her Sunday finest, and walk three miles to church in the freezing Michigan dark.

I started to thank Margo, but she stopped me.

"I thought my life was crumbling," she said, "that I'd wasted years for nothing. I couldn't lie in bed crying anymore, so I just threw something on and went driving. I didn't know what I was going to do. That's when I saw her."

"Mom?"

"We had the most incredible conversation. She said she knew how I felt, that things may seem dark now, but they will get better because God is always near. And she was right. They did. Your mom was such a kind soul and good listener. I will never, ever forget that night."

Mom's been gone now for a few years. I sometimes wonder about her need to get to church when the hour was darkest. I think she knew what she was about more than we might have suspected and maybe not quite as lost as we assumed. She was searching for something in that cold dark, something she knew was there. My old school friend said she'd never forget that night. Neither will I.

Lord, I search for You when the hour is darkest and I am most lost. Direct my steps to You.
—Edward Grinnan

Digging Deeper: Pss 73:28, 139:7–8; Jn 1:5

REMAIN IN ME

Sun 13

Most of the crowd spread their garments on the road, and others cut branches from the trees and spread them on the road. And the crowds that went before him and that followed him shouted, "Hosanna to the Son of David! . . ."
—Matthew 21:8–9 (RSV)

PALM SUNDAY: REMAINING FAITHFUL

It's graduation day at the University of Pittsburgh. It's thrilling, watching the young men and women I've taught go forth and do all of the world's work, but there's a nagging disquiet.

Like many weighty truths, their education is accompanied by an equally weighty lie. I've told my students they're unique and capable of wonderful things (true); I didn't warn them of the attendant difficulties that lay ahead. I've long stopped betting on their futures. Who am I to tell them about the odds of a successful life, the weird dance of hard work and good luck, the slings and arrows of outrageous fortune?

Luckily, today is filled with smiles, flowing robes, hugs, funny hats. In ancient times such celebrations would be marked by palm fronds, like Jesus' entrance into Jerusalem. And then is no different from now, where celebration can suddenly turn to trepidation, where young lives quickly discover that speaking the truth may lead to trouble, betrayal, or worse.

But today they'll throw their hats into the air with faith in the future. And when asked, I'll pose with them for photos. Years from now they'll wonder about the teacher with the gray hair and wan, anxious smile, who looks as if he might be praying.

Lord, we often praise You one day, then betray You the next.
Let us overcome our fickle nature and be faithful
companions to You and our brothers and sisters.
—Mark Collins

Digging Deeper: Mt 21:1–11

REMAIN IN ME

Mon 14

"Then shall the maidens rejoice in the dance, and the young men and the old shall be merry. I will turn their mourning into joy, I will comfort them, and give them gladness for sorrow."—JEREMIAH 31:13 (RSV)

MONDAY OF HOLY WEEK: SMALL GIFTS

I was comparing notes about middle age with a friend. We brought up the usual complaints of men in their fifties: bad knees, complicated relationships, uncertain futures. "Sometimes I feel like I'm out at sea," I said.

"Which one are you?" my friend asked. "The *Titanic* or the iceberg?"

I laughed, but I'm not sure why. Which one am I, the engineering marvel full of doomed lives and hubris, or the shadowy iceberg lurking in the night, small on the surface but holding so much more underneath? Does destiny control me, or am I able to navigate what lies ahead?

Lent is a time for preparation, but it's also a time of renewal. There's some question about what Jesus did right before His last, fateful trip to Jerusalem; I'll go with the story in the Gospel of John—that Jesus was relaxed and renewed, anointed with oil. The oil was a small gift but the right gift. Jesus seemed to have a knack for foresight—surely He knew what was awaiting Him—but it was not the time to dwell on the week ahead.

For myself, I dunno. I hope I am neither the iceberg nor the ocean liner. Instead, I want to be known as the bass player in the *Titanic* dance band. Right now we're playing a nifty swing number and the crowd is merry as we toast our collective voyage. Soon enough we'll be playing "Nearer, My God, to Thee," but for now we relax, we dance. It's a small gift, but sometimes small gifts are all we have.

Lord, suffering awaits all flesh. Let me appreciate the small, joyful gifts of Your bounty as we prepare for what lies ahead. Amen.

—MARK COLLINS

Digging Deeper: Pss 100, 106:1

REMAIN IN ME

Tue 15 *And being in an agony he prayed more earnestly: and his sweat was as it were great drops of blood falling down to the ground.* —LUKE 22:44 (KJV)

TUESDAY OF HOLY WEEK: A TRUE CROWN

As soon as the opposing player's hockey stick accidently nicked my noggin, I knew I was headed to the emergency room. The angle of the blow had opened a nifty gash above my forehead.

It was not a good time to be in an ER. Finally, a frazzled doctor saw me. She apologized that I had to wait. While she worked her needle, she gave a short recap of her difficult night: a fireman who had fallen answering a call, a fight between brothers, a diabetic dad in a losing battle with his blood sugar. Suddenly, she stopped. "I forgot to give you a topical anesthetic," she said.

This was true. From the moment she inserted the needle, I realized that a little lidocaine would've been welcome. I almost said something, but two things stopped me: warped machismo and some serious introspection. I'd received a venial cut from playing a sport I love, not from fighting a fire or fighting my brother. I wasn't forced to think about a pancreas transplant in the hope of seeing my children grow up. "No problem," I said. "Keep sewing." I didn't want to delay her anymore.

When I left, I caught my reflection in the paper-towel dispenser. The blood had marched across my hairline, paralleling the new set of railroad-track sutures. From that angle it looked like a crown of thorns . . . but it wasn't, of course. That kind of crown is carried by Someone Who has the weight of the world on His shoulders.

Lord, my contribution to humanity that night was freeing up the time of the genuine saints among us. It was trivial, really—a small thing. But I know even the small things are sacred to You. —MARK COLLINS

Digging Deeper: MT 27:11–31

REMAIN IN ME

Wed 16

And as they came out, they found a man of Cyrene,
Simon by name: him they compelled to bear his cross.
—MATTHEW 27:32 (KJV)

WEDNESDAY OF HOLY WEEK: GOD IS IN THE DETAILS

Which cliché do you abide by: The devil is in the details or God is in the details? No matter; something extraordinary is in the details.

Take for instance that single line about Simon of Cyrene. Maybe the Romans forced Simon to help; maybe he would've offered this small gift anyway. In either case, Jesus accepted. A cynic might note that Jesus didn't have much choice, but that misses the point: Jesus had *lots* of choices. He could have wiggled out of the whole mess with Pilate. He could have chosen a quicker execution. He could have skipped the whole proceeding. He did not.

Our youngest daughter, Grace, has talked about becoming a hospice worker when she grows up. She's seen two grandparents die in hospices. She has seen the kind of people who work there: kind people. Maybe it's a job; maybe economic circumstances compelled them to work there—does it matter? Fact is, they're *there*, in someone's time of need, to assist others on their journey, to make their passing less difficult.

Are we compelled to help others or do we offer? I'm guessing that the person whose burden is suddenly lightened by our presence doesn't really care what brought us to that moment. Those are just details . . . and I think God is, most assuredly, in the details.

Lord, You said that what we do for the least of our brothers and sisters
we do for You. Help us to see You in everything we do in
our everyday lives, even in the tiniest details.
—MARK COLLINS

Digging Deeper: Ps 147:4–5; Lk 12:6–7

REMAIN IN ME

Thu 17

They went to a place which was called Gethsemane; and he said to his disciples, "Sit here, while I pray."
—MARK 14:32 (RSV)

MAUNDY THURSDAY: LEARNING TO SAY YES

I'm sitting in a car in the rain with my friend Linda, looking out over the Pacific Ocean, eating chicken satay. This will be our last meal forever, at least on this earth. Actually, I'm the only one eating. Linda is—as discreetly as possible—using a paper bag to, *um*, unload some of the chemotherapy from her stomach.

When we arranged this trip—my flying in from Pennsylvania to California—we didn't know it was the good-bye tour. Check that: I suspected but said nothing. Linda had been declining for two years. By the time I arrived, it was obvious this would be it.

Ordinarily, I'm not an obedient servant nor a fully engaged human being. I am scattered, sarcastic, selfish, and way too proud. But for two days now I have answered her every wish the same way: *Yes.* I agree to even strange requests, like tossing back chicken satay while she tosses her cookies. Part of me can't think of anything more tragic; another part of me realizes every moment of this visit is fully lived, fully engaged, and will be fully remembered for the rest of my life.

Long ago, in centuries far away, another Last Supper took place among friends. I won't pretend to know what that Passover meal felt like, but I can tell you it was fully lived and fully remembered. I can tell you that Someone said *yes* to what was asked that night, a sacrifice beyond sacrifice. But that's what loved ones do for each other, something that redeems even the most scattered and selfish and proud among us sinners.

Lord, help me to say yes more often—to You and to others.
—MARK COLLINS

Digging Deeper: IS 53:5; 2 COR 5:21; HEB 10:1–14

REMAIN IN ME

Fri 18 *And there followed him a great company of people, and of women, which also bewailed and lamented him. But Jesus turning unto them said, Daughters of Jerusalem, weep not for me. . . .* —Luke 23:27–28 (KJV)

GOOD FRIDAY: MORNING IS COMING

My sister Cindy died three years ago, and I have yet to cry. I've cried about other tragedies, other deaths, but not about my sister.

"Strange" does not begin to describe this behavior. Cindy was quadriplegic—had been for forty-five plus years. I could say she suffered (she did); I can say her death was a release (it was); I can even whip out the funeral clichés: "She was needed in heaven" (I wouldn't know). But none of that explains my dry-eyed grieving.

Late one night, my ever-patient wife said, "You know, you already mourned your sister." I assumed Sandee wanted to start a large fight with a large insult. I hadn't even *begun* to mourn. Then she added, "You mourned when she was alive. You celebrated who she had become, but you mourned the loss. You mourned that Cindy couldn't walk. You mourned that she was in pain. It's okay. You were a good brother. You *are* a good brother."

I realize this revelation was Sandee's small gift to me. No one can tell you the right time to cry. Grief follows its own etiquette; death is rude and, lacking dignity, tramples timetables.

I doubt Jesus' gentle admonishment to the daughters of Jerusalem worked (Do you really think they stopped crying?), but now I get the point: It's okay to mourn and it's okay to finish mourning because morning is coming.

Lord, Your death overcame sin but did not overcome sadness. Teach us how to grieve our losses as we celebrate Your victory. Amen. —Mark Collins

Digging Deeper: Ps 30; Is 25:8

REMAIN IN ME

Sat 19 *May God who gives patience . . . and encouragement help you to live in complete harmony with each other. . . .*

—ROMANS 15:5 (TLB)

HOLY SATURDAY: LIVING IN HARMONY

Depending on which source you consult, Americans spend forty-five minutes to an hour each day waiting: waiting in lines, waiting for files to download, sitting in traffic . . . waiting.

If you ever spy me waiting in traffic, I look patient. I am not. My demeanor masks a very angry man who is contemplating mayhem. I once sat in my car in a highway construction zone on a hot summer afternoon beside a flashing sign that read, SLOW DOWN! YOUR CURRENT SPEED IS 0 MILES AN HOUR. I thought the long wait might cause overheating and then a blown gasket—and I don't mean the car.

It takes a special kind of person to be given a life of unfathomable gifts (food, drink, leisure time, central air) and then complain about occasional delays in living that life. I could, for instance, spend that time enjoying music or praying or pondering my existence rather than pondering mayhem, but no. I have chosen to seethe. Meanwhile, somewhere a child waits for rice from the back of a UN truck. A mother waits for a husband missing in Afghanistan. A couple waits for word about an adoption. A young man in a faraway time waits for the welcome death to end His suffering, accompanied by nothing but two thieves and vinegar mixed with some gall.

Lord, I realize that's what I have: gall. To grumble with such pettiness takes a lot of gall. Perhaps I've found something else to ponder the next time I await Your return when I have lost sight of You.

—MARK COLLINS

Digging Deeper: Ps 27:14; Mi 7:7

REMAIN IN ME

Sun 20

. . . The children of God, being the children of the resurrection. . . . For he is not a God of the dead, but of the living: for all live unto him. —Luke 20:36, 38 (KJV)

EASTER: CELEBRATE

I'd like to think that, unlike Peter, I wouldn't have denied Jesus three times, but my faith is tepid, sketchy, uncertain. I wish it were different. I wish, like my mother, I could hold on to my faith, no matter what.

Weird thing is, I can accept the bizarre claim that an itinerant preacher in first-century Palestine was crucified like a common criminal, was dead and buried . . . but not buried for long. I can buy that—which, you gotta admit, is a pretty large story to swallow. And I can believe His message is a living one—not because I have that much faith but because it makes sense to me: We're here to help others so that "whenever you cared for one of the least of these, you did it for me." Yessir. Roger. Understood.

But that Someone could forgive *my* trespasses, *my* myriad shortcomings, *my* irrational fuming, *my* weak-willed nature so that I *can* help others by forgiving them . . . no. No can do. My ego won't allow it.

This Easter, I think I've figured out at least one gift inherent in the Jesus story: It's about letting go of ego, that ridiculous remnant from our hominid past, that lying leftover that says we're in control, we need neither the world nor each other, thank you very much, that we don't require (and therefore don't deserve) forgiveness . . . my God. Just let it go. Let. It. Go. Bury the past; then roll away the stone and celebrate what's risen in its place.

Lord, this Easter, help rid me of my selfish ego. Granted, ego is easy and forgiveness is difficult . . . but today, of all days, I'm willing to try the hard way. —Mark Collins

Digging Deeper: Mt 28:8–10; Lk 24:1–12; Jn 11:25–26

Mon 21

Blessed are those who trust in the Lord. . . .
—Jeremiah 17:7 (NRSV)

"You're *sure* you know where you're going?" My wife's voice made it obvious she had her own answer to that question. And she was right. I was lost.

We were in Cambridge, Massachusetts, staying with friends before Kate ran the Boston Marathon. The last time she'd run it, five years before, we'd stayed in Boston and spent a morning wandering around Cambridge. I thought it might be fun to find the café where we'd had lunch that day.

Actually I had another reason for this search. A freak heat wave was forecast for marathon day; officials were warning runners susceptible to heat to drop out. Kate was determined to run. I didn't try to dissuade her. Instead, I channeled my nervousness into seeking something familiar.

"Maybe it's down this street," I suggested. Kate frowned. She was supposed to be taking it easy today, not trudging all over town.

Suddenly, a few blocks away, I spotted it. "There it is!" We stood outside, peering in at the rickety old tables and racks of pastries. We smiled at each other.

"Wasn't it great when we found this last time?" Kate said.

I thought back to that rainy day and how God had cared for us, bringing us to this warm, dry place, guarding Kate through the cold, wet race. God had been with us then; He'd be with us now.

"Shall we go in?" said Kate.

"Definitely," I said.

Help me to trust You in all things, Lord.
—Jim Hinch

Digging Deeper: Ps 56:3; Na 1:7

Tue 22

O Lord, how many are Your works! In wisdom You have made them all. . . . —Psalm 104:24 (NAS)

In her intriguing book *What's Your God Language?* Dr. Myra Perrine explains how, in our relationship with Jesus, we know Him through our various "spiritual temperaments," such as intellectual, activist, caregiver, traditionalist, and contemplative. I am drawn to naturalist, described as "loving God through experiencing Him outdoors."

Yesterday, on my bicycle, I passed a tom turkey and his hen in a sprouting cornfield. Suddenly, he fanned his feathers in a beautiful courting display. I thought how Jesus had given me His own show of love in surprising me with that wondrous sight.

I walked by this same field one wintry day before dawn and heard an unexpected *huff.* I had startled a deer. It was glorious to hear that small, secret sound, almost as if we held a shared pleasure in the untouched morning.

Visiting my daughter once when she lived well north of the Arctic Circle in Alaska, I can still see the dark silhouettes of the caribou and hear the midnight crunch of their hooves in the snow. I'd watched brilliant green northern lights flash across the sky and was reminded of the emerald rainbow around Christ's heavenly throne (Revelation 4:3).

On another Alaskan visit, a full moon setting appeared to slide into the volcanic slope of Mount Iliamna, crowning the snow-covered peak with a halo of pink in the emerging light. I erupted in praise to the triune God for the grandeur of creation.

Traipsing down a dirt road in Minnesota, a bloom of tiny goldfinches lifted off yellow flowers growing there, looking like the petals had taken flight. I stopped, mesmerized, filled with the joy of Jesus.

Jesus, today on Earth Day, I rejoice in the language of You.

—Carol Knapp

Digging Deeper: Pss 24:1, 145:5; Hb 2:14

Wed 23

"You did not choose me, but I chose you and appointed you so that you might go and bear fruit . . . that will last. . . ."
—John 15:16 (NIV)

Hi, Dad," the voice on the phone said, a bit muffled and faraway. "Oh, it's you, Will." You can always recognize your children's voices, even as they grow older and more mature.

"Can you hear me better now?" It sounded like he was in the office next door. I went through a quick mental calculation. Today was Monday. That meant he was in Singapore, part of a weeklong trip for his job.

"Yes, it's very clear. What time is it there?" I looked at the clock: 5:30 PM in New York City.

"Five thirty in the morning on Tuesday. Singapore is twelve hours ahead. I'm still jet-lagged."

"How was your trip?"

"I had a seventeen-hour layover in Tokyo. I took the train in from the airport and the train back, so I saw a little of the city."

"Sounds great."

"Maybe I'll go back sometime and see more of it. I can't stay on the phone long, Dad. I have a meeting soon with the office in California and wanted to be sure I could get good reception, so I had to choose somebody to talk to. I chose you."

I chose you. "I'm glad you did. I hope the meeting goes well."

"It should. Love you, Dad."

"Love you, Will."

I put down the phone and pondered his words for a moment: "I chose you." It's often said our families are given to us, but our friends we get to choose. It occurred to me we choose our families too. We make choices about being close to them, staying in touch, nurturing relationships that run deeper than blood. There's a lot to be said for a two-minute conversation from across the world.

Let me always choose to love, Lord. —Rick Hamlin

Digging Deeper: Jn 15:1–17

April

Thu 24

So I saw that there is nothing better for men than that they should be happy in their work, for that is what they are here for, and no one can bring them back to life to enjoy what will be in the future, so let them enjoy it now.
—ECCLESIASTES 3:22 (TLB)

Recently, I learned that a book on friendship that I'd written with my best friend, Melanie, was rejected by a publisher who had been very positive about it for over two years. I was devastated. All those months and years of writing, rewriting, and then reworking it again . . . only to have it rejected in the end.

I was ready to give up my career altogether, retire, and concentrate on biking, swimming, kayaking, and traveling.

Then I read something my pen pal Oscar had written about his own retirement twenty-five years earlier. He wrote that in retirement we must have direction and purpose, accept change, remain curious and confident, communicate, and be committed. The longer I looked at his list, the more it spoke to me. *Why, those are the very attributes I need to be a good writer*, I thought. So I decided to buckle down and rework other unsold manuscripts I'd written over the years. Using Oscar's plan of direction, purpose, confidence, and commitment helped me to stop telling people that I didn't have any marketing genes and to keep busy rewriting and looking for different publishers.

I may never sell all of my work, but I'm living a life filled with purpose. And I'm a whole lot happier in my semiretirement than if I was just playing every day, all day.

Father, give me purpose in life whether it's volunteer work,
pursuing dreams, reworking an old career, or finding
a new way to use the talents You've given me.
—PATRICIA LORENZ

Digging Deeper: PRV 16:9; ROM 12:3–8

Fri 25

"Let your light shine before others, so that they may see your good works and give glory to your Father in heaven."
—Matthew 5:16 (NRSV)

For more than a year, I've dedicated an hour a day to an eight-year-old neighbor with special needs. She's afraid of my cat, so we play outside.

Last spring I stood at the bottom of the front steps and waved my hands like a choir director. "This Little Light of Mine," she belted from the landing. Then, "Miss Evelyn, now you!" We switched roles. Later I donned her backpack, and she walked *me* to the bus stop. *Oh, what are the neighbors thinking?*

On summer days, in the only available shade, we strewed the public sidewalk with puzzles and pencils. Like a gatekeeper, she asked every pedestrian, "Where are you going?" Most people smiled; everyone gave us a wide berth.

In the fall, we crossed the street to collect acorns and rake leaves before the maintenance crew swooped in.

Over the seasons, it's become increasingly obvious that the neighborhood sees her need and notices our routine. Late August, as I walked around the block, a man I hardly knew handed me a bagful of school supplies "for that girl you work with." Remembering the kindness, she and I signed a handmade Christmas card to "Mr. and Mrs. Neighbor" and slipped it inside their mail slot.

A few days later I found a package at my door. "Miss Evelyn, Merry Christmas." The signature on the card cited the house number of the strangers. I unwrapped a selection of fruits and a necklace that left me speechless: a delicate gold cross. *So this is what the neighbors think.*

Lord, my neighborhood needs this little light of mine.
Help me to let it shine.
—Evelyn Bence

Digging Deeper: Mt 5:13–16; Lk 8:16–17

Sat 26

"I have not stopped giving thanks for you, remembering you in my prayers." —Ephesians 1:16 (NIV)

How do you express gratitude to someone who has shaped your life? I pondered this recently when I attended the seventy-fifth wedding anniversary of my uncle Clarence and aunt Shirley Walker.

My grandfather Eddie Walker was a successful rancher on the high plains of eastern Colorado. One day in 1933, he asked my father, Al, to ride with him to pick up supplies. Walking into a store, my grandfather suddenly collapsed. His stomach ulcer had perforated in an age prior to antibiotics. Within three days, he was dead, leaving his wife, Callie, a sixteen-year-old son, Clarence, and my fourteen-year-old father to run a ranch at the height of the Great Depression. It seemed an impossible challenge.

However, Clarence dropped out of high school and poured his energy into saving the ranch, insisting that my father remain in school and help only as time permitted. Later, Clarence encouraged him to attend college. Over the next eight years, my father earned a PhD in theology and became a minister, teacher, and missionary.

As I flew to Colorado, I promised to say thank you. Clarence and Shirley are frail and live in an assisted-living facility. Both are deaf, and there would be few private moments for conversation. However, the time came on the evening following the anniversary celebration. Sitting quietly by Clarence's bed, I placed my hand on his and quietly said a simple prayer of thanksgiving for a good and loving man. I know he heard me and God did too.

Father, may I say thank you to people I love
while there is yet time and day. Amen.
—Scott Walker

Digging Deeper: Rom 1:8

Sun 27

But he said to me, "My grace is sufficient for you, for my power is made perfect in weakness". . . .
—2 CORINTHIANS 12:9 (NIV)

I had built a sparkling white pedestal in my mind for my church to stand on. Righteous. Holy. Perfect. A place where people check any baggage they may have at the door and enter into God's perfect presence in perfect harmony, in perfect fellowship, in perfect love. And the pastor? Well, he was anointed by God to lead, wasn't he?

My pedestal started to crumble a few weeks ago. A staff member left the church in a less than perfect fashion, and people began to take sides. Things got messy. Unkind words were said. Feelings got hurt.

I confess, I didn't like this dingy new pedestal. I wanted the old facade back. But, interestingly, as the church I knew changed around me, *God's* power, *God's* majesty, *God's* holiness became more evident as they were transposed against the backdrop of human sin. And as all of my preconceptions about what a church should be, and how a pastor should lead, were tested, I was able to take my church off of the sparkling white pedestal and place it on the rock where God intended it to be.

Lord, thank You for reminding me that the best place for any church is on Your rock, not my pedestal. Amen.
—ERIN MACPHERSON

Digging Deeper: PSS 18:2, 62:6–7

Mon 28

For you make me glad by your deeds, Lord; I sing for joy at what your hands have done. —Psalm 92:4 (NIV)

My golden retriever, Millie, and I were walking home from the dog park, where Millie socialized for a bit but mostly sat sedately next to me on a bench while I read. At five, Millie doesn't play as rambunctiously as she once did. She has a few select friends whom she will cavort with, but her inner puppy rarely emerges anymore.

Except when we pass Clement Clarke Moore Park, which is teeming with children. There is nothing my dog loves more than kids. She gives me a plaintive look as if to ask, "Can we go inside and have some real fun?" There is a sign, though, that says the park is only for kids and their parents or guardians. No dogs allowed.

I gently tug on her leash. She is reluctant to go, dawdling and glancing longingly over her shoulder, her tail drooping. *Lord,* I wonder, *do dogs know that they break our hearts?*

"Sir? Excuse me, sir?" A woman stood at the park's gate, pushing a baby in a stroller trailed by two older kids. She waved at me. "Can my kids say hello to your dog?"

Before I could answer, Millie was on the move, prancing and pulling me back. First she said hello to the baby, giving it a kiss, her tail flying. Then she bumped up against the older kids, letting them hug and pet her, all the while with an ecstatic look on her face. Finally the woman maneuvered her kids back into the park. "Thanks," she said, "they really wanted to see a dog today."

Thank You, Lord, for giving us what we need, even a maturing golden retriever whose inner puppy still wants to play.

—Edward Grinnan

Digging Deeper: Ps 84:11

Tue 29

The disciples were together, with the doors locked for fear....
—John 20:19 (NIV)

After eighteen years, Pastor John preached his last sermon at our church. We honored him and his wife, Diane, with music and skits based on a popular radio program. As the host, I closed by saying, "Please come back next week! Even though two key players are leaving, make no mistake: God will always be the star of our church and He isn't going anywhere. We all have access to Him through His Son and agent Jesus Christ. The entire production, every week, is guided and directed by the Holy Spirit."

Several members of our congregation thanked me for reminding them that a pastor, no matter how beloved, is not the Messiah. I spoke those words confidently, and yet seeing John's empty office was unsettling. Was it like an empty tomb? Or was it just an office waiting to be filled by another key player who is not a star? There is a definite Good Friday feel to our church this week, even though Easter has come and gone.

Attendance had doubled within four years of John's arrival at our church. He eventually welcomed over seven hundred new members. Some moved away, some died, and many others will probably leave now that John is gone. To many of us, John was our church.

But I hope we look to God first in our search for new leadership. I hope Jesus gives us that access. I hope the Holy Spirit directs us not just to a new pastor but to a new understanding of what we can be without John. I hope.

Dear God, please allow us to become the humble leaders we are searching for.

—Tim Williams

Digging Deeper: Acts 20:28; 1 Cor 12:12–26

April

Wed 30

"When she finds it, she calls her friends and neighbors together and says, 'Rejoice with me; I have found my lost coin.'" —LUKE 15:9 (NIV)

If this spring had been a fighter, it would've been a heavyweight contender. My husband, Brian, and I had faced losing family friends to sickness, and our siblings were grieving over friends dying in car wrecks. At one point, I stood in our closet and sobbed. "I just can't do this anymore."

The next day, Brian got an e-mail that read, "Someone contacted us saying that they found your lost ring. Would you like it back?"

We looked at each other, speechless. He'd lost his wedding ring in the ocean two years ago. While it hurt to lose the ring (we'd only been married six months), its return felt like a crashing wave resounding with God's strength and presence. I could almost hear Him whisper, "Do you not know that I'm here?"

I didn't need God to return the ring to us to know He was there, but the fact that He did reminded me that we're never alone and that the challenges we face are anything but insurmountable.

"Trust Me. Feel Me. Follow Me," God seemed to say to us. We called our parents, and over and over again we heard, "It's a miracle!"

While getting the ring back felt wonderful, it was the reminder of God's presence that we needed most.

Lord, when I need it most, You send a sign of Your everlasting faithfulness. Forgive me for ever doubting.

—ASHLEY KAPPEL

Digging Deeper: PSS 89:8, 91:3–6; LAM 3:22–23

DAILY MERCIES

1 ______________________________

2 ______________________________

3 ______________________________

4 ______________________________

5 ______________________________

6 ______________________________

7 ______________________________

8 ______________________________

9 ______________________________

10 ______________________________

11 ______________________________

12 ______________________________

13 ______________________________

14 ______________________________

15 ______________________________

April

16 ______________________________

17 ______________________________

18 ______________________________

19 ______________________________

20 ______________________________

21 ______________________________

22 ______________________________

23 ______________________________

24 ______________________________

25 ______________________________

26 ______________________________

27 ______________________________

28 ______________________________

29 ______________________________

30 ______________________________

May

Let thy mercy, O Lord, be upon us,
according as we hope in thee.

—Psalm 33:22 (KJV)

Thu 1

They go out to their work, searching for food....
—Job 24:5 (NKJV)

My husband, Keith, and I decided to drive down to Tulip Town and wander the fields of vibrant color the Skagit Valley is famous for. Enchanted, we ordered about twenty different varieties for our half-barrel planters. I loved deciding between the American Dream and the Peking Red, the Black Diamond and the Purissima, the Monte Carlo and the Gudoshnik.

We planted the bulbs in September, but it was a bad winter. When spring came, I saw only about one-tenth of the tulips we'd planted. Closer inspection revealed squirrels had lived off our bulbs when other food was really scarce. I was upset and complained loudly, angrily, to Keith, but he only said, "The squirrels needed food."

I grumped about that for a while but slowly came to realize that he was right: Providing nourishment should trump surface beauty every time. I came to see the squirrels as survivors and was glad that the tulips had helped them get through the winter.

Lord, help me to understand more quickly that being part of the balance of life means I don't always get to do things my way.
—Rhoda Blecker

Digging Deeper: Prv 18:17; Ez 34:18

Fri 2

He took up also the mantle of Elijah that fell from him, and went back, and stood by the bank of Jordan. —2 Kings 2:13 (KJV)

I am preoccupied thinking about my eighty-year-old friend and Scrabble nemesis, Lizette Williams. Sitting in my car alone, I think random thoughts so I will not fret about Lizette: about the clouds, the sky, how there used to be so many butterflies but I can't remember the last time I saw one. Now, mostly, I see them in the summers when I am away at camp—the camp where I visit with Lizette, the woman I have nicknamed my Roomie.

My Roomie has been gravely ill, and it troubles me that I am not able to be at her side to say good-bye. She and I have had many talks and shared some hard-fought Scrabble games. I don't want to imagine the camp in Pembroke, Illinois, without her jetting around on her golf cart, working in the kitchen, or stopping to hug the children. She made all of us feel loved and welcomed—I want to do the same. Selfishly, I don't want her to pass without personally saying good-bye.

Suddenly, though it is a cold, blustery spring day, there is a parade of butterflies fluttering before the windshield. They are all kinds—big ones, tiny ones, purple, yellow, blue, white—like a child would draw. I laugh in spite of myself, especially at one large one, comically flapping her wings as the wind blows her about.

No one else is around to witness the butterflies. I smile more, thinking of my Roomie. Then my friend Mary calls to tell me her mother, my Roomie, has passed. I inhale, ready to be sad, especially since I couldn't be with her. Then the butterfly flutters by and catches my eye again. I smile.

Good-bye, Lizette. Good-bye, Roomie. Until we meet again.

Lord, thank You for such wonderful people in my life. Thank You for my Roomie. I pray that my light and love will shine like hers.

—Sharon Foster

Digging Deeper: 1 Sm 18:1–3; Prv 17:17, 27:17

Sat 3

Who hath despised the day of small things?...
—Zechariah 4:10 (KJV)

When I awoke on Saturday, I didn't have a clear plan for the day. Even so, I asked God to guide my steps.

What varied paths did I take? A neighbor girl is learning to count by tens; in the morning I taught her how to stack (ten, twenty, thirty . . .) and roll pennies in red paper sleeves. I baked and froze a batch of blueberry muffins. I skimmed the newspaper and addressed a birthday card. After paying some bills, I changed the bed linens and towels and trudged across the apartment complex to the laundry room.

I searched diligently for—but never did find—the upholstery remnant needed to repair a couch pillow. I phoned my friend with Alzheimer's. Does he remember my name? I don't know; I regularly touch base with him anyway. I ran into an old friend, and we chatted in the parking lot. When I came home, a neighbor asked if I could take her to the drugstore. "Give me a few minutes and then, yes."

By dinnertime, I repeated a puzzlement I'd often heard from my mother: "I don't know where this day went!"

At bedtime I picked up *A Blossom in the Desert*, written and illustrated by Lilias Trotter. A particular entry captured my attention and quickly retired my complaint: "Such a day of small things still, but on God's terms, and that is enough."

I closed the book and turned off the light, confident that God had answered my morning prayer.

Lord, I don't know exactly how each new day will unfold.
Even so, I ask You to guide my steps.
—Evelyn Bence

Digging Deeper: Pss 27:11, 37:23–24

Sun 4 *And a little child shall lead them.* —Isaiah 11:6 (AMP)

The first time Jack climbed the mountain behind my house, he was only six years old. He was climbing with his dad and me one day after church.

Jack spent the hour of our walk locating large sticks that had fallen off of trees and then whacking them against other trees. He had a great time. Jack's dad and I talked about Jack's emerging illness. No one knew what to make of it. Jack's symptoms were baffling his doctors and all of the specialists he'd seen thus far.

"Our lives are on hold," Jack's dad began. "I feel like I'm holding my breath. I don't know what to do."

Deep in the woods, we sat down on a log for a rest and for lunch. When we were done, Jack asked if he could roll the log over. "Why do you want to?" his dad asked.

"Just to see the worms," Jack replied.

My friend gave me a look: *This is a kid thing.*

Sure enough, there were worms everywhere.

"Do you like worms?" I asked the boy.

"Yes!" he said as he picked one up. "And my Sunday school teacher told me that they know they will keep on living in a new way, even if you pull them apart."

Holy One, help me to live for Your kingdom this day,
as this wise child has modeled for me.
—Jon Sweeney

Digging Deeper: Mt 5:3, 6:33

Mon 5

Fear ye not, stand still.... —Exodus 14:13 (KJV)

Help, God! I'm overwhelmed!

In the middle of creating a real estate brochure, my computer paused for what seemed an eternity each time I dropped in a new photo. *"Hmm,"* said the technician when my computer reacted to his touch like a really slow-moving snail, "let's check your apps." The technician tapped my home screen twice, and a stream of intriguing icons appeared at the bottom of the page. He swiped them with his finger. There were my mailbox, weather, news, Google, Mapquest, calendar, contacts, two word games, solitaire, a poetry book. On he swiped, past real estate, camera, some magazines, alarm clock, dictionary, Bible. "You haven't turned off your apps in a while," he said.

"I didn't know I was supposed to," I answered.

"If you leave them on, there's too much information vying for space," he explained. "Then everything slows down. A computer is like a person... can't handle everything at once."

Hey, God, have You brought me here to tell me something?

The tech showed me how to turn off the apps I didn't need. Now my computer was brochure-ready and humming at full speed.

As I left the store, I was humming too. Standing still, I turned off all the extra programs in my head and focused on the task at hand!

Father, in a complicated world, You bring me back to what's always true:
"Be still" and know... one thing at a time!

—Pam Kidd

Digging Deeper: Prv 3:5–6; Is 40:28–31

Tue 6

Let every thing that hath breath praise the Lord. Praise ye the Lord. —Psalm 150:6 (KJV)

The e-mail came from my brother-in-law Mike to a long list of addressees. "It's official," he wrote. "I am now bike safe! I'm back. I got approved by my therapist. Praise God!"

Ten months earlier Mike had been the only survivor in a devastating plane crash. He ended up in a burn unit for two months. Since then he'd been in physical therapy five days a week. He'd been passionate about cycling before the accident, going on long rides with friends. We'd prayed and prayed for his recovery. Now he was back.

"Great, Mike," I wrote. "What an answer to prayer." I hesitated for a moment then hit reply-to-all.

For the next two hours the messages kept coming, reply-to-all: "You are incredible, Mike!" "We love you and continue to be in awe of your accomplishments." "Great news, Dorky!" "The Mule is back!" "Looking forward to your jokes on the morning rides!" "You are an inspiration to us all!" Every time I'd go to open one e-mail, there'd be another one in my in-box.

The names were mostly Mike's cycling buddies, guys I didn't know. But as I read their messages, it dawned on me that this was the same community that had been supporting him and my sister Diane and their kids for the past ten months. They were the ones bringing food, sending cards, visiting the hospital, running errands, and supplying prayers.

"Thanks for all your love and support!" Mike wrote back. "Praise God!"

Praise God, indeed. I've never been crazy about that feature "reply-to-all." It generates too much "me too" copy in my already crowded in-box. All those messages from all those people. But this time I wouldn't have wanted to miss one of them. All that praise ringing through cyberspace was a great chorus of thanksgiving.

Let the praise multiply, Lord. —Rick Hamlin

Digging Deeper: Ps 150; Heb 13:15

Wed 7

Follow God's example, therefore, as dearly loved children . . . .
—EPHESIANS 5:1 (NIV)

Sally Ann is a TV anchor on a popular morning news show in New Orleans. She arrived early at an event in our school district, so I was tasked with keeping her company until it was time for her to speak.

She was gracious and kind. It was obvious by her heartfelt stories that she was a woman of deep faith who believed in the power of role models. She spoke of Miss Ellie, a woman who had made a difference in her mother's life, which had, in turn, made a difference in her own life. Sally Ann had gone on to cofound a mentorship organization called Each One Save One that pairs mentors with at-risk children.

After she had left, a colleague asked, "Do you think we were good role models for our students when we were teachers?"

"I don't know," I said, shaking my head. "I prayed often to make a difference in the lives of my students. I sure hope I did."

Later that week, while shopping, a young woman walked up to me. "Remember me?" she asked with a big smile. "Jenny, class of 1994? You taught me American history."

"Yes," I replied, giving her a hug, "so good to see you!"

"You know, I never liked history until I took your class." She paused for a moment and beamed proudly. "Guess what? I'm a history teacher now!"

Even though it's not necessary, Lord, it's sure nice
to know that what we do matters.
—MELODY BONNETTE SWANG

Digging Deeper: LK 6:43–44; JAS 2:17–18

Thu 8

Give me relief from my distress; have mercy on me and hear my prayer. —PSALM 4:1 (NIV)

My friend, who lives in another state, phoned me on the eve of her husband's serious surgery. She was calling for prayer . . . for her computer! My friend works from home, and her computer kept freezing up, even though a technician had spent five hours installing a new drive. "There's work I *have* to get done today before my husband's surgery," she said. "I'm desperate!"

"You've called the right person," I told her. What I didn't say is that I'd never prayed with anybody about getting a computer to start working. But my friend needed help, so I told her to lay her hands on her computer and I would lay my hands on mine. I prayed for the computer and that God would supply the words my friend needed to write so her work would get out on time. Then I prayed about my friend's stress level and asked for God's help and presence.

My friend thanked me, but I wasn't exactly optimistic that her computer would start up properly as a result. Five minutes later I received an e-mail from her saying that her computer was up and running. I was amazed. I'm certainly no expert on the theology (or technology) behind the healing of computers, but I do know God loves and cares for my friend. Maybe she needed one recent, memorable answer to prayer to hang on to during the next few weeks when her husband was hospitalized.

Dear God, when daily glitches overwhelm me with stress,
I thank You that You hear my prayers. Amen.

—KAREN BARBER

Digging Deeper: Ps 66:16–20; Mt 6:7; Jn 15:7

May

Fri 9

"But when you are praying, first forgive anyone you are holding a grudge against. . . . "—MARK 11:25 (TLB)

Forgiveness is difficult for me. I know I hurt myself by nursing a grudge—my stomach churns, I can't sleep, and my prayers seem to hit the ceiling and bounce right back—but I still struggle to forgive.

After a recent incident, my "Help me forgive!" plea bounced back with an unrelated thought: My grandson Ryan's dog Ryker, a year-old husky, got out of the yard and disappeared. Ryan searched for two days without success, although he found an older husky at a nearby animal shelter. He was getting ready to place a lost-dog ad when he saw that another man had also lost a husky. The man lived seven miles away, making it unlikely the shelter dog was his, but Ryan called anyway.

That evening the man phoned to thank Ryan. The dog was his, and they had a joyful reunion. Then he said, "I'm not sure, but I think I glimpsed a husky in an alley behind my house." Ryan drove over and found a filthy, thirsty, delighted-to-be-found Ryker.

Ryan got his dog back because he stopped thinking about his loss long enough to help someone else. Would focusing on other people help me to forgive? It wasn't quite the same, but I decided to try. I sent a card to a relative, visited a homebound friend, and ran an errand for my husband.

My resentment didn't immediately disappear, and neither did the knot in my stomach. But doing things for other people did help me move beyond myself, and in time I was able to forgive.

Forgive my sins, Lord, as I forgive those who sin against me.
—PENNEY SCHWAB

Digging Deeper: EPH 4:32

Sat 10

"Whoever belongs to God hears what God says. . . . "
—JOHN 8:47 (NIV)

I sat in my car, ready to go to a workshop, yet frantically fumbled through my purse, looking for my cell phone. This had become an all-too-familiar routine. I'm ready to pull out of the garage and realize I don't have my phone. So I rush back into the house to look for it: the closet, by the bathroom sink, on the kitchen counter. My last resort is to call myself on another phone and wander around the house, hoping to hear it ringing.

That's how I found it this morning, buried under some papers by my computer. I hurried back to the car and went on my way—late, stressed, and frustrated.

It's my children's fault, I rationalized. They communicate mostly by texting and I began missing their messages, so I started carrying my cell phone around the house with me. *No wonder I lose it.*

By the time I arrived at the workshop, I'd rationalized my cell-phone frustration . . . until the topic of blaming others came up. "We often blame others to dispel our own frustration," I heard, which made me wonder if someone told this speaker what to tell me.

Later, I considered the way God connects words and thoughts into timely, personal messages. My frustration with my dependence on my cell phone is about me, and I'm the only one who can change it. I don't know what that might look like yet, but the message couldn't have been any clearer if God texted it directly to me on my cell phone.

Lord, I know I need to take responsibility for my own frustrations.
—CAROL KUYKENDALL

Digging Deeper: LK 12:47–48; GAL 6:1–5

May

Sun 11

"For six days work is to be done, but the seventh day is a day of sabbath rest, holy to the Lord. . . ." —Exodus 31:15 (NIV)

Day of rest? Yeah, right. I'm sure it'd go over really well if I plopped down on the couch, put up my feet, and refused to do any work for a day. Breakfast? How about some animal crackers and cereal? Laundry? Just wear yesterday's underwear. Can't you see Mama's resting? Oh, and the baby doesn't really need to have his diaper changed every time it's wet, does he?

All sarcasm aside, the last time I took a day off was before my first son was born. Just thinking about relaxing for a day makes me shudder at the thought of what I'd have to tackle the next day. But even God rested on the seventh day.

So I'm going to do it. On Mother's Day, I'm going to dedicate the day to God and my family. I'm going to put my laptop on its charging station and leave my phone on the bedside table. I'm going to go to church to enjoy the service. I'm going to have lunch with my kids without worrying about whether they've eaten their vegetables. I may even take a nap when the baby does. Because if God can do it, I can too.

Lord, give me the courage to put You and my family first this week so that I can tackle each day refreshed, rejuvenated, and ready to do Your work. Amen.

—Erin MacPherson

Digging Deeper: Gn 2:3; Mk 2:23–28

Mon 12

And if by grace, then it cannot be based on works; if it were, grace would no longer be grace. —ROMANS 11:6 (NIV)

I couldn't help noticing something on the dashboard of the cab I was riding in this morning: a snapshot of a college grad with mortarboard and gown, holding a diploma, smiling proudly; maybe the driver's son.

"Congratulations," I said. "Your son?"

"No," he answered, "that's me."

Momentarily mortified, I found myself thinking, *Tough luck, driving a cab with a college degree.* I got a better look at the driver. Middle Eastern, middle-aged. *Probably has a PhD in astrophysics back in his home country.*

"Well," I said awkwardly, "congratulations all the same. That's great."

"An education is the best thing this country has given me. I just got an accounting degree and pretty soon I will find a job in my field, God willing. But meanwhile I have a family to support. Want to see them?"

"Sure."

He flipped open the glove box where there were pictures of two boys and a girl, all in caps and gowns, all recent grads of high school and college. "I try to set a good example for them," he said with a laugh. "God willing, they will find good jobs too. Education is the key to everything."

As we pulled to the curb, I thought of my own family coming to this country and struggling to reach the American dream, just like this man and his family. I thought of all the opportunities I'd been blessed with and how I can take it all too much for granted at times. "It was an honor to ride in your cab," I said, handing the driver his fare.

"Have a good day, sir," he replied.

"I shall," I said, "God willing."

Jesus, they called You "Rabbi," which means teacher. This month please bless all those who have worked so hard and so long for that great key to the future, a diploma. —EDWARD GRINNAN

Digging Deeper: PRV 4:13, 16:3; ECCL 7:12

Tue 13

"But I have called you friends. . . "—John 15:15 (RSV)

I shoved down a feeling of panic when my car stalled as I exited a shopping center. I phoned my husband, Gene, and explained the situation. I knew it was silly, but I felt a bit, well, abandoned. It's a strange sensation I've battled all my life.

After thirty minutes, my cell phone rang. Gene, only ten minutes away, asked, "Are you on your way home?"

"What?" I bellowed, fighting tears. "Didn't you understand? I'm stranded here and . . ."

"Oh, I'm sorry, honey. I thought the car was just flooded. I'll get dressed and be there in a few minutes."

A snail could dress faster than my husband. Why hadn't he come immediately?

Just then, someone tapped on my car window. He was homeless and needed money. In my anger at Gene and my feelings of abandonment, I shook my head. He tipped a worn hat and gave me a toothless smile.

Glancing in my rearview mirror, I saw him join a woman and a young man a few feet from my car. They sat close together on a large wooden box up against a brick building. We were all stuck in the narrow alley on this cold, windy day.

I desperately needed companionship. Pulling money out of my purse, I opened the car door and approached them. Three genuine smiles greeted me. I put the bill in the woman's cold, rough-looking hand. "Thank you, ma'am." They all stood, and we introduced ourselves as though at a social gathering. The older man offered me a seat on the wooden box, and we sat down, scrunched up together. The sun warmed me, and my loneliness melted as my new friends and I made easy conversation.

Father, I saw You in their kind smiles. Teach me to see You everywhere.
—Marion Bond West

Digging Deeper: Eccl 4:9–12

Wed 14

And Jesus said to him, "'If you can'! All things are possible for one who believes." —Mark 9:23 (ESV)

My neighbor Irene's dog, Stray, is seventeen years old, they guess. Stray limped down the road scared and bone-thin fifteen years ago. Irene put out a bowl of food and led the dog to the shade of her back porch. Hours later, the dogcatcher came by asking if she had seen a mutt. Irene shrugged her shoulders and shook her head, feeling a need to protect the napping dog. She had already fallen in love.

In the last few years, Stray's black fur has grown gray around her deep brown eyes. Her gait is labored and difficult. When I saw Irene's husband digging a hole in the side yard, I thought the worst and went over to see if there was anything I could do.

"Stray probably won't make it through winter," he said. "Irene loves that dog so much. Always has. We just have to prepare."

"I'll pray for her," I said. And I did. Every time I looked out the window and saw the plywood covering the hole I prayed, "Please help Stray live a long happy life."

For most of the winter, snow covered the board. Each morning when I opened the blinds, I looked at the spot of the empty hole and prayed.

On a warm spring morning, I went out to get the paper. On the far edge of the neighbor's property, Stray wandered on top of a hill. I hadn't seen her that far away from the house in years. I yelled out to Irene, "Looks like you better fill that hole back in!"

"Oh that," she said. "Amazing, isn't it? I forgot all about that hole."

Dear Lord, help me to remember that when others prepare for the worst,
I can still pray for the best.

—Sabra Ciancanelli

Digging Deeper: Rom 12:12, 15:13

Thu 15

Now faith is the substance of things hoped for, the evidence of things not seen. —Hebrews 11:1 (KJV)

It was long past bedtime when I heard footsteps approaching our bedroom. Without opening my eyes, I knew who it was. Ten-year-old Maggie always has trouble falling asleep.

"What's the matter, Maggie?" I asked, trying to keep the irritation out of my voice.

"I want to ask you a question."

"Can't it wait until morning?"

"No."

I took Maggie to the living room. As we sat down on the sofa, she asked, "How can we be happy if people we love are in hell?"

I shook the cobwebs out of my head and sent up a quick prayer. "That's a very hard question," I said.

"Well, how can we?"

I told her that God was perfectly just and also perfectly merciful, and that we would see this in heaven and be content with everything He's done. I could see that Maggie wasn't convinced.

Maggie lives her faith; she's active in church, generous-hearted to those around her, concerned about the problems of the poor. And she's looking forward to two weeks at Bible camp this summer. I'm thankful for that. And I'm thankful that she feels she can come to me with her questions, even if I'm not very good at answering them.

Holy Spirit, give me the words to answer the questions I can and the humility to admit there are some that I can't.

—Andrew Attaway

Digging Deeper: Is 55:8; Jas 3:17

Fri 16

"Remain in me, as I also remain in you. No branch can bear fruit by itself; it must remain in the vine. Neither can you bear fruit unless you remain in me." —John 15:4 (NIV)

I've always been a high-intensity, high-ambition kind of person. I got straight A's in school. I became a professional ski racer and went to the Paralympics. I own an electric toothbrush and scrub my teeth each day till they sparkle.

But to the extent that ambition and drive are good things, I'm also a textbook example of the fact that you can have too much of a good thing. I've recently been struggling with a debilitating stress-related illness—and I don't mean headaches. I mean not-getting-out-of-bed-for-days-on-end debilitating. Once I figured out, with the help of some doctors, that it was my personality and lifestyle that were to blame instead of a rare virus, I knew I had to change. But change is hard.

I discussed my situation with my brother Matt and told him I didn't know how to slow down. "It's going to be difficult," he said, "because it will feel counterintuitive. Your whole life you've always been successful by being determined and persistent, by fighting hard. But this is a battle you can only win by fighting *less* hard."

It is, indeed, counterintuitive, I thought, *but Matt is right.* And in giving my body the time and space to heal, I've learned there are a whole host of things that can only be achieved with less effort, not more: peace, patience, loving relationships. And that includes my relationship with God, because it's only through His efforts, not mine, that I can know Him. The best things in life are not earned; they are given. But only if I pause long enough to receive them.

Lord, please help me to know when to fight and when to slow down and abide in You.

—Joshua Sundquist

Digging Deeper: Ex 34:21; Ps 127:2; Mt 11:28–30

Sat 17

I have much to write to you . . . so that our joy may be complete.
—2 John 1:12 (NIV)

I saved all the letters I received from my nieces and nephews over the years. There weren't many at first, but eventually my parents had twenty grandchildren.

All of them were affected by my mom's death ten years ago. I lived in Colorado, over a thousand miles away from most of my family, so I didn't really know any of my nieces and nephews well enough to understand the extent of their sorrow. It seemed to me that Rachel was especially saddened. Her pain reminded me of mine when my grandfather died, a pain so deep I gave up on God for years. I tried to comfort Rachel at the funeral and then wrote to her after I returned home. I was a father who had raised two sons. What could I say to help a young girl? I prayed and wrote and hoped God would give me words to bridge the wide gap created by age, gender, and geography.

I recently received a letter from my niece and lovingly placed it in a folder labeled Rachel. Her letter included these words: "I was eleven or twelve when I started writing you, and I remember vividly just what a letter from an adult outside my immediate family meant. And I remember how I memorized every word and kept all the letters."

Whenever I feel sad, I can always get out the Rachel folder and soon my joy is complete. Maybe God and love can bridge any gap, however wide.

Dear God, please bless my family as much as they have blessed me.
—Tim Williams

Digging Deeper: Ps 23:4; Zep 3:17; Jn 14:16

Sun 18

We may throw the dice, but the Lord determines how they fall. —Proverbs 16:33 (NLT)

A predawn visit to the gym found me crossing an empty parking lot on a rainy Sunday morning. I planned a quick workout before heading to church to preach the sermon I'd preached the night before. I spotted one other person, rummaging through trash cans for recyclables.

Two weeks earlier, I had loaded my car with four large bags of bottles and cans. I planned to redeem them but hadn't gotten around to it. There they sat, clinking and rattling at every turn.

What are the odds that one man was looking for recyclables while another man had a car loaded with them? And what are the odds that the one with the recyclables had preached a sermon the night before, saying, "Always be willing to do the next thing God prompts you to do" and was on his way to preach that sermon again?

My self-protective instincts told me to avoid eye contact and walk fast, but the Lord prompted me: "Help him." At first I missed His prompt—too busy, too anxious. I kept walking. Then it hit me. God wanted me to live what I was about to preach.

"Hey, buddy," I called out, "do you want some bottles and cans?"

"Yeah, sure." He eyed me warily and came my way. I opened the car and loaded him with all he could carry. "This is awesome," he said. "God bless you."

"Yes," I said, "it is awesome. God bless you too."

Thank You, God, for orchestrating Your mercies into my coincidences.
Awaken me to Your gentle promptings that I might
better share Your grace.
—Bill Giovannetti

Digging Deeper: 1 Kgs 19:11–12; Jas 4:17

Mon 19

I went down to the grove of nut trees to look at the new growth in the valley, to see if the vines had budded. . . .
—Song of Songs 6:11 (NIV)

I was pretty sure, in our first year of homeownership, that we'd managed to kill the roses, the yard, the crape myrtles, and the vine, which had fallen prey to some much-needed foundation repairs. My husband and I spent the winter looking out the window. "Are you supposed to water in winter?" I asked. "Or mow?" We watched our neighbors and decided not to.

I was preparing for a wedding shower in early spring when my mom arrived to help. The first thing she did was turn on our sprinklers full blast. "When the plants are growing, flowering, and making leaves, that's when they need the most water," she said.

Overnight, our yard transformed. The scratchy yellowed grass went "to seed," my mom said, sprouting tiny nubs at the tip of each blade, which she assured me meant new growth. The weeds I'd so diligently and ineffectively plucked from the beds bloomed into beautiful tulips. The roses lit up our backyard, not to be outpaced by the abundance of mint that crept along the fence. And that gnarled, woody vine exploded with crisp green leaves and dainty white flowers that drew big fat bumblebees, never failing to make me smile.

I always feel like my house is teaching me something. Often the lesson of the day is patience, but in this case, I learned the importance of nourishment, endurance, and rebirth. As I sit in my backyard, surrounded by blooms, buds, and bright green leaves, I'm reminded of God's tender mercy, His Resurrection, and His life-giving blood, which, like the water to my plants, brought new life in a seemingly hopeless space.

God, thank You for rebirth and renewal. Remind us that life moves in seasons. Help us enjoy every moment.
—Ashley Kappel

Digging Deeper: Rom 6:8–11; 2 Cor 5:17; 1 Pt 1:3–8

Tue 20

"The one who had received the one talent went off and dug a hole in the ground and hid his master's money."
—MATTHEW 25:18 (NRSV)

My husband, Kris, and I are of different bents regarding planning. He loves considering best case, worst case, and likeliest case scenarios. I, in contrast, despise planning. Planning evokes all the terrors fermenting below the surface of my faith. I don't even like thinking about retirement or the loan needed to pay for the girls' schooling, much less talking about it. My go-to response is fear! In my view, the guy in Jesus' parable who buries his master's money is not lazy but terrified. If it were up to me, we'd never discuss the future at all.

Not, mind you, that I'm more trusting than Kris. When problems arise—as they inevitably do, despite our plans—Kris's mustard seed is definitely bigger and more robust than mine. "God will take care of us," he says. And he believes it. Planning, paradoxically, is part of letting God do just that.

Kris likes a joke in which a drowning man turns down help from a rowboat, then a speedboat, then a helicopter, saying, "God will rescue me." Later, in heaven, he asks God why He didn't answer that prayer.

"Well," God responds, "I sent you a rowboat, then a speedboat, then a helicopter. . . . "

Planning, Kris argues, is good stewardship of the opportunities God sends. I fear I'll never learn this, but I keep trying.

Father, help me remember not only Your provision
but Your expectations of us as its stewards. Replace my fears
with good judgment and ever-growing trust.
—PATTY KIRK

Digging Deeper: 2 TM 1:7; 1 PT 4:10

Wed 21

"If you, then, though you are evil, know how to give good gifts to your children, how much more will your Father in heaven give good gifts to those who ask him!"
—MATTHEW 7:11 (NIV)

Things boiled over again last night. The daughter left the back door open and the dog escaped, and we all had to spend an hour tracking him down in the rain. Everyone is annoyed with her, and so she is annoyed and guilty and grim.

The younger son bugged the older son one too many times and the mother popped a gasket and the father roared and all retreated and the house simmered—and it took hours for everyone to apologize.

In bed, my lovely bride says for the thousandth time that if nights like this happen, we have not done well enough as parents, and for the thousandth time I reply that stuff happens, and bucolic families only exist on TV. But later in the dark I too am dark and sad that I have roared at my children, that perhaps I did not teach them the crucial essence of kindness and empathy they need in the bones of their hearts; but then in the morning I hear the daughter arise to make the coffee, and I hear one son in the shower without being reminded it is his turn to get up early, and I hear the other son murmuring affectionately to the dog, and I think, *Yes, oh yes, God's compassions never fail; they are new every morning, yes, oh yes . . .*

All too soon there will be no bicker and burble in the house, the children will be gone to college and maturity, and I know I'll weep and mourn and know better what I dimly realize now—that even their sneer and snarl is a mysterious gift from the Maker, Who granted us children to teach as best we can.

Dear Lord, yes, I know I begged for them. I remember that well, the wheedling and pleading, and You gave them to me! Not a day goes by that I do not lie here smiling that You listened, that You granted them, that they drive me crazy! Thank You!
—BRIAN DOYLE

Digging Deeper: Ps 127:3–5

Thu 22

A soft answer turns away wrath, but harsh words cause quarrels. —PROVERBS 15:1 (TLB)

Before Jack broke up with me in 2010, I'd written a long list of reasons why I never wanted to marry him. I didn't let him read the list, but I had told him about it.

Two months after the breakup, I wrote a list of all the things I missed about him. I didn't show him that list either because pride got in my way. The new list had forty-three things on it including: his hugs during the day; having a calm soul next to me to chat with daily; going to Mass together, knowing we are each praying for the other; holding hands during the sermon; fixing meals together; Saturday date night; swimming in the Gulf together; playing canasta, even when I lost; traveling together in the car; shopping with him, knowing it would be short; when he'd bring my mail and sit in my office for a visit.

I wonder what would have happened if I'd given him that list of forty-three things I missed about him the day I wrote it. However, he was dating another woman at the time and I didn't even want to speak to him then.

Eight months after we got back together, I found the list in my computer and forwarded it to Jack. He was touched and told me nearly everything on that list was a reason he, too, wanted to get back in the relationship.

These days when I think of something I particularly like about my husband, I tell him immediately. I think the sweet words are definite happiness enhancers for both of us.

Father, never let me hold back when I have something nice to say about someone, and always help me to keep the not-so-nice things to myself.
—PATRICIA LORENZ

Digging Deeper: PRV 12:18, 16:24; EPH 4:29

Fri 23

Let your eyes look directly ahead and let your gaze be fixed straight in front of you . . . and all your ways will be established. —PROVERBS 4:25–26 (NAS)

Recently, I hiked in the Rocky Mountain National Park in northern Colorado. Never have I seen color so vibrant, lakes so bracing, or more serene majesty of mountains brushing cumulous sky.

Leaving the park with a firm resolve to return, I drove along the northern Trail Ridge Road, which weaves and twists as it climbs above 12,400 feet. The road grew more narrow and treacherous as I edged around hairpin turns and stared down steep valleys. I gripped the steering wheel firmly as sweat broke out on my brow.

Fighting panic, I riveted my eyes straight ahead and refused to look down into the chasm of fear. Seconds seemed like minutes and a mile an infinite distance. Forcing a weak smile, I thought, *Walker, you'd never make a paratrooper. They'd have to kick you out the door.*

Well, I survived and carefully descended to Grand Lake, enormously grateful for flat land, lush prairie, and broad highways.

Life teaches us that there are days when we simply have to stay focused, ignore panic, and ascend the mountain. We learn that even though fear is raw, God is with us. We discover that there is no courage devoid of fear; no faith without challenge.

Father, fix my eyes on the road ahead. May I not be afraid of fear. Amen.
—SCOTT WALKER

Digging Deeper: DT 31:6; JO 1:9; HEB 12:1–2

LIFE LESSONS FROM THOSE I'VE MET

Sat 24

It was not you who sent me here, but God....
—GENESIS 45:8 (RSV)

JUAN, CUBAN PASTOR

It was 1986 in Communist Cuba when I met Juan, a graying fifty-one-year-old with a merry smile that was hard to understand as he told his story.

After the revolution, his engineering firm demoted employees who wrote "Christian" on a new questionnaire. With his salary halved and their fourth baby on the way, he and his wife applied to leave the country. For that, he was sent to work in the sugarcane fields. "To feed our children, my wife and I would go to bed hungry."

It was two years before the exit visa came and they could make the daylong bus trip from Santiago to Havana. Their luggage was already aboard the plane to Miami when an official spotted the word *engineer* on Juan's papers. "Engineers are not permitted to emigrate!"

"But I'm not allowed to work as an engineer."

"The law is the law."

They got back to Santiago to find strangers in their house. Juan's family moved into a single room in a friend's apartment where Juan began again filling out forms for emigration. It was in the fields one day that everything changed. "It was like a voice inside my head: *It isn't the law that keeps you here. I have work for you to do.*"

Juan withdrew his application to emigrate. His citizen status was restored, and he was offered his old engineering post. He turned it down to lead a dozen small house-churches. As he took me to meet some of those he ministers to, I knew I'd never seen a man more fulfilled.

Let me learn from Juan to ask, when my own small plans are blocked, "Lord, is this You?" —ELIZABETH SHERRILL

Digging Deeper: JOB 42:2; ROM 8:28–29

May

Sun 25

When Jesus spoke again to the people, he said, "I am the light of the world. Whoever follows me will never walk in darkness, but will have the light of life." —John 8:12 (NIV)

Over the past eighteen months, I've been working on a reporting project that has taken me to dozens of churches. Of all the ones I've visited, my favorite is a pile of rocks in western Ireland. The Gallarus Oratory is a dry-stone construction, which means that it doesn't have mortar holding it together. It looks a little like a small boat turned upside down, and nobody knows exactly who built it or when it was built—maybe it was the eighth or ninth century.

When I visited the oratory, I walked around it and noticed there are only two openings: a man-size one that serves as a way in and, opposite that, a square-size hole that functions as a small window, letting in a single stream of light. This house of worship is purely that, without seating or an altar or a baptismal font or stained glass or crucifix or any of the things that might stereotypically signal "church."

How simple this piece of architecture was! How focused and how appropriate. As I stood there, just inside the doorway, all I saw was that lone window through which the sun shone, breaking the room's dimness. All I saw was darkness pierced by one solitary and powerful light.

Lord, we thank You for illuminating our lives.

—Jeff Chu

Digging Deeper: 2 Cor 4:6; 1 Jn 1:5

Mon 26

Jonathan said to David, "Go in peace, for we have sworn friendship with each other in the name of the Lord, saying, 'The Lord is witness between you and me, and between your descendants and my descendants forever'". . . .
—1 Samuel 20:42 (NIV)

Retired major general and former chief of chaplains Gaylord T. Gunhus and I spend a lot of time on the road, visiting with military chaplains. Gunhus is the military adviser for Guideposts' outreach ministry. While on one of our trips to Fort Lewis in Seattle, Washington, Gunhus asked me to accompany him to visit his longtime friend, retired four-star Major General John, at the assisted-living community.

Upon our arrival, the two men embraced. John had suffered a stroke that impaired one side of his body but told Gunhus, "Earlier today I was at the golf course. I took a swing from the cart with one hand."

These two men caught up on each other's life, talking about the troops and the country they love so deeply. They remembered the different military installations, places of service, and colleagues who had gone home to be with the Lord. I thought to myself, *What a blessing it is for me to experience such a display of love, care, and respect between friends.*

As we were getting ready to leave, Gunhus asked John, "May I say a prayer for you?" The general nodded. Chaplain Gunhus got down on one knee next to the reclining chair where the general was seated, and prayed for the well-being of his dear friend. Little did we know that it would be the last time they would see each other.

Lord, teach me to treasure my lifelong friends through my love and actions.
—Pablo Diaz

Digging Deeper: Mt 6:19–21; 1 Thes 5:11

Tue 27

I thank my God in all my remembrance of you, always offering prayer with joy in my every prayer for you all.
—Philippians 1:3–4 (NAS)

My sister-in-law had lost her brother and father close together and suddenly. Now, only months later, her mother was recovering from serious cancer surgery, wondering whether to try chemo pills in her eighties. The family seemed inundated with grief.

Thirteen of us agreed to pray each Tuesday. I e-mailed a weekly "Remember!" letter that included an array of both immediate and ongoing family prayer needs. I added a brief meditation, along with a Bible verse.

From Alaska to Colorado to Washington, DC, from Minnesota to California, we prayed for one another as one voice. Amazing things happened! The cancer patient did exceptionally well with chemotherapy, astounding her doctors, and remains cancer free. Our son-in-law, leaving a communications company to begin studying veterinary medicine, received an unusual and generous severance package.

Our son and daughter-in-law, unable to afford to finish shipping their personal goods long distance to their new residence, cringed as huge storage fees accrued. When the freighting agent finally decided to auction their things, he saw their wedding photo—packed on top at the last minute. He contacted them, saying it "broke his heart" and he was waiving all fees. They were able to complete the shipping.

Not only did we see God's magnificent answers in our prayers for one another, we also drew closer as a family. Ask us our favorite day of the week; it's Tuesday!

Listening Father, You are a God Who responds to heartfelt prayer seven days a week.
—Carol Knapp

Digging Deeper: Mt 18:19–20; Jas 5:16

Wed 28

Grace to you and peace. —1 THESSALONIANS 1:1 (RSV)

At first, I thought he was a construction worker on a lunch break. He was sitting on the curb, with food almost gone from a plastic plate. But as our eyes met, he asked, "Spare change?" I dug in my purse and hurriedly gave him a few coins; I was on my own lunch break.

About to walk on, I was startled when he patted the curb. "Sit a minute, please." I did, and he said, "They kicked me out of there." He jerked his thumb toward a fast-food place down the street. "I picked up a plate or two that people had left, and they told me to get out." I was horrified, unsure what to say, when he continued: "People in a church I used to go to always used to worry about shut-ins. But what about us shut-outs?"

Dear God, what have I gotten into here? I wondered what it would be like to be kicked out of a fast-food restaurant, and thought of several times in my life I'd felt shut out: from being last to be chosen for a team to not being invited to a baby shower and even to being disowned by a family member. It's a lonely, unhappy, isolating feeling.

Still... I've got to go back to work, I thought, torn.

But he then stuck his hand out. "I'm Kevin."

I shook his hand. "I'm Linda," I said.

"Thanks for shaking my hand, Linda," Kevin said. "You're probably in a rush," he said. "Everyone is."

I started to rise and then stopped. "I have a little time," I told him. "Work can wait."

Lord, today let me not exclude another human being from my circle.
After all, You don't shut anybody out.

—LINDA NEUKRUG

Digging Deeper: MT 25:31–40; ROM 12:15

May

Thu 29

Being confident of this, that he who began a good work in you will carry it on to completion until the day of Christ Jesus. —PHILIPPIANS 1:6 (NIV)

The Internet wasn't working, and I needed to get online to send out some important e-mails. "Ryan," I called downstairs, "are you on the Internet?"

We had a weak router. Usually, if my husband got on from his computer, it would knock me off mine. "No!" he called back.

Frustration stirred. How was I supposed to get any work done with such spotty service? I stomped downstairs and looked up the number for our provider. I made the phone call, and the longer I waited, the stronger my irritation grew. Finally, a female voice came on the other line. As she walked me through the different trouble spots, my tone was impatient.

When I got off the phone, I didn't know what I was more annoyed with: my Internet or my attitude. Ryan came upstairs, popped his head into our office, and found me sitting with my elbows on my knees, my face in my hands. "Did you get it fixed?" he asked.

"Yes."

"Then what's wrong?"

"I was really rude to that woman." My memory verse from the week scrolled through my mind: *Love . . . does not demand its own way. It is not irritable* (1 Corinthians 13:4–5). I felt like such a failure—so far from the person I longed to be. "Sometimes I feel like a lousy Christian."

"You're a work in progress." Ryan rubbed my shoulders. "We all are."

Thank You, Lord, for beginning a good work in me and for Your unending grace when I mess up. I'm so glad that You are not done with me yet.
—KATIE GANSHERT

Digging Deeper: GAL 6:9; PHIL 1

Fri 30

So the next generation would know them, even the children yet to be born, and they in turn would tell their children.
—Psalm 78:6 (NIV)

A friend asked me to stop by her house to see the antique mahogany china cabinet she'd inherited from her grandmother. With its large, antique, double glass doors, you could see the delicately etched crystal stemware, fine heirloom china, and sterling silverware placed just so.

"What a beautiful cabinet!" I exclaimed. I carefully opened it and picked up a dinner plate that was trimmed with tiny lilac flowers and soft green leaves. "Your china is lovely too," I said. I turned over the plate and read the back: Haviland.

"All the women in my family for three generations have picked Haviland as their wedding china," she said. "It's a legacy in our family."

"How wonderful," I replied.

"Is there a china pattern passed down from generation to generation in your family?" she asked.

"Oh no," I said. "My mother and grandmother never owned any china. They struggled just to make ends meet. My grandmother worked hard her entire life as a waitress. My mom quit school when she was a teenager to help her family. When she became a single mom with the five of us, she worked two jobs." I placed the dinner plate back in its place. "No," I said, "there was no legacy handed down in my family."

"No legacy?" she asked. "Well, it sure sounds like your grandmother and mother worked very hard, sacrificed a great deal, and did whatever they had to do to keep the family going. If you ask me, that's a pretty awesome legacy."

Thank You, Father, for a family who lived their faith through difficulties and hardships and who inspire me how to live.
—Melody Bonnette Swang

Digging Deeper: Pss 78:4, 103:17–18

Sat 31

They trusted in thee, and were not confounded.
—PSALM 22:5 (KJV)

It was spring break—a time for joy—but my mind was in turmoil. Some big changes at the college threatened my income and clouded my future.

We were on our way to visit our daughter Teresa in Kansas City, and as we crossed the flooded Missouri River, I could see my own tumultuous future in its roiling waters.

We had a nice visit in the city of fountains, but as we packed our suitcases to return home, my mind still raced with doubts. "I think I'll take a little walk," I said to Teresa, "before we hit the road."

"Okay, Dad, but stay off of Troost Avenue. That's a rough neighborhood."

I strolled through pretty residential areas with perfect gardens and glorious dogwoods in bloom. But it was all a little too perfect and somehow irritating, so I turned east, then headed back by Troost, in spite of my daughter's warnings. Somehow Troost matched my mood better. It was noisy, chaotic, even scary, with graffiti scribbled on every building.

Teresa's house was in view, when some graffiti on the back of a garage caught my eye: "Let the muddy water settle and then you will see clearly."

I plopped down on a bus stop bench and took a deep breath. "That's the problem," I said to myself. "I keep stirring up the waters with my questions. I just need to let things settle down."

It wasn't easy, leaving my future alone, but in a few days I began to feel much better. Now, months later, I can see exactly what I need to do.

Thank You for taking away my confusion, Lord, and
for teaching me to trust You with my future.
—DANIEL SCHANTZ

Digging Deeper: PRV 3:5–6; JAS 1:5

DAILY MERCIES

1 ______

2 ______

3 ______

4 ______

5 ______

6 ______

7 ______

8 ______

9 ______

10 ______

11 ______

12 ______

13 ______

14 ______

15 ______

May

16 ______________________________

17 ______________________________

18 ______________________________

19 ______________________________

20 ______________________________

21 ______________________________

22 ______________________________

23 ______________________________

24 ______________________________

25 ______________________________

26 ______________________________

27 ______________________________

28 ______________________________

29 ______________________________

30 ______________________________

31 ______________________________

JUNE

He hath shewed thee, O man, what is good; and what doth the Lord require of thee, but to do justly, and to love mercy, and to walk humbly with thy God?

—MICAH 6:8 (KJV)

HOPE IN HOSPICE

Sun 1 *"This is my blood of the covenant, which is poured out for many for the forgiveness of sins."*—MATTHEW 26:28 (NIV)

GIFT OF COMMUNION

Lay Eucharistic Visitor—the title scared me. The responsibility felt heavy. But the need was there, and I had raised my hand.

"Here's what you need," said the minister. He handed me a small black box with a leather handle. I was tongue-tied as I took out the tiny silver chalice, the flask of consecrated wine, the box of wafers, and the small white cloth embroidered with a cross. *Can I do this? Suppose I lose my place or drop the chalice? Suppose I am asked questions I can't answer?*

I felt shy about offering Communion, but then how could the hospice patients know it was available unless I told them? Mike, a volunteer with many years of experience, was cheerfully reassuring. "It's a gift you have to give." Many were obviously grateful. A few, he said, declined but thanked him for the offer.

So I took the plunge with Anne, a patient who had been active in her church but now was growing weaker each day. "Would you like to receive Communion?" I said with a smile.

"Oh yes, please," she replied immediately.

I spread out the white cloth and began rather hesitantly: "Jesus said to them, 'I am the bread of life; whoever comes to me shall not hunger, and whoever believes in me shall never thirst'" (John 6:35, ESV). Right then I realized, without any doubt, that though I might be the messenger, the message was a gift far beyond my shaky fingers.

Thank You, Lord, for the gifts of Your Communion table
that keep us always in Your sight.
—BRIGITTE WEEKS

Digging Deeper: MT 26:26–29

Mon 2

He sent a wind over the earth, and the waters receded.
—GENESIS 8:1 (NIV)

Most of the biblical references to "wind" are associated with destruction. There are scorching winds in Genesis, locust-bearing winds in Exodus, and rock-shattering winds in 1 Kings. In the book of Acts, 276 people go without food for fourteen days because the winds have kept them "in suspense."

I dislike wind. It dries our gardens and covers everything in dust. If the gusts continue into the night, I am both awake and hungry. Until this winter, I rarely welcomed the wind.

We have an evaporative pond beyond our septic tank instead of a leach field. We didn't choose the pond; our soil doesn't leach, so we needed a pond. This winter the trees south of our pond grew tall enough to shade our pond, and it didn't evaporate. The deepening water eventually was higher than our septic tank, and our pipes quit flowing. I limbed the trees but thought my wife and I would have to shower sparingly and do laundry in town for a few weeks. Instead, God sent some unusually dry and persistent winds over our pond, and the waters receded.

The winds grew even stronger this spring. I ate many suspense-free meals and thanked God for the winds' water-wicking power.

Dear God, help us to see the blessings hidden in Your storms.
—TIM WILLIAMS

Digging Deeper: Ps 107:29; Is 25:4

Tue 3

The Lord is close to the brokenhearted and saves those who are crushed in spirit. —Psalm 34:18 (NIV)

It had been a year since my wife Julee's brother Mick took his life after a long and only occasionally hopeful struggle with alcohol, drugs, and depression. It ended one June day with a bottle of pills. No note. No more pain.

Julee would sometimes talk about finding the manuscript to some masterpiece Mick left behind and getting it published. Then she would catch herself; that book had been buried with him. Her voice, like her dreams for her brother, would trail off.

On this first June day without Mick, I found Julee sobbing on the bed. Not healing tears, not good tears. Tears of anguish and anger and bitterness. "I'm so mad," she said. "I don't even know who I'm mad at. Mick? Maybe God? Who says there are stages of grief... like there's some sort of GPS for your pain? There isn't. Don't believe it. There's just hurt and confusion and loss that I will never ever understand!"

I didn't have an answer for Julee. I don't think she expected one. She needed to say what was in her heart, and her heart would change with time. I was sure of that. She would always love her brother, and sometimes God is the only one big enough to be mad at in the face of such pain. A wise old-timer in an AA meeting once told me that life doesn't get easier, but it does get better. It took me years to understand that. Julee understood it too, even if she didn't feel it on this first June day without her beloved brother. But she would, in God's time.

Lord, life is not always easy, but when we walk with You it is always good.
Please be with Julee and those whose hearts grieve. The greater
the loss, the more You are there.

—Edward Grinnan

Digging Deeper: Ps 147:3; Mt 5:4; Rv 21:4

Wed 4

"And when it reverts in the jubilee, the field shall be holy to the Lord, like a field set apart...." —LEVITICUS 27:21 (NAS)

I turned sixty about the time Queen Elizabeth II celebrated her Diamond Jubilee reign over the United Kingdom in June 2012. There was a big lunch for the nation's families, friends, and neighbors; a flotilla on the Thames; a national service of thanksgiving at St. Paul's Cathedral; and Jubilee beacons lit around the world to honor the queen's years on the throne.

In researching the event, I learned the royal Diamond Jubilee celebration was condensed from seventy-five years to sixty during the time of Queen Victoria. Hers was commemorated in 1897, to draw the country together in a time of turmoil.

Jubilee is found in the book of Leviticus. God commanded Moses: "You shall have the fiftieth year as a jubilee" (Leviticus 25:11, NAS). Fields were to lie fallow, property restored to its original owner, and Hebrew indentured servants allowed to return home. God declared that the year "be holy to you" (Leviticus 25:12). *Jubilee* has come to mean spiritual rest and restoration and renewal. It is a time to go deep with God.

When I turned fifty, I thrilled to the idea that it was my jubilee year. However, in the years following, I experienced an intense crisis of spirit. God "went deep" with me through it all, reviving me again in the gifts of jubilee.

That's why turning sixty with the queen brought more excitement than I'd known at fifty. I celebrated with God His rightful reign in me. You might say I had my own Diamond Jubilee—with the King!

High King of heaven, to Thee be the kingdom and glory
and power forever and ever!
—CAROL KNAPP

Digging Deeper: Ps 103:19

Thu 5

Therefore, as we have opportunity, let us do good to all people, especially to those who belong to the family of believers.
—Galatians 6:10 (NIV)

When I resigned as pastor of a congregation, one of the most disappointed folks was Bob, a good friend of several years. He couldn't understand why I was stepping down. On several occasions I felt his frustration, hurt, and annoyance and was saddened by his behavior toward me. We were not able to talk about our feelings before I left.

One afternoon while I was at my new job, I learned that Bob was in the hospital. I tried unsuccessfully to contact members of the congregation to learn more about his status. I even called him, but he didn't pick up. Finally, I sent him a text message: "Bob, thinking of and praying for you."

Early the next morning, I saw that Bob had responded to my message: "I am leaving the hospital today. Thank you for your prayers." I wanted to see him but felt like I had missed the visiting window since he was being discharged. My wife encouraged me to go.

When I arrived, Bob was surprised and happy to see me. Tears rolled down the corners of our eyes as we hugged. We talked, laughed, and caught up on family, church, and work.

I stayed with him and his wife until he was released from the hospital. On my way home, I thanked God we were able to put our disappointments behind us and reconcile our differences.

Lord, give me the courage to reach out to those
who have been disappointed or hurt by me.
—Pablo Diaz

Digging Deeper: Mt 5:23–24; Eph 4:32; Heb 12:14

Fri 6

Now abideth faith, hope, charity, these three; but the greatest of these is charity. —1 CORINTHIANS 13:13 (KJV)

I was walking my dog Max on the village green when I saw two men working high in the maple trees, hanging from ropes, cutting branches. Their truck sat below them, parked on the street.

I was pondering and praying over how to help a friend in need. *Should I reach out to him, God? Is it the right time to offer help? Or does he need time and space to handle this on his own?* I didn't want to intrude.

Then a loud noise jerked my head around. I looked to see one of the men reaching for a branch that wasn't there. A second later, he fell, landing on the grass twenty feet below. "Oh, God!" he screamed. You don't often hear a man scream.

A split second later, his coworker, still hanging safely in the trees above, suddenly let go. I watched as he slid about ten feet down the trunk of his own tree, then jumped, landing on the ground with two feet. Now at his friend's side, he immediately began examining him, asking what sort of help he required.

What an act of friendship and caring I had just witnessed! God had answered me.

Lord, give me the courage today to love without fear.
—JON SWEENEY

Digging Deeper: PS 56:3–4; 2 TM 1:7; 1 JN 4:18

Sat 7

Therefore, if anyone is in Christ, he is a new creation; the old has gone, the new has come! —2 CORINTHIANS 5:17 (NIV)

Solomon, Henry, and I walked to the front of the grocery store to the special shopping-cart cars. For years, the boys have been riding in kid-friendly carts that have a riding car in the front with steering wheels, seatbelts, and horns.

Henry, five, ran to the closest car cart and slid in. He put on the seatbelt and turned the wheel. Solomon, nine, put one leg to the side and squeezed. He tried another angle. "I don't know, Sol. I think the day has come. I think you're too big," I said.

Solomon shook his head and tried to go through the front. No use.

"How about pushing the cart? Would you like that?"

Solomon put his hands on the steering bar. I walked beside him as he struggled to maneuver the extra long and heavy cart. I walked to the onions, and Solomon veered toward a fruit display. I ran to rescue him, but he reached out and pushed away my hand. "No, I'm driving, Mom!"

Throughout the store, Solomon pushed the cart with a prideful smile. By the time we reached the checkout, my nerves were frazzled by the dozen near-misses of running into products or people.

"You're a good helper," the cashier said to Solomon. He smiled.

When we got in the car, I looked in the rearview at the boys. I thought about how cute Solomon and Henry looked when they were younger and could both fit in the car cart. *Soon Solomon will be in middle school,* I thought. *The days of him even wanting to come shopping with me are numbered.*

"Henry, some day you'll be big like me!" Solomon said. "Some day you'll get to push the cart!"

Lord, help me see the changes ahead with the same joy as a child getting older. —SABRA CIANCANELLI

Digging Deeper: Is 40:31; Mt 6:33

Sun 8

I press toward the mark for the prize of the high calling of God.... —PHILIPPIANS 3:14 (KJV)

The sermon, based on Philippians, was a moving story recalling the struggles early Christians faced. Unfortunately, sitting there in the pew, I found myself losing focus. As an investment adviser, I was struggling with a tough investment environment. My mind floated around, bouncing between life's challenges, and suddenly moved to something incredibly unimportant: golf.

"How hard can it be?" I had scoffed at my best friend Ben. "The ball isn't even moving when you hit it."

So armed with my razor-sharp reasoning and a new set of clubs, I toiled away, until my shirt was soaked with sweat and I was madder than a hornet. Things only got worse when I played a round with my father-in-law. "Brock," Lee said in the kindest possible way, "you should consider taking lessons from Virgil. He's the best in town."

"Golf is difficult," were Virgil's first words to me. "It takes a lot of practice and patience, but I can help if you stick with it." After months of struggling through lessons, I made a breakthrough. The path of my swing wasn't right. That corrected, my game improved and I began to enjoy the sport more than ever.

Suddenly, I was back in the pew and connecting the dots. "The path we take is a constant work in progress," the minister continued, "but Paul teaches us that there is always hope for those who press on."

I can't control the stock market and I'll never make the PGA tour, but as I walk along the course of life, I can keep my focus on the great truth that God spreads before me: No matter what our challenge, it's pressing on and finishing the round that makes life well worth any struggle.

Father, help me stay focused as I work to stay on course and press on toward Your goals for me.

—BROCK KIDD

Digging Deeper: PHIL 3

Mon 9

Choose my instruction instead of silver, knowledge rather than choice gold. —Proverbs 8:10 (NIV)

I got married in the "silver candy dish era" of wedding presents and now, some forty years later, I'm wondering what to do with them and many other assorted pieces of silver that have been passed down in our family. My friend Marilyn owns an antique store and recognizes the value of such things, so we sat down at my dining room table where I'd spread everything out.

"These silver spoons meant something to our grandmothers who displayed collections on their walls. I tell people to pick out a couple of unique ones and I make bracelets out of them," she said, showing me how she bends them into a circle with the help of some special tools.

She looked at glassware, silverware, and other pieces. "See if your children or grandchildren want any of these. They might surprise you. Any family attachment is way more valuable than what you might get if you sell it."

The next day I showed my nine-year-old granddaughter a tarnished spoon engraved with a K, which is her initial, from the silverware set. She took it in her hand and slowly turned it over a couple of times. "I really like this," she said softly.

Lord, let me learn the value of those things with meaning beyond what I see today.

—Carol Kuykendall

Digging Deeper: Prv 13:22; Mt 6:19–21

Tue 10

"Why did you bring us up out of Egypt to this terrible place?. . . "—NUMBERS 20:5 (NIV)

Maggie's been moody lately. Her naturally expansive personality easily stretches from pure joy to profound grumpiness, and at nearly eleven years old she's now able to hit both extremes several times a day. I love this about her. Maggie's got grit and range and passion. She's a thinker. She's dramatic. Though she's a thin, leggy preteen, there's something big about her. She's going to grow into an amazing woman.

Maggie, of course, doesn't feel that way. She only sees that her emotions zing back and forth, that life is a roller coaster and the ride isn't always thrilling. I tell her it's normal to feel this at her age, and that the ups and downs will settle into a gentler pattern with time. It's okay if she doesn't want to grow up. It's okay that she yearns for the freedoms of teenagers too. It will all happen eventually. God will give her plenty of time to grow into being the Maggie He created her to be.

But then I sense my own world shifting. I think about all the unknowns of having a house full of teens, and it feels uncomfortable. So I remind myself that the thing that matters is God is with me today. He'll be with me tomorrow and with every step I take, every day of my life. Even in the wilderness of not knowing, I'm never alone. The only truly bad thing that can happen is to forget He is there.

Father, even if it takes forty years in the wilderness to teach me to trust You daily, teach me.

—JULIA ATTAWAY

Digging Deeper: MAL 3:6; HEB 13:8

Wed 11

"One thing I do know. I was blind but now I see!"
—JOHN 9:25 (NIV)

Our son Jeff unearthed a little picture book out of our basement entitled *My First Bible*, which had been his when he was a preschooler. The book had drawings of Bible scenes with brief stories about them.

Jeff opened the book to a picture of Jesus and handed it to his eighteen-month-old daughter Kendall. She sat right down in the middle of the kitchen floor, put the book in her lap, opened the next page, pointed her finger to the printed words, and pretended to read. "I see, I see," she repeated over and over.

At first I thought this was an amusing phrase for a baby to say as she pretended to read. But then I realized that she was used to books where she was asked to see things like stars and puppies, and point them out to learn new words. As Kendall continued to repeat, "I see, I see" after every sentence, she succeeded in summarizing the Bible in a simple yet very profound way that babies—even adults—can understand.

The Bible is indeed a place where we *see* things. We see God and Jesus. We see ourselves. We see God's kingdom. We see our faults and our need to repent. We see how to live. The list is endless. The following day when I finished reading a passage in the Bible, I closed it and said, "I see, I see."

Father, there is so much I need to see about myself and my life today.
Open my eyes and illumine me as I open Your Word. Amen.
—KAREN BARBER

Digging Deeper: Ps 119:1–18

Thu 12

"Therefore be merciful, just as your Father also is merciful."
—Luke 6:36 (NKJV)

The antique Pinwheel quilt was tattered on the edges and stained. Still, I fell in love with it. After I babied it and got the stains out of the sage-green background, I mailed it to Steve, who lives in Elkton, Kentucky, and rebinds old quilts by hand.

But when I received the quilt back from Steve, it was in a smaller box and felt lighter. His puppy had gotten ahold of it and chewed the sides and top. In an effort to salvage it, Steve had cut down the quilt and rebound it. He offered to repay me for my vintage quilt.

A friend advised, "That quilt was one of a kind and you loved it. Take the money."

My mind told me every reason why I shouldn't wipe Steve's slate clean, but my heart had other plans. I recalled beloved puppies of mine like Thunder, the one who gnawed the leg on a neighbor's table. I tried to reimburse her, but she said, "I wouldn't think of it, honey. We've all had puppies."

The situation with Steve called for mercy. I could hear the relief across the miles when I telephoned him. And that quilt that used to fit a double bed? It makes the most darling little table topper.

Thank You, God, for those who point us to the path of mercy. Amen.
—Roberta Messner

Digging Deeper: Lk 6:27–36

June

Fri 13

"I create new heavens and a new earth. . . ."
—Isaiah 65:17 (RSV)

When the topic of building a brand-new public library first came up, I couldn't imagine there would be any dissension about funding it, but there was. Shocked that some people were just stick-in-the-muds, I wrote a letter to the editor, talked up the project to friends, and did all I could to promote the new library, including praying that others would see the need to embrace it. "New books, gleaming bookshelves, a separate children's section with colorful furniture for kids to enjoy while they read. And scores of computers!" *Why are some people against progress?*

Now, about a year later, I settled into one of the library's comfy chairs in front of a computer. I reached into my Friend of the Library tote and pulled out my floppy disk to insert in the computer . . . and couldn't find the floppy disk drive. I called over the reference librarian, who said, "It doesn't have one."

A man sitting nearby looked up and said briefly, "No one uses floppies anymore. It takes a CD or flash drive."

So I went home and gave my friend an earful.

She just laughed. "I guess God answered your prayer pretty fast! Remember, you said you wanted people to learn new things."

"I guess I didn't mean me," I said shamefacedly.

My friend joked, "You know what they say: When you point a finger at someone else, a flash drive points back at you!" So I bought a flash drive, and after an hour of self-torture, I taught myself how to use it.

Lord, thank You for poking and prodding me into the new world when I am desperately trying to hang on to the old!
—Linda Neukrug

Digging Deeper: Prv 22:4; Rom 12:3; 1 Pt 5:5

Sat 14 *Make a joyful noise unto the Lord*. . . . —Psalm 98:4 (KJV)

Last June I started reading the Bible straight through . . . out loud. It was a good way to wake up my voice box in the morning, and it helped me stay committed to this daily regimen, keeping me focused.

I read through several chapters every day, but I got bogged down in the lengthy, complicated—and let's face it, downright boring—series of "begats" in the Old Testament. I understand the importance of the Israelite ancestry—this is their personal heritage that underlines the promise from God—but the unfamiliar names were tricky to pronounce. I was tempted to drop the oration. *It would be much faster to read this part to myself*, I thought as I stumbled through lists of temple workers.

Most of the names I had to attempt a few times before I was happy with the pronunciation. Then came "Eliphelehu" (1 Chronicles 15:18). Who in their right mind would name a baby Eliphelehu? I sighed and tried to go on in spite of feeling discouraged. "Eely. No, Ellee . . . fellee . . . ah . . . he . . . who. No, that's not right."

Suddenly, I was giggling uncontrollably. Eliphelehu came out "Elly-felly-who." God alone knows if I mispronounced it, but in an instant the names became a game, not drudgery: Jobab (good ol' Joe Bob) and Hurai (Hooray!) and Guni (he invented the gunnysack) . . .

Lord, thank You for showing me the fun in Scripture. I will make a joyful, if somewhat imperfect, noise unto You.

—Erika Bentsen

Digging Deeper: Ps 100:1–5; Col 3:16

Sun 15

"Behold, children are a heritage from the Lord . . . "
—Psalm 127:3 (NKJV)

Today is Father's Day, so I ask myself a crucial question: "What is worth my one precious life?" My answer is clear: "My children are worth my life, my labor, and my love."

Drew, Luke, and Jodi are now young adults. When I began writing for *Daily Guideposts,* they were small children. Time has flown by. Each has graduated from college. Drew is now married and an attorney in Columbia, South Carolina. Luke is single and working in computer security sales in Washington, DC. Jodi is also unmarried, lives five blocks from Luke, and works for the National Association for the Education of Young Children.

When my life comes to its conclusion, I know that I will be measured in many ways. But the most important criterion is how I loved, shaped, affirmed, and blessed my children.

It is important to remember that God is the Father of all human beings. But God needs our help. Father's Day is when every man must ask, "Am I living in the image of my heavenly Father? Am I helping God raise and support His children?"

Dear Lord, help me to be a parent to Your children. Amen.
—Scott Walker

Digging Deeper: Is 64:8; Mt 5:43–48

Mon 16

Teach us to number our days and recognize how few they are; help us to spend them as we should.
—PSALM 90:12 (TLB)

I come from a family of long livers. Great-uncle Charlie lived to be 104. Aunt Helen was ninety-six; Grandpa Knapp was ninety-two. My dad, born in 1919, is going strong, lives in the house he built in 1946, and still does his own yard work and most of the household repairs. No one in my family smokes; no one is obese. We all exercise and try to eat right.

I'm not saying I haven't fought the battle of the bulge off and on my whole life, because I have. In the spring of 2012, a few months before my wedding to Jack, he and I both went on the "wedding diet" because we were twenty pounds overweight. I started fixing more salads than either of us had ever eaten before. We ate fruit for dessert instead of ice cream and cookies.

I have to say we both looked and felt much better on June 16, 2012. And we're still cutting our portion sizes, taking half of our restaurant meals home, eating lots of fresh foods, and exercising every day. I know that's God's plan for us. After all, these bodies that were given to us at birth are an amazing gift and I, for one, feel a great responsibility to keep Jack's and mine in tip-top shape.

Father, You have given me family members who lived long, healthy lives. Help me to respect Your creation by doing my part to keep my body healthy.
—PATRICIA LORENZ

Digging Deeper: 1 COR 6:19–20

June

Tue 17

"Come to me, all you who are weary and burdened, and I will give you rest. . . . For my yoke is easy and my burden is light."
—MATTHEW 11:28, 30 (NIV)

Last night, on the phone, my sister commented that God's purpose isn't for people to be happy. "Everybody thinks it is, but it's not. God wants us to do the right thing."

Sharon's bleak assessment inhabited me this morning as I dithered around trying to make myself go down to my mother-in-law's house to wash, dress, feed, and spend time with her. *Sharon's right*, I told myself. *God simply wants me to do the right thing, however reluctantly.*

Reflecting on my mother-in-law, though, it felt just wrong. She's always done the right thing, as far as I can tell. Sure, she has her faults. In the grocery store, she never failed to point out people who were "large," as she put it. She herself has always been tiny. And there were other things. Mostly, though, she's been selfless and kindhearted all the years I've known her. Motivated, it seems, by a keen desire to be helpful. And always cheery.

Nonetheless, her mealtime prayer—the prayer she'll pray before breakfast today—is for forgiveness: "Dear Lord, please forgive my sins. Help me do the right thing." And even now, her brain frayed by Alzheimer's, she seems, above all, happy.

God's purpose is that we be like my mother-in-law, I think. Reliant on His help to do the right thing. And thus, happy.

Dear Lord, please forgive my sins and help me
to do the right thing. Cheerfully, happily.
—PATTY KIRK

Digging Deeper: Is 1:17; Mt 7:12; Lk 6:45; Gal 6:7–10

Wed 18

"And what does the Lord require of you but . . . to walk humbly with your God?" —MICAH 6:8 (NRSV)

Have you ever had one of those days when things don't go as planned? How did you handle it? I hope better than I did, as you will see.

I'd been asked by a church group torn by severe disagreements to mediate the situation, something I'd done a number of times before. I knew how this worked and what to do. Except this night, what I knew wasn't working. And the harder I tried—my original process, then Plan B and C and D—the more recalcitrant the participants got. Finally, I said, "We're going to take a break. Let's come back in fifteen minutes." But I didn't have a Plan E.

Outside, half-angry, half-crushed under the weight of my own failure, I said to God, *What do I do?*

The stars shone brightly, and for the longest time I just looked into the great expanse of heaven. As my shoulders sagged and my eyes teared, I found Plan E. I went back into that tense room and invited those people outside to look up. "I've been trying too hard to solve your problem and have simply gotten in the way," I said. "What if we start over? But this time let's remember how we fit in God's world."

We didn't fix everything that night, but, in the next few weeks, tensions started to ease and enemies began to reach across the aisles. I got out of the way and let God be present.

God, show me where I can step out of the way
and instead point to Your glory.
—JEFF JAPINGA

Digging Deeper: I CHR 16:24; PSS 3:3, 8:1

Thu 19

It is pointless that you get up early and stay up late, eating the bread of hard labor, because God gives sleep to those he loves. —Psalm 127:2 (CEB)

Did you get enough sleep?" I asked my wife in the predawn darkness. "No," Carol said. She turned off the alarm and flipped on the light.

This was the second Friday in a row that I had an early morning flight out of JFK; this one we'd board together. I never sleep well before an early flight. I'm too worried about missing the alarm or, worse, my flight.

"How'd you sleep?" she asked.

I rubbed my eyes and began to recollect a dream—a sweet, peaceful one. "Pretty well," I said, surprised. I got up and went to the bathroom, wondering why I felt so rested. I washed my face, shaved, and got dressed.

Carol was in the kitchen pouring a second cup of coffee. "I can never sleep when I have to get up early to catch a flight. I wake up every half hour and check the clock," she said.

"I know what you mean." That's the way it usually goes for me. Like the previous Friday when I was flying without Carol, I tossed and turned and checked the alarm. But not this time when we'd be on the same flight . . . suddenly I felt a little guilty.

"I slept well because of you," I said. "I knew you'd get up in time, so I didn't worry about it."

"Oh," Carol said, not particularly gratified.

"Don't worry," I said. "I'll watch the clock when we have to fly back."

"Thanks." Another division of labor that helps a marriage work. One does the cooking and one the dishes. One keeps track of the budget, and the other the checkbook. One takes charge of the alarm; the other sleeps.

We got to the airport in plenty of time, thanks to Carol.

God, I am forever grateful for those who share my life's burdens with me.
—Rick Hamlin

Digging Deeper: Eccl 4:9; Gal 6:2

Fri 20

Sing to him a new song; play skillfully, and shout for joy.
—Psalm 33:3 (NIV)

I really don't know what got into me. I had meant to go out there to stop the mayhem as I watched my kids taking flying leaps off of the porch into a giant mud puddle. I had wanted to call them inside before I ended up spending hours scrubbing mud-splattered clothes and days drying out soaked shoes. But then I saw those big, wonder-filled smiles and forgot all about worrying about things like bleach and muddy footprints tracked across my clean floors.

I walked slowly to the edge of the porch and jumped off. Joey's and Kate's faces registered fear (*Mama has gone nuts*!); then shock (*What has gotten into her*?); then pure joy.

For the next half-hour, we played outside. We sang silly songs. We splashed in the puddle. We laughed as the baby discovered the feeling of rain on his face. I reveled in the smiles on my children's faces, in the way that their innocence and delight mixed together into a beautiful and messy joy—a joy that I would've missed had I been too busy being an adult.

Lord, help me never to let the business, the messiness, or the heaviness of life cause me to stop shouting for joy at Your greatness.
—Erin MacPherson

Digging Deeper: Ps 100

Sat 21

And she opened a bottle of milk.... —JUDGES 4:19 (KJV)

One of the things I always look forward to during my visits to the monastery is the milk. I never drink milk at home, but their milk is fresh from the Jersey cows the monastery raises and hand-milks. Sales of the bottled milk is one of their sources of income, and for more than thirty years, drinking it has been a dependable part of life there.

So when I opened the refrigerator my first morning, cereal bowl in hand, I was flabbergasted not to find a bottle of fresh milk but a carton of store-bought milk. I stared at it, thinking, *Impossible!*

I cornered Mother Prioress, who did the milking, convinced there had to be something very wrong. "Oh," she said calmly, "the two cows we'd be milking are going to have calves, so they're dry now."

I searched for the right words to commiserate with her for the loss of income, but before I could say anything else, she continued, "It's so wonderful not to have to get down here in the cold every morning. I thank God every day for the extra sleep, especially this time of year."

I bit my tongue and used the other milk on my cereal, which was still very tasty.

Don't let me forget, Lord, that You see the whole picture and know what is needed better than I do.
—RHODA BLECKER

Digging Deeper: DT 11:14; PS 111:5; MAL 3:10

Sun 22

For Christ's love compels us. . . .
—2 Corinthians 5:14 (NIV)

In our marriage, I'm usually the first one to say, "I love you." Maybe that's why I longed for us to take part in a "renew your wedding vows" ceremony.

After celebrating thirty-three years together, we attended a marriage series at church. On the final Sunday, the pastor planned to offer marriage vows.

On the way to church that night, I almost asked if we were going to participate, but it seemed pushy. Rick probably thought saying our vows once was enough. Besides, what if he didn't want to? I sighed.

After the preaching and final song, the pastor slipped on a black jacket and moved underneath an archway of flowers. "For those of you who'd like to renew your wedding vows, please stand and repeat after me." All around us, people rose to their feet.

Lord, will You move in his heart if it's the right thing to do? I just can't ask him.

"You ready?" Rick asked, grinning at me like so many years ago.

My heart pounded as though I were eighteen again standing beside him at the altar. He looked so handsome with flecks of gray in his dark hair, same trustworthy brown eyes.

"I, Rick, take you, Julie, to be my wedded wife."

This time, we knew a little bit more about what marriage meant. We'd experienced seasons of better and worse, sickness, health, richer, poorer.

Thank You, Lord. Your love remains faithful.

Speaking the age-old promises for the second time, I heard my words resound in choppy whispers and joyful tears . . . cherished by God and my husband.

Lord, our marriage lives because of Your compelling love.
—Julie Garmon

Digging Deeper: Gn 2:24; Mk 10:9; 1 Cor 13:4–8

LIFE LESSONS FROM THOSE I'VE MET

Mon 23

This is the day which the Lord has made....
—PSALM 118:24 (RSV)

ROBERT FROST, AMERICAN POET

Robert Frost opened the door of his hotel room, wearing a white shirt open at the neck, his white hair a wild aureole around his head. My husband and I set up the machine in the corner, a bulky reel-to-wire recorder that was state of the art in 1954. We switched it on as Frost talked about his youth as a bobbin boy in a textile mill and about turning down the headmastership of the school in New Hampshire where he taught: "It would have killed the poetry in me."

At the end of our time together, he picked up a book and, turning the pages, began reading the tragic final segments of "The Hired Man." The eyes beneath the great brows, I noticed, never looked down at the book; he was reciting from memory. *And we have this recorded!* I kept thinking. My mind raced ahead to all the times we would listen to it again, all the people we would share it with.

He'd reached the end of the long, dramatic narrative when I glanced at our recorder. A great steel spaghetti-snarl sprawled across the floor, the wire had skipped its track. I'd scarcely listened to this private, once-in-a-lifetime recital. So intent had I been, fantasizing about some future event, that I'd missed the unrepeatable moment itself.

It's been a reminder to me ever since that *now* is the only time we ever really have.

Help me live this day, Father, as if there were no other.
—ELIZABETH SHERRILL

Digging Deeper: Ps 118

Tue 24

Every good and perfect gift is from above. . . .
—James 1:17 (NIV)

Here we go! I thought as I got on my newly purchased, used bicycle and started pedaling down the street. There was a little fear, especially near the cars, but once I reached the bike path near New York City's Hudson River I was zooming and squealing like a kid.

I breathed in the smell of the water and watched the small boats sail by and smiling people sprawled out on picnic blankets on the grass. I stopped along the way to hear a band, but for the most part I just rode my bike! As I felt the sun and wind on my face, I thought of all those days I spent locked away in my own sadness that terrible year of my pending divorce and the struggles of parenting alone. Each day felt like a prison sentence, and often I wished God would just take away my life. It took months of healing; the process was long and slow.

"Thank You, Lord, for my life!" I repeated over and over again.

A few months later, my bike was stolen, but I didn't wait long to get another one. Nothing can stop me from living now.

This life You've given me is such a gift, Lord. Thank You!
—Karen Valentin

Digging Deeper: Ps 37:4; Jn 10:10

Wed 25

The Lord's lovingkindnesses indeed never cease. . . .
—Lamentations 3:22 (NAS)

I awakened early the morning of my breast biopsy. My husband, two daughters, and I would be driving into Atlanta for the surgery. Family, friends, and I had prayed for a good result. But in the predawn hours before my procedure, I knew I needed a friend with me—back where family couldn't go.

Father, would You let someone who loves You be there with me? I need an instant friend.

At the hospital, I hugged my husband and daughters before going back to the large surgical area. A smiling nurse greeted us. "We'll take very good care of her," she told my family.

They say that to everyone, I thought.

Even though I kept an eye out for the person I'd asked God to supply, it now seemed like a foolish prayer. Inside my small, curtained cubicle, the nurse said my name with unusual excitement, I thought. She pulled up a chair very close to my bed. "I've been praying for you since I saw your name on the schedule. I could hardly wait for you to get back here."

I looked puzzled.

"We met fifteen years ago, Marion," she explained. "You were speaking at a women's meeting about your life, struggles, fears." She leaned over and gave me a genuine hug. In a few minutes, my instant friend and I sat close together on my small bed, talking like old college chums—even laughing.

As she took my blood pressure and temperature, put an IV into my hand, and gave me slip-proof socks, my instant friend and I remained connected by our Father.

Lord, teach me to anticipate Your mercy.
—Marion Bond West

Digging Deeper: Pss 13:5–6, 23:6, 25:6–7

Thu 26

Here is a list of some of the parts he has placed in his church, which is his body . . . Those who can help others . . . .
—1 CORINTHIANS 12:28 (TLB)

What are you doing to serve Jesus since you retired?" a pastor-friend inquired. The question caught me off guard.

"Well, I, uh, I'm keeping busy," I stammered.

That was certainly true. I did a bit of writing, served on community projects, and played the organ for church. I took my turn baking cookies for Joy Club, a weekly afterschool ministry, and helped with vacation Bible school. I had time to visit a couple of neighbors in retirement homes and provide occasional rides to appointments.

I was busy, but I couldn't shake lingering doubts that I wasn't doing all God wanted me to do. After all, baking cookies was a far cry from running a food bank like I'd done at my full-time job. Visiting elderly friends didn't have the same impact as raising funds for medical ministry. But after retirement, the big, important things I tried hadn't worked out: Committee for a Christian women's group wasn't a good fit, and the distance to meetings for a Justice for Immigrants group was a barrier.

One evening, I was sitting in my car and hemming a pair of slacks for a friend while I waited to pick up my granddaughter from school. As I stitched, I pictured my friend wearing the slacks and was glad I could be of help. Then my granddaughter thanked me for being her "taxi," so she didn't have to wait until her mom could pick her up after work. Little things, but they made me happy. And at this stage of my life, helping out is what God calls me to do.

Lord Jesus, thank You for letting me be one of Your helpers. Amen.
—PENNEY SCHWAB

Digging Deeper: 1 COR 12:4–31

A NEW WAY TO SERVE

Fri 27 *"Blessed are you who weep now, for you will laugh."*
—Luke 6:21 (NRSV)

VALUED

After Bill, my friend and cofounder of the St. James Literary Society, died, I knew I had to plan some kind of memorial service. The idea of it, combined with my shock and grief at his death, just about buried *me*. But this was not something I had to do only for Bill and his sister, a lovely, fragile woman who contacted us after he died. I had to do it for all of the homeless people I'd met, and all who had known Bill, so that they would know that his life—and their lives—meant something; that they were of value, not only in the eyes of God, but in the eyes of other human beings.

God was allowing something else to unfold. God was giving others, some who didn't know Bill or other homeless people, the opportunity to acknowledge him and them. A local funeral director took charge of Bill's remains; he himself dug Bill's grave. Our pastor offered the church and service at no cost. Judy, a volunteer who ran a flower shop in her spare time, provided a gorgeous arrangement. The newspaper printed a memorial and donated a photo of Bill taken a year earlier.

And when I stepped onto the altar to talk about Bill, I looked out on a gathering that included a range of New London, Connecticut's citizenry, from every member of our book club to a former mayor and his wife. At that moment, when it came to this funeral, I saw the point.

Father, in every heart-wrenching loss, help us to see ahead, as You see.
—Marci Alborghetti

Digging Deeper: Pss 19:1, 139:13–16; Rv 21:4

Sat 28

He will cover you with his pinions, and under his wings you will find refuge.... —PSALM 91:4 (NRSV)

"Daddy, watch me."

I watched, but I didn't want to. At age five, Frances had discovered the monkey bars. She and her friends spent every recess trying ever more daring feats of dangling and flipping. Naturally, she wanted to show off to Mom and Dad.

"Great job, sweetheart. You're sure that bar's not too high?" I called out.

"Nope," answered Frances, her hair trailing down as she hung by one knee. It was all I could do to keep from hovering.

Not long before, Frances had made her first foray into the neighborhood without parents. Some kids were riding their bikes around the block. "Can I go?" Frances pleaded.

"Um, okay," Kate and I said. Fifteen minutes later Frances was back, flush with pride and excitement.

I tried to remain excited about all these new developments. But, worrier that I am, I pictured Frances barreling into a big, mean world all by herself.

Just then another little girl dashed onto the playground. "Hi, Austen," said Frances. The two girls hoisted themselves onto the bars and dangled.

I laughed. *All by herself?* The only reason Frances was becoming independent was because she was never alone. All day she was surrounded by friends, teachers, parents of friends. The world is big and it can be mean, but God is serious when He says we are His workers in the world. His protection is no abstraction. It exists in the eyes, hands, and hearts of those who know and care for us.

"Daddy, watch me," said Frances. And I watched.

Today I will be confident, Lord, because You watch over me.

—JIM HINCH

Digging Deeper: Ps 121

Sun 29

The next morning he was up long before daybreak and went out alone into the wilderness to pray. —MARK 1:35 (TLB)

My husband, Jack, and I don't go to church on Sunday. Jack's the head usher at St. Jerome, and we always attend Mass on Saturday at 5:30 PM, one of the busiest of the seven weekend services.

Sunday mornings seemed to get lazier for us, often sleeping in and reading the paper until noon . . . unlike my friend Brenda who can find more things to do than I could in a month: craft classes, mah-jongg, art projects, long walks, boating, movies, visiting her sister, plays, discovering new restaurants with her husband. Brenda is always on the go on Sundays, and I kept thinking Jack and I should stop being slugs and find something energizing to do with our Sunday mornings.

Then I discovered a new bagel store in our neighborhood and talked Jack into a Sunday-morning adventure. Now we often jump on our bicycles and head for that little store, buy an egg-ham-cheese bagel sandwich, and then bike over to a small park where we walk the boardwalk through the mangrove trees out to a big covered pavilion that stretches out over the Intracoastal waterway. There we dine in peace, while watching boats go by as the seagulls, pelicans, ospreys, cormorants, egrets, and herons delight us with their antics. We usually discuss how blessed we are to have such a glorious nature-filled place to enjoy each other's company. Now I pray in church on Saturday evenings and outdoors on Sunday mornings. Works for me!

Father, thank You for blessing me with friends who encourage me to get outside, so I can appreciate all You have created.

—PATRICIA LORENZ

Digging Deeper: Pss 24:1–2, 66:1–4

Mon 30

My times are in your hands.... —Psalm 31:5 (NIV)

I'm one of those people who feel compelled to arrive early everywhere I go, but long to slow down, enjoy the little things, and stop checking my watch so often. I decided to try to change. I stopped wearing a watch.

I loved my new freedom but had an upcoming conference in St. Louis. *How will I stay on schedule? Make flights? Keep appointments?* Nevertheless, I left my watch at home.

Feeling unhindered, I chatted with friends after meals and had longer quiet times in the mornings. I only checked the clock on my cell phone a couple of times.

My return flight was scheduled to leave at 5:55 AM. Several conferees were already waiting outside the hotel lobby. The shuttle driver arrived and called the names on his list. He boarded the steps to close the door. "What about me? Julie Garmon."

"Sorry, this shuttle's full. Another driver will be here soon."

My heart lurched. *Oh no! I'll never make my flight!*

As I boarded the next shuttle, the driver received a text. He announced that we were waiting on someone who'd overslept.

"What am I supposed to do? I have a 5:55 flight."

"Miss Julie, I'll get you there in time. Relax."

I had a choice to make: panic or trust. I decided to breathe deeply and trust God and the driver. Several minutes passed and the tardy passenger joined us. We arrived at the exact time the driver had predicted. "Have a blessed day," he said, smiling.

Sitting at the gate, I enjoyed a banana, a cup of coffee, and witnessed a glorious sunrise—all in God's perfect timing.

Lord, You hold time in Your capable hands.
Don't let me waste a single second by hurrying.
—Julie Garmon

Digging Deeper: Prv 12:25; Jas 4:13–15

DAILY MERCIES

1 ______________________________

2 ______________________________

3 ______________________________

4 ______________________________

5 ______________________________

6 ______________________________

7 ______________________________

8 ______________________________

9 ______________________________

10 ______________________________

11 ______________________________

12 ______________________________

13 ______________________________

14 ______________________________

15 ______________________________

16 __________

17 __________

18 __________

19 __________

20 __________

21 __________

22 __________

23 __________

24 __________

25 __________

26 __________

27 __________

28 __________

29 __________

30 __________

July

The Lord is merciful and gracious,
slow to anger, and plenteous in mercy.

—Psalm 103:8 (KJV)

Tue 1

And regardless of what else you put on, wear love. It's your basic, all-purpose garment. . . . —Colossians 3:14 (MSG)

I needed a new outfit for a fancy banquet. I'd be meeting people and making connections. I wanted to appear put-together, sophisticated, and stylish in my semiformal attire. Mother helped me choose a knee-length black dress with turquoise and silver jewels around the neckline. She suggested dangling silver earrings with a matching bracelet, and then we headed to the shoe department.

"Shoes make such a statement," she said.

I tried on a pair of silver sandals. Mother said they looked "just darling."

Saturday night arrived; time for the gala event! I dressed carefully, grabbed my silver purse, and as I stepped off the elevator, the strap to my sandal snapped in two. I hobbled across the lobby to my friend Lynne, whom I'd met the night before.

Lynne hugged me. "Not a problem. Wait here, honey." She returned with a roll of duct tape. Lynne had worked in theater and taught acting classes. She fixed my sandal in seconds, though part of the duct tape showed. "Smile real big and nobody will notice your feet."

Miraculously, as I moved through the crowd doing what Lynne suggested, the most amazing thing happened: I completely forgot about my dilapidated shoe and focused on others. When I greeted people in genuine love, everyone smiled back.

Lord, the secret to my confidence didn't come from my bejeweled dress and sparkly silver shoes. It was Your love shining through me.

—Julie Garmon

Digging Deeper: I Jn 4:9–12

Wed 2

When my anxious thoughts multiply within me, Your consolations delight my soul. —Psalm 94:19 (NAS)

For most of my life, I've been a worrier. I worry about arriving on time for an appointment, the precarious state of the world economy, and everything in between. Medication has helped, but I still find my worries cropping up when I'm working or reading or doing household chores or spending time with our children—even in the middle of my prayers. Then, the other day, it occurred to me that there's one activity of mine that's entirely worry-free.

At noontime most days, I take our dog Amsterdam out for a walk. We amble (well, I amble; Amsterdam mostly sniffs) north to Fort Tryon Park and make our way past the New Leaf Café (with time out for squirrel gazing), down the steps and under the road to the dog run. Amsterdam greets his friends Charlie and Gracie and Ollie and Brody and little Mickey.

After he's run awhile with the pack, Amsterdam will usually indulge me with a game of fetch. He's very good at running after a tennis ball, pretty good at finding it, and improving at picking it up and bringing it back to me. Then he'll ramble around the run, stopping to explore a pile of wood chips (I have to be careful that he doesn't start eating them) or catch the scent of the groundhog that lives just east of the run. He takes from each moment what it has to give and then moves on, secure in the knowledge that he's loved and provided for.

When we leave the dog run, I'm rested and refreshed and reminded that I, too, am loved and provided for. I guess the Lord knew what He was doing when He created dogs.

Lord, help me to remember that You're always walking alongside Amsterdam and me.

—Andrew Attaway

Digging Deeper: Mt 6:25–34; Col 3:15

Thu 3

If there is any excellence and if anything worthy of praise, dwell on these things. —PHILIPPIANS 4:8 (NAS)

I am a moment-maker. I like to pause an experience—step out of the moment and see it, glean from it—in order to step back in and value it. Last October, I sat with a friend before a fire in her hearth, sipping hot chocolate and watching falling maple leaves swirl past the window. An ordinary moment, alive suddenly with perfection, as I saw how it embodied autumn in its hunkering down.

When my eight-year-old granddaughter Ruby visited last summer, the moments practically tripped over themselves. There was the evening she rode her bicycle, no hands, down our quiet street, arms lifted high like she might leave terra firma and pedal across the sky. I embraced in that moment the wide-open invitation of childhood.

The day we arrived at the zoo, Ruby exclaimed, "Hallelujah!" I responded, "Halle*zoo*jah!" We wilted through the humidity from one animal enclosure to the next, got sticky from melting bubblegum ice cream, swam with the brown bear on the *outside* of the tank—almost, but not quite, wishing we were inside cooling off. The whole day was one big "halle*zoo*jah" moment as we celebrated generational joy and discovery.

To make a moment is to inhale the very breath of my Creator Savior. It is to see Him in all that He has established, and breathe it back to Him.

Master of all moments, You reveal to me things eternal...
moment by moment.
—CAROL KNAPP

Digging Deeper: PHIL 4:4–9

Fri 4

O give thanks unto the Lord, for he is good. . . . And gathered them out of the lands, from the east, and from the west, from the north, and from the south. —PSALM 107:1, 3 (KJV)

It's the savory smell of tri-tip barbecuing over mountain mahogany. It's the sight of long tables loaded down with countless macaroni or potato salads, baked beans, casseroles, fruit and veggie platters. It's an overflowing basket of rolls. It's the pies and homemade ice cream waiting on ice in the shade. It's the boisterous din of conversation among country neighbors, almost clannish and isolated the rest of the year, coming together en masse to celebrate Independence Day.

It's that brief, pivotal lull between irrigating and haying season in our valley; the last chance for neighbors to get together and socialize before the long, arduous process of gathering and storing forage against the coming winter. Most of us won't see each other for months, if not until next year.

As the dinner triangle clangs, there's a whoop of joy and laughter. We bow our heads as one for the blessing. I steal a glance over the assembled crowd: cowboys and Indians. Retirees from California. Ranch kids. Old-time families and recent imports. Dear friends and complete strangers. Rich and poor. All races and all walks of life. Each of us came to this valley in pursuit of the American dream. My heart swells with pride at our great nation.

Dear Lord, thank You for giving our forefathers the dream to live in freedom and unity, and for the men and women who are constantly fighting for our right to keep it alive.

—ERIKA BENTSEN

Digging Deeper: 2 COR 3:17; GAL 5:13

Sat 5

Light in a messenger's eyes brings joy to the heart. . . .
—Proverbs 15:30 (NIV)

"Umm . . . I think I look a little overdone," my daughter Lindsay texted me one morning. I smiled because I, too, looked overdone.

The day before, my two daughters and I had tried out a new spray tan applicator that Lindsay got for her birthday. The color seemed fine when we finished, but all three of us woke up shocked to see how our fake tans had grown darker overnight.

It would have been simply funny if we were not all headed to the same event that morning where we were bound to triple the effect . . . and feel self-conscious. That's why we started a three-way texting conversation. "Google how to lighten us up," I begged.

"Use baby oil," one responded.

"I heard you can use lemon juice and baking soda."

"Of course that will work because it takes off the top layer of skin."

Later, as we walked into the event, we got the predicted responses. "Have you been to the Islands?" "Wow! What happened?" "You look great! What have you done?" which only made me feel more self-conscious because "looking great" obviously meant I didn't look like myself.

Over the next several days, the color came off slowly . . . on my towels, clothes, pillowcase. Mostly I now smile at the memory of the experience, which challenged me to lighten up while walking around with an overdone tan.

Lord, when I do silly, dumb, harmless things,
help me to lighten up and laugh at myself.
—Carol Kuykendall

Digging Deeper: Prv 15:13, 17:22

Sun 6

God blessed the seventh day and made it holy, because on it he rested from all the work of creating that he had done.
—Genesis 2:3 (NIV)

My husband and I are polar opposites on many fronts, one of which is our capacity to nap. He is a world-class Sunday-afternoon napper, while if I am idle for ten consecutive minutes, I consider myself to be slacking off. There are e-mails to return, schedules to plan, meals to prepare, countless ways to "get ahead," and somehow these things always win out.

Recently I was reading a children's book to my daughter Prisca that told the story of God creating the world, and as if reading the account for the very first time, I was captivated by the pattern I saw. In seven days flat, He *formed*, He *filled*, and He *reflected* on all He had done. The pattern was good enough for God, but I'd deemed it utterly substandard for me.

For the past three Sundays, I have forced myself to give God's pattern a try. The forming and filling part on the first six days was a breeze, but that seventh day—the reflection day—definitely took some work.

I haven't resorted to napping just yet, but instead of using Sundays to blast into the week ahead, I'm spending the hours looking back. I think about the week that has just passed—where I went, whom I talked to, how I felt, how I grew in the depths of my own inner world. I review the evidences of God's faithfulness that I don't soon want to forget. And then I slow my pace long enough to tell Him thank You for the work He has done.

Father, in the same way You reflected on Your creation,
help me take time to stop and reflect on mine.
—Ashley Wiersma

Digging Deeper: Mk 2:23–28; Heb 4:1–10

Mon 7

The fruit of the Spirit is . . . kindness. . . .
—Galatians 5:22 (NIV)

Dianne, my wife, can tolerate a lot of pain, but her arthritic hip finally forced her to accept that it was time for surgery. She was in the hospital for three days after her hip-replacement operation. I was with her much of the time, but several dedicated nurses were with her all the time, one of nine spiritual gifts listed in Paul's letter to the Galatians.

Yes, we are grateful for the skills of the surgeon and for nurses who can expertly find a vein when inserting a needle for an IV. And, yes, competence should be the tenth fruit of the Spirit. But in the course of the minute-by-minute duration of recovery, there is nothing more important than kindness.

"I'm just doing my job," Nurse Kelley gently chided me after I thanked her more than once for taking care of my wife. How wrong she was! Kindness is a gift, not an obligation. Kelley, Bonnie, James, Lisa, and others whose names I've forgotten gave us that gift, again and again, until Dianne was able to come home.

Thank You, God, for the kindness in others. Please bless those who share such a precious gift.
—Tim Williams

Digging Deeper: Prv 11:17; Col 3:12

July

Tue 8

"Therefore, if you are offering your gift at the altar and there remember that your brother or sister has something against you, leave your gift there in front of the altar. First go and be reconciled to them; then come and offer your gift."
—MATTHEW 5:23–24 (NIV)

A cyber-apology? I plunked down my coffee mug and took a second look at my computer screen. There it was: an apology delivered via a private message on a social media site.

"This is an official apology to you," she started. She said the offense had "haunted her" and "kept surfacing" in her mind.

I took a deep breath. I never expected this. The offense happened twenty years ago. It was public, painful, but very long ago. Decades-old humiliation rose easily in my heart. The wound was still there. I was haunted, too, by embarrassment and pain.

"I've grown over the years," she wrote. "I need to soften my heart and tear down some walls."

My nine-year-old son chose this moment to come downstairs from his bedroom. A few hugs and kisses later, he was playing a video game. "It's too loud!" I barked. "Turn it down."

Too sharp. His eyes welled with tears. I'd blown it. Apologies are hard. "I'm sorry, buddy." He smiled and went back to his game.

I looked back at my laptop. Yes, apologies are hard. I could only imagine how hard it was to send this message. She'd hurt me, yes. But she was God's work in progress too. Besides, God has forgiven me far worse offenses. With moist eyes, I typed: "Thank you. This means so much to me. Consider your apology accepted and appreciated. Best wishes for you and your family." I clicked Send.

"Hey, Dad, I won!" my son said.

"Good job," I said. "Me too."

God, enable me to seek forgiveness, grant forgiveness, and receive forgiveness, just as You have forgiven me. —BILL GIOVANNETTI

Digging Deeper: MT 5:9; JAS 5:16; 1 JN 1:9

Wed 9

And he shall be unto thee a restorer of thy life, and a nourisher of thine old age.... —RUTH 4:15 (KJV)

I regularly get a copy of *Boatman's Quarterly Review*, the newsletter for and about the men and women who row rafts and guide motor rigs on the Colorado River through the Grand Canyon. It's been twenty years since I did a trip, and I've been wondering why I still read the newsletter. The river is a young person's game, and I no longer qualify. I've been growing envious of the people in the pages of *BQR* because I can't be like them any longer.

In the most recent issue on page twenty-five was a picture from 1987 of Martha and Suzanne, two "boat-hags" my husband, Keith, and I loved. They were just as I remembered: happy and young, strong, and confident.

I used to be like that, I thought. I wondered where they were now, what they were doing, and then it occurred to me that they were more than likely still happy, strong, and confident. The mere absence of youth wouldn't have changed that.

"They're probably just the same now as they were then!" I said to Keith, trying to keep the resentment out of my voice.

"So are you," he said, grinning. "You just can't see it because you're so hard on yourself."

I started to deny it but knew I'd always been my own worst critic. The difference between Martha and Suzanne and me was that they didn't compare themselves to anyone else. Neither should I.

Thank You for giving me Keith, Lord.
He is such a better mirror for me than I am for myself.
—RHODA BLECKER

Digging Deeper: PRV 13:14, 20

July

Thu 10

Start children off on the way they should go, and even when they are old they will not turn from it.
—Proverbs 22:6 (NIV)

A colleague was upset to learn that I enforce gender-inclusive language in my courses. Everyone knows that *he* includes *she* and *man* means *human*, he argued. So began a series of debates that gradually evolved into what was really at issue: the Bible.

"What would you say," he asked, "if a student said she couldn't read the Bible anymore because it excluded her?"

"I'd recommend a gender-inclusive translation," I answered.

"But what if one didn't exist?" he persisted. "Would you tell her to just quit reading?"

I imagined my daughter Charlotte taxing me with harder questions. "Mama, how can you believe in the God of that book? How can you read about women abused—cut into pieces, sacrificed as burned offerings—by men praised for their faith? Or Paul saying women can't teach? How can you be a woman and accept what that book says about women?"

Out of this vision, I answered my colleague: "I hope some student does ask. I certainly hope my daughters do. I hope they vie against every passage, every word, that seems to expose a God Who excludes them—even if it means they reject the Bible altogether—because their faith can't be real unless they do."

Considering these eventualities has shaped my prayers ever since, sending me back into Scripture in search of promises.

Oh, Father, whatever the means, make Your love as clear to Your daughters as it has historically been to Your sons.
—Patty Kirk

Digging Deeper: Rom 8:37–39

Fri 11

You will . . . turn and comfort me.
—Psalm 71:21 (CJB)

My husband, Keith, and I agreed to put the cat bed on one corner of my desk because our greyhound was too rambunctious in the house and the cats were afraid they'd be trampled. Chi and L.E. took turns sleeping in the bed, running across my desktop and, it turned out, knocking all my papers onto the floor. When the sunlight slanted over my desk, they stretched out in it. What I was working on was of no importance to them; my desk had become their property.

By the time I figured it out and tried to banish them, it was too late. I tried to shoo them away, even yelled at them. And I wasn't getting enough work done, so I seethed.

Then I took a call on my desk phone. It was from a high-school friend telling me about the unsuccessful surgery of another classmate. I hadn't seen her for a long while, but we had spent a lot of time together back in school. I hung up the phone and started to cry. Those bothersome cats immediately came over, rubbing against me and butting their heads under my chin. Chi rested her paw on my arm; L.E. licked the tears on my cheeks.

I never again thought about moving the bed. The cats belonged in that place.

You entrust Your task of comfort to small creatures with fur,
Lord, and I love You for it.
—Rhoda Blecker

Digging Deeper: Dt 31:8; Ps 145:9–10

Sat 12

For the trumpet will sound, the dead will be raised imperishable, and we will be changed.
—1 CORINTHIANS 15:52 (NIV)

When my friend went on hospice care, she said, "I've never liked surprises, not even good ones. I want to know what dying and heaven are like." She'd certainly given me a challenging assignment! Fortunately, I found a book by a chaplain that described what people saw, heard, and felt during near-death experiences.

The next weekend our family traveled to the coast. When my son John and I were walking along the beach, we noticed that the lowering tide had stranded hundreds of helpless starfish on the shore. "You'd think that the starfish would know better by now not to get so close to the beach," John remarked.

As he tossed a starfish back into the surf, I got to thinking that starfish don't know to avoid the shore because they have no grasp of the fact that there's a parallel world of dry land that isn't filled with water like the one where they've lived all their lives.

I thought about how, although I'm made of physical working parts, I haven't been left clueless that there's a very real, unseen spiritual world that exists. I smiled as I thought, *My friend has done an excellent job of living in both the physical and spiritual worlds all her life. She'll probably be quite surprised when she reaches heaven that she's not really surprised after all!*

Dear heavenly Father, help me as I live this day on earth to become no stranger to heaven by becoming much closer to You. Amen.

—KAREN BARBER

Digging Deeper: PHIL 1:21–23, 3:20–21; 2 PT 3:13

Sun 13

And he said to them, "Follow me, and I will make you fishers of men." Immediately they left their nets and followed him.
—MATTHEW 4:19–20 (RSV)

I am in the church I'd grown up in, sitting with Mom in the familiar pews. I look up to the vaulted arches with their wooden beams and the warm timber ceiling. That ceiling reminds me of Dad's sailboat, the varnished planks stretched along the wooden ribs in the hull. All at once I'm a kid again, sitting on a canvas cushion next to my father. An orange life jacket rises up around my ears, and the salt spray spills over the bow.

Dad points to the trembling sail. "You see that?" he asks. "We call that *luffing*. It means we're not taking full advantage of the wind. But look what happens if I pull in the mainsail." He pulls the rope in his hand. "We've caught the wind again. Or if I push the tiller toward the sail it can have the same effect."

"How do you know where the wind is coming from?" I ask.

"You can feel it. Can't you tell?"

I rub the back of my neck and then point in that direction. "Good," Dad says. "Soon you'll be able to sail on your own."

It would be a couple of years before I handled the tiller by myself or held the mainsail in my hand, but Dad had given me his trust of wind and waves to go by.

Now Dad is gone, his boat a distant memory. But his lesson still reverberates in my soul. I know how to sail, looking for the wind, steering through the waves, keeping my hand on the tiller. And I know how to sit in church, listening for the spirit. That the place looks like a boat is no architectural accident. The church was meant to launch us all on a journey, one I am still on. "Doesn't the ceiling remind you of Dad's boat?" I ask Mom.

"He loved to sail," she says.

Keep the wind in my sails, Lord, and let me know where to turn to find the breeze. —RICK HAMLIN

Digging Deeper: Ps 119:105

Mon 14

A glorious throne, exalted from the beginning, is the place of our sanctuary. —JEREMIAH 17:12 (NIV)

It was work time. The baby was napping, both of my older kids were at school, and I had a big deadline looming. But as I pulled out my laptop, I just sat there staring at the screen.

I was stuck. Frozen, really. For twenty precious minutes, my thoughts raced around in my head as my to-do list threatened to overwhelm me. Yet I was unable to type a single word.

"What is going on, Lord?" I prayed. "I only have a small window of time to get a lot done. Why am I wasting the precious minutes that I have just sitting here?"

Then my Bible, which had been unopened for at least a week, caught my eye. Instantly, I knew. I had been so preoccupied with getting my work done, in checking another task off of my ever-growing list, that I had forgotten to schedule time with God.

I picked up His Word and opened it to the last page I had bookmarked. I spent twenty precious minutes with Him, pouring out my heart and letting His truth soak into the fibers of my busy life. As I drew closer to God, my frozen mind started to thaw. Ideas started to flow. And words started to pour out of my heart.

Lord, even when life threatens to pull me away from You, bring me back. Remind me of the sanctuary that I have in You. Amen.

—ERIN MACPHERSON

Digging Deeper: Ps 73

THE PATH TO ADOPTION

Tue 15

"Everyone assembled here will know that the Lord rescues his people, but not with sword and spear. This is the Lord's battle, and he will give you to us!" —1 SAMUEL 17:47 (NLT)

WILLING

I got down on my knees and told God this whole thing was way over my head. We didn't have the money. Not even close. So what in the world were we doing? I was sure the lines got crossed somewhere. I was sure God meant to ask somebody else. Somebody wealthier. Somebody more equipped. This was way over our heads. Way, way over.

Those were the words I repeated to God again and again. Those were the words I spoke to my husband as well. Then we went to church, where our pastor stood up in the pulpit and said, "If you want to be filled with the Holy Spirit, if you want to see God at work in your life, then get in over your heads."

I looked at my husband. Neither of us said much on the drive home. We were both lost in our thoughts. When we pulled into the driveway, he turned off the ignition and sighed. "We can't let finances stop us."

So we didn't. We filled out the adoption application. Some people looked at us like we were nuts, irresponsible. Occasionally, I found myself wondering if they were right. Until that first check came. "To help with the adoption," the note said.

More followed, and somehow, without even lifting a finger, we had ten thousand dollars. It was like a promise from God that humbled and bolstered me all at the same time.

Thank You, Lord, that You don't look for the strongest or the richest to carry out Your will. You simply look for the willing.
—KATIE GANSHERT

Digging Deeper: MT 20:27–28; JN 15:9–17

Wed 16

But Jacob was a peaceful man, living in tents.
—Genesis 25:27 (NAS)

There is a wonderful scene in Genesis 32 where Jacob, having left his father-in-law and striking out on his own with his family, servants, and livestock, encounters the "angels of God." He overnights there and names the place *Mahanaim*, saying, "This is God's camp" (Genesis 32:2).

One interpretation of this name is that Jacob saw two angels. Another is that it denotes two camps: Jacob's and God's. For someone who has tented in campgrounds from childhood, God's tent pitched alongside mine makes a powerful image.

I don't camp much anymore, but I do have my tent set up all summer on our acreage. It's an outdoor sanctuary where I go to think and pray and read my Bible. I find it uncommon that my close friend Cheryl also has a tent hideaway. Not many women get excited over having their own private tents!

This year Cheryl is moving from her secluded property and wonders where she'll pitch her tent. I've invited her to stake it beside mine. We grinned at the idea of being side by side, quietly companionable in our "forts."

There's something immensely reassuring about two camps. Jacob had eyes to see the angels making camp with him. I wonder how often God's tent has been right next to mine and I didn't know it. Maybe a summer of tenting with my friend beside me is just the visual I need.

Two tents, my Friend—Yours and mine—that's all I ask.
—Carol Knapp

Digging Deeper: Gn 32:1–21

Thu 17

"My grace is sufficient for you, for my power is made perfect in weakness".... —2 CORINTHIANS 12:9 (NIV)

Yesterday morning, as I took coffee on the deck overhung with maple branches where I am house-sitting, a chartreuse glimmer caught my eye. A tiny inchworm dropped out of the air, paused, then dropped some more to hang in space with no visible support. A wisp of a breeze revealed its suspension thread when it swayed and flashed silver. This inchworm hung about ten feet off the ground and about twenty feet below the nearest maple branch. It remained still for only a few minutes, then began to hump and stretch, and hump and stretch, literally inching up its lifeline as insubstantial as a hair. I sat hypnotized by the determination and trust of this speck of life.

I can relate to its precarious existence.

About a year ago, I gave up my apartment, stashed my furniture and other belongings in my daughter's basement, and embarked upon my Year of Houseless Living, the better to afford international travel and writing retreats. By renting rooms, house- and pet-sitting, staying with relatives, and visiting friends, I have enjoyed shelter, companionship, and productive creativity. Though I calculate that over the past twelve months I have slept in twenty-five beds, not once did I fear that I would have no shelter. Nor do I fear it now. Why, just this week, more monthlong house-sitting invitations—and new creative ideas to pursue—have come my way!

Though to the casual observer, both the inchworm and I may appear to live high-risk, insecure lives, we know better. God's boundless grace supports us every moment.

Lord of all Grace, how You amaze me!
—GAIL THORELL SCHILLING

Digging Deeper: 2 COR 12:1–10; PHIL 4:19

July

Fri 18

Our mouth was filled with laughter....
—Psalm 126:2 (RSV)

God, *can You open the ground and let me disappear?* As embarrassing moments go, this was one of my biggest. I'd been angrily waiting for my girlfriend Sheila and had a feeling that it would be a long wait. To give you an idea, Sheila's license plate frame says, "Always late... but worth the wait." As I waited on a street corner, tapping my foot impatiently, I silently rehashed my negative thoughts: I told her that I only had forty-five minutes for lunch today since I had a meeting at 1:00 PM sharp.

Another friend was able to shrug off Sheila's lateness as just one of her quirks, and so could I... sometimes. *Oh, why couldn't she be more considerate?* Still, I knew praying for someone else to change was a losing proposition, so instead I prayed, "God, help me be more tolerant!" And when I saw Sheila racing toward me down the street, I felt calmer and shouted, "I'm not mad at you! Stop running!" Which she did. Immediately.

That's when I saw that the woman who stopped running was not my friend but a complete stranger, who was now walking very slowly past me, giving me an odd look along with plenty of space. And several minutes later, there was Sheila, strolling along as if she didn't have a care in the world. She gave a big smile when she saw me. "Aren't you proud of me? I'm only ten minutes late. Why are you laughing?" But I couldn't answer her because I was laughing too hard, thinking of that stranger's face. And since laughter and anger don't mix at all, I thanked God for answering my prayer in such a funny way.

Lord, help me see the humor today in something
that would ordinarily make me mad.
—Linda Neukrug

Digging Deeper: Job 8:21; Prv 17:22

Sat 19

Now to him who is able to do immeasurably more than all we ask or imagine.... —EPHESIANS 3:20 (NIV)

Strolling along the edge of Mother Ocean for hours at a time the last few days has refreshed yours truly as regards the Maker's profligate generosity, *new every morning* indeed—not only excellent things to eat (and my enterprising children have harvested crabs, mussels, and perch from these waters for our meals, saving the old man some serious coin), but in gaping wonder at the incalculable numbers and forms of life: eagles the size of tents, sea lions the size of cars, inquisitive seals in the surf like wet-whiskered grandfathers, and then the herds of skittering small children loose on the beach, shrilling and thrilling; swallows and minks along the creek, beach roses and sea rocket in the dunes; and as many blackberries along the trail back to the cabin as a man can eat and carry home for pie in his now-permanently-purple baseball cap.

We take this for granted. You know we do. We stare at the immeasurable miracles of the Maker and we worry about the car. This is foolish.

When I feel especially foolish, I recruit a child and go down to the shore and count sand crabs at low tide. In one square yard of sand, we dig up more than a thousand, many smaller than a thumbnail, the manufacture and operation and spark of which are utterly beyond the ability of the greatest geniuses among us. We take this for granted. You know we do. I'm the chief fool in this vein. Except sometimes, in summer, when I'm reminded, usually by a child; then we walk back to the cabin, picking berries, unabashed and thrilled.

Dear Lord, ah, the ocean is the mother, isn't she? From whence we came, in this form, all of us one percent salt, like the sea used to be when life sparked in it so long ago. Do we ever stop and thank You for the spark? Such a generous flick of Your love, to set us swimming.

—BRIAN DOYLE

Digging Deeper: Ps 19:1; Jn 1:3

LIFE LESSONS FROM THOSE I'VE MET

Sun 20

Blessed are they which are persecuted for righteousness' sake. . . . —MATTHEW 5:10 (KJV)

REBMANN WAMBA, PRESBYTERIAN PASTOR

It was a typical noisy market scene in Kenya, except for the sudden silence surrounding the stall where Rebmann Wamba had stopped to bargain over a stalk of matoke bananas. It was the same at the poultry vendor's, where he purchased a chicken (live), and the tea seller's, where he counted out the coppers for two tea bags.

My husband and I were interviewing Wamba about his transformation from violent Mau Mau chieftain to ordained Presbyterian pastor. Once hailed as a freedom fighter, he'd told us, he'd become a despised outsider. We saw this now ourselves as hostile eyes followed him on his errands.

The chicken and tea were luxuries in our honor. Wamba had invited us to Sunday dinner with his wife and eight children in their mud-and-wattle home in Ngecha, and afterward to the service at his church. Walls were all it had. No roof. No floor. But a congregation overflowing the wood-plank benches. A drummer beat out the rhythm of a joyous opening hymn. For two hours, Wamba preached in Kiswahili while we watched the rapt faces of this embattled minority.

With the closing hymn, a collection was taken. The congregation's offerings, Wamba had told us, were the church's only support. I looked into the basket, which held a few penny coppers, two eggs, and an ear of corn. *How long*, I wondered, *till a roof rose over these walls?* And how long had I taken for granted the roof over our lovely stone church at home? How long had I tranquilly called myself a Christian and never encountered the hostile gaze of a neighbor?

Remind me, Lord, of all those who have paid the price for following You.

—ELIZABETH SHERRILL

Digging Deeper: JN 15:18; 2 TM 3:12

Mon 21

Inasmuch as ye have done it unto one of the least of these my brethren, ye have done it unto me.
—Matthew 25:40 (KJV)

We wanted a donkey to help ward off coyotes on our family ranch. Word got around, and a man contacted us with a real deal. Mr. Hyde was free and delivered, so we agreed. How could we go wrong? However, one look at the ancient donkey and we knew he wasn't up to the task. We'd keep him anyway. We were appalled when the previous owner claimed he'd used him for roping practice. Mr. Hyde was shaggy, thin, and obviously neglected.

His gentle demeanor was partially masked by his overwhelming shyness. It was apparent he'd known love previously in his life, but that was ages ago and he'd long since given up expecting to see it ever again.

My heart went out to the lonely donkey. "Lord, let him remember love," I whispered.

We kept Mr. Hyde near the ranch house with heifers for company. At first I could barely approach him, even with alfalfa hay. He'd tense up or walk away when I tried to pet him. Gradually, he started to trust me. The first time he followed me home, I could barely contain my elation. Now when he sees me, he comes up to me for attention and nuzzles my hands for treats. In his eyes, I'm starting to see the love returned to me.

Dear Lord, thank You for showing me it's better to give love,
even when it doesn't seem to matter. The richness of love
in return is above all earthly value!
—Erika Bentsen

Digging Deeper: I Jn 4:19

July

Tue 22

Commit to the Lord whatever you do, and he will establish your plans. —PROVERBS 16:3 (NIV)

Our trip to the Museum of Natural History wasn't turning out as I hoped. The train was crowded, so we couldn't sit together for the ninety-minute ride to the city. We got lost in Penn Station, and walking to the museum, my son Henry tripped and ended up on his face, crying. By the time we got to the museum, we were pretty worn-out.

We walked through the exhibits of dinosaur bones and had fun in the solar system area. We ate lunch and walked through more halls.

"I'm tired," Henry said. "I want to go home."

"We have three more hours before our train leaves," I explained.

We found a bench in the Hall of Human Origins and sat down to figure out what to do. I thought of my sister Maria. The last time I was at the museum was with Maria and her daughter. We always did family trips together, and even though it's been four years since my sister died, I could feel myself going to a sad place of *If only she were here*. I pushed it away and remembered our last trip together.

A woman approached us. "Would you like to go to the Imax movie? We bought tickets for our college class, and there's a dozen or more no-shows. I'd hate to see them go to waste."

"Sure!" We perked up and headed over to the movie that would start in ten minutes. Inside the theater, we sat in the comfortable velvet seats.

"Look, Mom," Solomon pointed to the bronze plaque on his armrest inscribed with a person's name. "What does yours say?"

I read the inscription: "Remembering my brother and the glorious days we had in this grand museum."

Dear Lord, thank You for times like this when I find myself exactly where I'm meant to be . . . in the comfort of Your loving care.

—SABRA CIANCANELLI

Digging Deeper: Pss 13:5, 52:8

Wed 23

Return to Me with all your heart.... —JOEL 2:12 (NAS)

I've wondered through the years if I could have done anything in my son Jeremy's life during his childhood to have made a difference. Probably not. Decades of addictions and then bipolar disease made life difficult.

Jeremy stopped by our house recently. I had just obtained a recording of one of my all-time favorite songs, "I Have Returned" by Kenneth Copeland, and I had no idea Jeremy had come in. He stood quietly watching me swaying back and forth with my eyes closed, listening to the powerful words that spilled out into our living room. When it was over, I opened my eyes. "Oh, I didn't know you were there."

"I was just remembering."

"Remembering what?"

"When I was a child, you played that song a lot. For years. The words sunk deeply into me—the beat of the music. Finally, as an adult, I had to do what the song says. It's a big part of my turnaround. I love it. Play it again, Mom."

Jeremy and I sat on the sofa, close together, and listened: "I have returned to the God of my childhood/To the same simple faith as a child I once knew/Like a prodigal son, I longed for my loved ones/For the comforts of home/And the God I outgrew/I have returned to the God of my childhood/Bethlehem's babe/The prophet's Messiah/He's Jesus to me...."

Lord Jesus, help me abandon impatience and return to absolute trust in You—especially when answers come slowly.

—MARION BOND WEST

Digging Deeper: Pss 28:7, 91:2; Lk 15

Thu 24

"But ask the animals, and they will teach you, or the birds in the sky, and they will tell you. . . . Which of all these does not know that the hand of the Lord has done this? In his hand is the life of every creature and the breath of all mankind."
—Job 12:7, 9–10 (NIV)

We'd stopped in at the corner grocery to pick up a few things. Suddenly, Millie flopped down on her belly, casting me a pleading look. After a long afternoon driving, I didn't feel like dragging a ninety-pound golden retriever all the way back to the dairy case.

Hassan, the owner, chuckled. "She fears Angelina," he said of his twelve-pound cat, sitting serenely in the back of the store.

I laughed and told Hassan the events of earlier that day. Millie and I were hiking East Mountain on the Appalachian Trail when she stopped at a bend in the trail and started barking furiously. I peered ahead, wondering why a hiker was wearing a black hooded sweatshirt on an eighty-degree morning. But it was no hiker; it was a bear!

Millie held her ground, barking and snarling, glancing back at me. *Don't run*, I remembered. *Don't ever turn your back on a bear*. "Millie," I said, keeping my voice calm, "come." She hesitated. "Millie, come! Now."

Millie retreated slowly until she got to me, not turning her back on the bear either. Then we backed up cautiously. The bear just stared.

I tried to move Millie ahead of me, but she insisted on staying between the bear and me. When we were far enough, we turned around and walked purposefully all the way to the spot where I had parked.

Now, back in New York City, a cat had Millie cowering like a puppy. Hassan gathered our items. "Sometimes it's the little things that get us," he said. "The big stuff we handle." I smiled and took my things. Millie looked up at me gratefully, relieved to be out of danger.

Father, sometimes I'm like Millie: I let the little things get to me and only bother You with the big stuff. I will remember to bring all my troubles to You. And thanks for giving me such a brave dog. —Edward Grinnan

Digging Deeper: 1 Pt 5:7

Fri 25

For I will restore health unto thee, and I will heal thee of thy wounds, saith the Lord. . . . —Jeremiah 30:17 (KJV)

I had dinner with two of my friends from college, Mirielle and Debbie. We met at a Tibetan restaurant and started catching up. We were all struggling to make ends meet and figure out what to do with our futures, but I saw quickly that Debbie had even worse struggles.

As she looked over the menu, she reached into her purse and pulled out a large color-coded card. "What is that?" I asked.

"It's the list of foods I can't eat," she said. She'd recently been diagnosed with rheumatoid arthritis, and it was seriously restricting her diet.

Only a few minutes later, she mentioned something about a lump on her neck. Her doctor thought it was probably thyroid cancer. At our dismay, she tried to assure us that it would be no big deal to handle.

Then she started talking about her trip to Israel and was bursting with stories about visiting holy sites like the Wailing Wall; sharing in religious rituals; and having conversations with the Israelis she met, whom she thought were deeply spiritual people. Debbie had so much to feel victimized about, but all she wanted to talk about was how close she'd come to God.

Since that day, I've prayed for her health, but I've also prayed for myself. I've prayed for strength like Debbie's, to appreciate God even when life is painful.

Thank You, God, for Your messengers who direct me back toward You.

—Sam Adriance

Digging Deeper: Ps 103:2–5; 2 Cor 12:9–10

Sat 26

"The kingdom of heaven is like treasure hidden in a field. . . ."
—Matthew 13:44 (NRSV)

"I don't see anything." I stared up into a Monterey pine, a tangle of branches and pale green needles. We were in Pacific Grove on the Monterey Peninsula, a long-anticipated family vacation. Monarch butterflies spend winters nestled in stands of pines and eucalyptus along the peninsula's fog-enshrouded coast.

Except we hadn't seen any butterflies. "Where are the butterflies, Daddy?" Frances asked. Benji lost interest and canvassed the ground for sticks.

So far this trip had been less than ideal, with rain forecast throughout our entire stay. The kids bounced off the walls of our small motel room. "It was almost better at home," Kate said.

Suddenly her face lit up. "I see one!" she cried. We all looked.

"There." She pointed to a branch. "The undersides of their wings are brown. When they're closed up you can hardly see them. There must be dozens of them."

The kids and I squinted. "I see them!" cried Frances. And then I did too. What I had mistaken for leaves were actually countless monarchs huddled on the branch. Suddenly, several of the butterflies launched into flight. Their orange wings flashed. They swooped and looped. The kids clapped.

Kate and I looked at each other. What other blessings had we been blind to on this trip? "Let's look at the other trees," Kate said to the kids. "I bet there are loads more butterflies around here." We looked, and Kate was right.

Open my eyes to Your constant presence, Lord.
—Jim Hinch

Digging Deeper: Pss 95:2, 140:13; Is 45:3

Sun 27

By the seventh day God completed His work which He had done, and He rested on the seventh day from all His work. . . . Then God blessed the seventh day and sanctified it. . . .
—GENESIS 2:2–3 (NAS)

In the creation account of Genesis, God makes the world in six days and then rests on the seventh day. Not only does God rest, but He sanctifies the seventh day of creation for the purpose of recuperating from labor.

If there is anything that plagues modern-day folks, it is chronic fatigue. Seldom do we get enough sleep. And rare is the day when we truly disconnect from work and worry.

A second observation may sound a bit strange coming from a man who spent thirty-five years as a pastor: The church or synagogue often does not respect the mandate to rest on the Sabbath.

For people who have a Judeo-Christian heritage, the Sabbath is not only a time of rest but a day of worship. As a pastor, I would often be up late on Saturday night, finishing my sermon and preparing for worship leadership. I would arrive early at the church on Sunday for the first of multiple services. I often taught a Sunday school class. Then, after lunch, I would attend committee meetings followed by an evening vespers service and Sunday night fellowship. Sunday was the most exhausting day of my week.

There is a need to regain balance on the equal claim of rest *and* worship on the Sabbath. Both must be experienced in fullness in order to retain spiritual and physical health.

Dear God, help me to know that if You need rest, I must rest too. Amen.
—SCOTT WALKER

Digging Deeper: MT 8:24; MK 6:31

A NEW WAY TO SERVE

Mon 28

For I will leave in the midst of you a people humble and lowly.... —Zephaniah 3:12 (NRSV)

GOD HEARS ALL PRAYERS

When I started the St. James Literary Society at the homeless shelter, I had plans for structure, rules, you name it. Reality soon set in. Our book club became as messy as the lives of those of us in it.

Everything was on the table!

Once I abandoned my hope for an organized, structured forum, I opened myself up more to these people than to anyone in my life. They honored me by returning the favor.

I insisted that we end every meeting with a prayer. Not everyone identified as Christian, although most were familiar with the higher power of twelve-step programs. It took a little doing to get them to hold hands. I tried to make the prayers personal, including each person's particular needs. There were men and women standing in the circle, heads bowed, eyes closed, hands clasped. They'd stood up, put out their cigarettes, stopped jittering. They were addicts, dealers, poor in spirit and body, ill, hungry, worried, ex-convicts, angry, hurt, victims of injustice. And because I'd asked them, we were praying.

Father, thank You for hearing all prayers, especially the wordless ones.
—Marci Alborghetti

Digging Deeper: Mt 7:7–11; Rom 8:26–27

Tue 29

Then the lame shall leap like a deer. . . . For waters shall burst forth in the wilderness, And streams in the desert.
—ISAIAH 35:6 (NKJV)

Last summer there was a drought in Missouri. I was walking downtown when it finally started to rain, so I ducked under a store awning. A car parked in front of me and a young father got out. He popped open his big, blue umbrella and held it over his little girl, but she would have none of it. She twirled out from under the canopy and began leaping and dancing in the heavenly downpour, her wet, black hair hanging down like a tail and her pink T-shirt clinging to her stick-figure body. She was laughing hysterically, and her father gazed at her with envy.

All at once I had a powerful urge to join her in the rain dance, to return to my childhood when rain was a miracle and not a bother. But before I could get up my courage, the rain suddenly stopped.

The next day I was walking when, again, it started to rain. I had no umbrella and there were no store awnings handy, so I just kept walking. It felt utterly wonderful to be soaked to the bone after a summer of dry heat. My shoes began to squeak, and I was laughing so hard that other walkers were staring at me.

Somewhere on my way to adulthood, my sense of adventure got crowded out by things like propriety and dignity. Maybe it's time for me to step out from the umbrella of maturity and do something a bit daring now and then, like go with my granddaughter on that roller-coaster ride or volunteer for that pie-throwing contest at the PTO.

Who knows what joys await me outside the range of dignity?

Lord, I am sometimes paralyzed by propriety. Teach me to leap with joy at the wonders of Your world.
—DANIEL SCHANTZ

Digging Deeper: PS 43:4; PRV 17:22; HB 3:18

July

Wed 30

Even the wilderness and desert will rejoice in those days, the desert will blossom with flowers. —Isaiah 35:1 (TLB)

My friend Dianne travels the world as a flight attendant for a major airline. One day she's in Rome, dining on exquisite Italian food and shopping for olive oil. The next week she's in Buenos Aires, visiting museums and enjoying the party atmosphere. When she had her large kitchen totally remodeled, then bought a brand-new convertible, I felt myself turning a little green around the edges. It made me wish I'd worked harder during my peak years so that I, too, could afford such trips and luxuries.

Then one day I was kayaking on the Weeki Wachee River with Dianne and two other friends. The water was so crystal clear we could see fish swimming all around us. An array of birds and turtles entertained us as we rode with the swift current, hardly having to paddle at all. Suddenly, a large eight-foot-long manatee swam up alongside our kayak and stayed with us for half an hour. As I reached down into the water to pet the magnificent creature, I understood that I had all the riches and perks and loveliness that life has to offer right there in that rented kayak.

Heavenly Father, steer me in the direction of the most glorious natural places that You have created and teach me to appreciate the richness of each one.

—Patricia Lorenz

Digging Deeper: Ps 104

Thu 31

"For my thoughts are not your thoughts, neither are your ways my ways," declares the Lord. —ISAIAH 55:8 (NIV)

Gary and I sat at the large wooden table with two copies of our divorce papers in neat white piles, His and Hers. I felt strong. I wasn't as fragile as the last few times we'd almost signed. For months there was always something that caused a delay: missing information, an item we forgot to bring, canceled appointments. Each time I wondered, *Lord, is this You? Are You going to turn things around?*

The mediator smiled sympathetically as we took our seats. "Shall we go over the document to make sure everything is in order?"

I knew there would be no restoration. There would be no more delays. The pen was in my hand, ready to sign away my vows. And although I now felt at peace with letting go, it suddenly seemed so final. The strength I felt that morning slowly faded, and on a crowded train on my way home, I had to disappear into my jacket to hide my tears and muffle my sobs.

Why didn't You intervene? my heart quietly asked God. *Why couldn't You make us a family?* After all those months of healing and acceptance, I now had to mourn all over again.

When I got home, my children ran to me. Their happy faces urged me not to dwell on what I'd lost. So I hugged them tightly, holding on to what I still had, to what is yet to come.

Help me to hold on to Your goodness and promises, Lord,
even when the answers to my prayers are not what I expect.
—KAREN VALENTIN

Digging Deeper: Pss 84:11, 86:15

DAILY MERCIES

1 ______

2 ______

3 ______

4 ______

5 ______

6 ______

7 ______

8 ______

9 ______

10 ______

11 ______

12 ______

13 ______

14 ______

15 ______

16 __________

17 __________

18 __________

19 __________

20 __________

21 __________

22 __________

23 __________

24 __________

25 __________

26 __________

27 __________

28 __________

29 __________

30 __________

31 __________

August

But the wisdom that is from above is first pure, then peaceable, gentle, and easy to be entreated, full of mercy and good fruits, without partiality, and without hypocrisy.

—James 3:17 (KJV)

HOPE IN HOSPICE

Fri 1 *My comfort in my suffering is this: Your promise preserves my life.* —Psalm 119:50 (NIV)

COMFORT IN GOD'S PROMISES

Hardcover, paperback, printed, electronic, or audio—I need books in my life. Always have. So I happily volunteered to create a book cart at the hospice unit and included copies of *Daily Guideposts*—especially valuable with its short and varied stories—and Bibles. I made part of one shelf for the children—there are often grandkids running through the hospice. I added novels to pass the long night hours. I even included a few poetry books that, to my surprise, were very popular.

Once the cart was filled, I wheeled it into the corridor and wondered whether anyone would be glad to find it there. No worries! Week after week I found it nicely jumbled and messy, needing tidying up and more books.

Far and away the most requested book is the Bible. Both the dying and their loved ones clearly derive such comfort from Scripture. These well-thumbed volumes are working their own kind of spiritual transformation, comforting the sick and reassuring their families. Familiarity is particularly needed at times of stress. Which Psalm is the most requested? Always the words of the Twenty-Third: "Your rod and your staff—they comfort me." And they do.

Thank You, Lord, for Your words of Scripture. May they always bring comfort and wisdom as we face change and farewells.
—Brigitte Weeks

Digging Deeper: Ps 23; Prv 30:5

Sat 2

Don't jump to conclusions—there may be a perfectly good explanation for what you just saw.
—PROVERBS 25:8 (MSG)

The other day, I went to the zoo with my girlfriend Ashley. Generally, when an activity involves my girlfriend and a lot of walking, it results in holding hands.

But on this particular day, I noticed that while we were searching for the Giant Panda Habitat, she didn't reach out for my hand like she usually does. So when we walked from there to the Great Cats exhibit, I reached out for hers. We held hands for a few steps and then she let go.

Yikes! I thought. *Is she mad about something? Doesn't she like me anymore?*

I have this tendency to take a little event and jump to the worst-case scenario. At this point, you should also know that I'm an amputee and walk with crutches. So holding hands is slightly more difficult for us because my hand is always at the fixed height of my crutch handle.

By the time we left the zoo, I was in full freak-out mode, assuming our relationship was over. I tentatively asked Ashley if she wanted to go out for a bite to eat.

"Definitely," she said, "but first can we stop by my apartment so I can change into flats? The heels on these shoes make me too tall to be able to hold your hand."

I laughed.

"What?"

"Nothing."

Because it *was* nothing.

Please help me trust You, God, rather than jumping to my own anxious conclusions.
—JOSHUA SUNDQUIST

Digging Deeper: PHIL 4:6–7

Sun 3

All discipline for the moment seems not to be joyful, but sorrowful; yet to those who have been trained by it, afterwards it yields the peaceful fruit of righteousness.
—Hebrews 12:11 (NAS)

I truly get what David Murrow talks about in his book *Why Men Hate Going to Church*. I don't exactly hate church, but it's more of a discipline than a delight.

For one thing, I am terribly restless. In church, I feel like a racehorse confined to a broom closet. I need to move! Sitting on a hard chair for an hour of Sunday school and an hour of worship stretches me to the edge of sanity. And when I am forced to be very quiet, I become overly aware of my minor maladies. My acid reflux begins to burn like a blowtorch. The floaters in my eyes turn into thunderclouds. The allergy tickle in my throat becomes a raging itch, and I cough uncontrollably until my wife pokes me. "*Sh*, people are staring at us."

Last, I am an introvert. Crowds of people make me as nervous as a duck in a gun shop, and I get claustrophobic with people sitting on all sides of me. I've never found a way to make church easier. It's a discipline, like going to the doctor.

What brings me back each Sunday is the payoff. I feel less lonely for having seen all my fellow-strugglers in the same place, looking for help. I make better decisions at work because my conscience has been sharpened by good preaching. And when I walk out the front door of the church, I feel fifty pounds lighter because I have left my sins in the hands of a merciful God.

It's worth the discomfort, I think.

Lord, You are the Great Physician. I don't like going to doctors and I chafe at going to church, but I thank You for the healing I experience every Sunday. —Daniel Schantz

Digging Deeper: Mt 9:9–13

Mon 4

Remember how short my time is. . . . —Psalm 89:47 (KJV)

Nana, look!" Hannah whispered. A silvery-blue common morpho had alighted on her shoulder in the Butterfly Garden atop the Boston Museum of Science.

The docent showed us cocoons inside a glass-fronted box, an incubator for more butterflies from the tropics of Central America. My ten-year-old granddaughter inquired about the morpho habitat and learned to identify the butterfly even when its brown side camouflaged it among dead leaves. We watched, fascinated, as it ate from a scarlet flower with its proboscis, a dainty, microscopic straw. "We saw these butterflies when we came last time," Hannah volunteered.

Our guide paused a moment, then said gently, "You probably didn't see *these* butterflies. You see, they live only three or four months." Both Hannah and I fell silent for a moment. We left the garden buoyed by Hannah's magical encounter, yet I felt a twinge of sadness. We would never see these same butterflies again.

When Hannah related her butterfly experience to her mother, her face again radiated joy. I, on the other hand, quietly obsessed over why such a pretty animal was fated to live such a short time.

Eventually, though, I recognized that neither the common morpho—nor any of us—knows the number of our days. Within whatever time God does grant us, however, we can generate much joy, just as a silvery-blue butterfly gave my granddaughter during its tiny, beautiful life.

Eternal Father, help us to recognize Your timeless gifts
in the midst of the fleeting ones.
—Gail Thorell Schilling

Digging Deeper: 2 Cor 4:16–18; Jas 4:13–15

Tue 5

I will always thank the Lord; I will never stop praising him.
—Psalm 34:1 (GNB)

I was pouting with God. For months, I'd asked Him for several things to take place. Nothing happened. My prayers were a passionless list of requests, all pleases and no thank-yous. I stared out the window toward our neighbors' trail through the woods. Years ago, they'd erected garden art at intervals along the path. *Why don't you walk the trail and pray?*

I doubted it was God speaking to me, but I pulled on my rain boots and trudged through the soggy grass toward the path.

Praise Me for signs along the trail, God seemed to say.

"Okay, but it's not going to change anything." Entering the woods, I spotted the first piece of artwork on display. "Thank You for the wind chimes tied to that pine tree," I mumbled.

Keep praising Me.

I paused beside a plastic cardinal perched on a limb. "Thank You. You're my Salvation." Farther down the path, I saw a yellow tin butterfly. I touched its dotted wings. "You're my Healer. You alone set me free."

Each time I praised God, the words came easier. I discovered a mama black bear and her cubs made of particle board. "You're my Defender." A ceramic cow. "You're my Provider." A long shiny row of metallic sunflowers. "You're the Alpha and Omega, Beginning and End." I turned near a towering oak tree and studied a collection of red and blue metal stars. "You're my Bright Morning Star."

Leaving the woods to head home, I stepped onto my gravel driveway. "You're my Rock." The trees parted overhead. A thin ray of sun peeked through the clouds. "Your Son sets me free." Amazingly, the more I praised God, the less crucial my list of requests seemed. God grew, and my problems somehow felt insignificant.

Thank You, Lord. Praising You changes my heart. —Julie Garmon

Digging Deeper: Pss 147, 150; Heb 13:15

August

Wed 6

A man that hath friends must shew himself friendly....
—PROVERBS 18:24 (KJV)

A crowd is congregating outside the gates of Village Hope in Zimbabwe. Here on this little farm, over twenty orphans have found a home with Paddington and Alice, a couple who God partnered us with several years earlier. As we help prepare a community-wide meal, I find myself wishing that we could see one another as one people. *Do our differences make this impossible, God?*

Among those who've walked miles over mountain paths to get here is a barefoot girl who seems lost in the crowd. She finds a place to sit on a rock wall. I move toward her, but she recoils, tears filling her eyes. She's terrified by my white face. To these children, I might as well be an alien.

My family is stirring sadza in steel barrels over a fire and setting out plates, cups, steaming vats of tea, and baskets of bread. We're doing our best to act on Jesus' words "I was hungry," but the separation lingers.

Now, my granddaughter Abby has spotted the little girl. She goes over and quietly sits beside her on the wall, keeping a bit of distance as the girl stares straight ahead. When I glance back a few minutes later, I see that Abby has edged closer. Is that giggling I hear?

After the adults are served, the children form a long line. Now Abby and her new friend are holding hands. Later, as women begin popping up to sing and dance in thanksgiving for the food, I smile, seeing that Abby and the little girl are dancing too.

Too soon, the day ends. The girl runs to Abby and gives her a hug before following her grandmother home. Later, I tell Abby how proud I am of her. "You seemed like best friends. What did you talk about?"

"Oh, Mimi," Abby says, "we couldn't talk. She only speaks Shona and I only speak English, so we just laughed and danced and played!"

Father, help me bridge the differences that divide us from one another simply and honestly, by "showing myself friendly." —PAM KIDD

Digging Deeper: JOB 2:11; PS 119:63

THE PATH TO ADOPTION

Thu 7 *Religion that God our Father accepts as pure and faultless is this: to look after orphans and widows in their distress and to keep oneself from being polluted by the world.*
—JAMES 1:27 (NIV)

TAKING CARE OF THE ORPHANS

"What if I can't love an adopted child as much as Brogan?"

It was a question I hated thinking, let alone expressing out loud. It was a question that kept me from saying yes to adoption for a long time. It was a question I needed to voice, even if it made me feel like a horrible person.

"Can you love a child who wouldn't otherwise be loved?" my husband asked.

"Yes, I can do that."

"Can we give a home to a child who wouldn't otherwise have a home?"

"Yeah, we can."

Suddenly, I got it. I was making this about me, when it wasn't about me. It's about the millions of orphans out there who need a family, who need love, who need somebody to take care of them. I was letting my fear keep me from obedience.

God says to take care of orphans. So I'm obeying. I'm opening my heart and my home to a child who needs a heart and a home. I'm trusting that God will equip me with everything I need to care for that little one. Already I feel a shift—an aligning—as God's love for the orphan takes hold of my soul.

Lord God, thank You that You are a God Who sets the lonely into families, that when we step out in obedience, You give us everything we need.
—KATIE GANSHERT

Digging Deeper: JN 15:14; GAL 5:13–14; 2 JN 1:6

August

Fri 8

"When you come looking for me, you'll find me."
—Jeremiah 29:13 (MSG)

My neighbor Dee works full-time for a ministry in town, in addition to raising three daughters and caring for her husband, who also works full-time. She is typically easygoing, low-key, measured in her words, faithful in her walk. But she'd stepped in a few recent messes at work, and now her team and her boss were miffed.

As I sat there listening to the blow-by-blow explanation of her weeks-long misery, I couldn't help but see myself in her description. I'd said similarly stupid things, reacted in similarly dumb ways, let myself play the fool on more occasions than I care to count.

But then, the conversation shifted from shared misery to seeking God. We asked the questions that can't help but grow us up spiritually, questions of His activity and purpose and plan: *What are You after in this situation, Father? What are we supposed to learn from this pain?*

We reminded each other of God's commitment to transforming us, even if the process sometimes hurts. And we reaffirmed our belief that good always comes, even from the wreckage we unwittingly cause.

Life feels so much easier when it's full of exclamation points—declarations and decisions and demonstrations of our having things under control. But when question marks punctuate our thoughts, it's only then that we seek hard after God.

Thank You for life's question marks, Lord. May the curiosities and confusions and problems and defeats only make me seek harder after You.
—Ashley Wiersma

Digging Deeper: Jas 1:1–18

Sat 9

Steer clear of foolish discussions which lead people into the sin of anger with each other. —2 TIMOTHY 2:16 (TLB)

Here in Florida, on the Gulf Coast, we're very careful of stingrays—those beautiful, gentle creatures who bury themselves in the warm sand next to the shore during mating season. If you step on one accidentally, it'll whip its long tail and jab you with the barb located halfway down it with such velocity that the pain is nearly unbearable.

The county even posts signs along the beaches to warn people to do the "stingray shuffle" where you keep both feet flat in the sand and shuffle them forward when you enter the ocean. The stingrays won't hurt you as long as you don't step on them. If you tread lightly and shuffle your feet in the sand, they can feel the vibrations and scatter before you come near.

Over the years I've had to learn to do a bit of shuffling, zip my lip, and tread lightly with my friend Brenda when it comes to a few topics of discussion. Our religious and political convictions are light-years apart, and rather than ruin a wonderful friendship when those subjects come up, I do the stingray shuffle until I can change the subject. It isn't always easy since I enjoy a good discussion, but I also know that neither of us is willing to stray from our convictions.

Brenda's willingness to do the shuffle too has maintained our close friendship to the point where she was my official witness when Jack and I married in 2012.

She's a keeper!

Heavenly Father, You are the Master Negotiator. Help me to tread lightly when it comes to words that can cause pain or disagreement.

—PATRICIA LORENZ

Digging Deeper: MT 5:9; ROM 12:18; EPH 4:1–6

Sun 10

And Moses hid his face, for he was afraid to look at God.
—EXODUS 3:6 (NRSV)

I wasn't too excited before the reconciliation/forgiveness service at St. Columba, a strong, spirited church that we attend in Oakland, California. At the entrance of the darkened, purple-draped church were ugly, fist-size rocks. We were to select one and take it inside.

Our pastor explained that the rock symbolized our sins. We were to feel the drag of its weight as we held it during the service and carried it when we went to one of the ministers to confess. Afterward, we were to drop our rocks in a large bin set on the altar. This was how we would release sin and accept God's forgiveness.

Easier said than done, I thought. I didn't believe it would be that simple to shed my sins.

While I waited to make my confession, I watched others. Some were crying; others smiling and laughing, relieved as the rocks slipped from their fists. Some bent to place the rock gingerly. A few triumphantly tossed in their rocks. One woman, victory etched in her features, hurled hers, the resulting clang mixing with our laughter.

I discovered that everyone felt the burden of sin differently and that many who'd released their rock looked truly surprised at the freedom they felt. Could I be one of them?

I stood up. I didn't know what would happen tomorrow or the next day, but right then I was eager to find out how it would feel to drop that rock.

Father, teach me to embrace Your grace and
forgiveness, for my need is great.
—MARCI ALBORGHETTI

Digging Deeper: ROM 5:1–2, 8:1–11

Mon 11

My mouth will speak the praise of the Lord. . . .
—Psalm 145:21 (NRSV)

I have favorite phrases I say a lot and, interestingly, many of them have to do with food. Something easy? "Can o' corn" or maybe "Piece a cake!" When I do something foolish, I'm a "meatball!" My colleague Jack often responds to ideas or actions he likes with the phrase "Cool beans!" Once I heard someone ask, "You got the spaghetti on the cranberries?" He meant, do you have information on the situation?

One day Jack challenged me. "Every time you say 'Can o' corn' in the next month, you owe your local food pantry a can of corn. Deal?"

Well, I couldn't pass up a challenge like that, but I added a twist. "I'll take that deal, if you'll donate a can of beans for every time you say 'Cool beans.'"

When some of our coworkers heard about what we were doing, unusual things began to happen. One person offered to match our totals, can for can. I'd find cans of corn in my mailbox or would be intentionally asked to do some easy task, hoping for my usual verbal response. By the time the month ended, a dozen of us had collected more than four hundred cans of vegetables for the local food pantry. Cool beans, huh?

You never forget those in need, God. By my words and deeds, help me to follow You.
—Jeff Japinga

Digging Deeper: Lk 12:7; Jas 2:14–17

August

Tue 12

Then the Lord said to Moses, "I will rain down bread from heaven for you. The people are to go out each day and gather enough for that day. . . ." —Exodus 16:4 (NIV)

"No, Kemo!" I scolded my golden retriever as he came in from the backyard, his face and front paws covered with wet dirt. He'd just dropped a huge, dirty bone at my feet. Wagging his tail, he picked it up and dropped it again, as if I should be thrilled. I was not.

He'd recently started this new habit of burying, then digging up, and then again burying the rawhide bones I gave him. I was baffled because I thought bone-burying was something only fictional Fidos did.

Later, I told a friend about this and she just laughed. "Burying bones is their natural instinct. Before dogs were domesticated, they buried their bones, so they wouldn't starve when the food supply got scarce. Bones are their treasures."

"So he's suddenly developed a hoarding habit?" I asked. "As if he's forgetting that I faithfully feed him twice a day?"

"Maybe that's the point," she said. "He wants to share his precious bounty, like a gift."

I just shook my head, but she continued in her sage gift-of-dog-wisdom voice. "Maybe you can't see the gift because you don't like the packaging."

That stopped me short because the meaning of her words went way beyond the dog. Back home, I apologized to Kemo and thanked him for the gift. Obviously, he didn't understand what I was saying, but I did . . . and God did.

Lord, open my eyes to recognize Your gifts wrapped
in many different packages.
—Carol Kuykendall

Digging Deeper: Ex 16

Wed 13

Now during these days he went out to the mountain to pray; and he spent the night in prayer to God.
—LUKE 6:12 (NRSV)

I sat down at the kitchen table and two-year-old Benjamin sat across from me in his high chair. He grinned. "It's just Daddy and Benji," he announced. "Not Mommy, not Frances," who were away visiting Kate's parents.

We ate our leftover soup and a salad, and talked through the meal, something Benji and I rarely get to do. While I washed up, Benji played with his tractors on the kitchen floor. We stretched out the bath, Benji delighting in being the only one in the tub. "How about we read two bedtime books tonight?" I suggested.

"Yeah!" said Benji.

We said prayers, and I laid Benji in his crib. The house was quiet. I missed Kate and Frances terribly. But suddenly I realized Benji wasn't the only one getting some much-needed alone time with his father.

After I finished making Benji's lunch, I'd have plenty of time to sit down with my *Book of Common Prayer* and say evening prayer. In the morning, I wouldn't be banging out of bed at 5:30 to exercise. I'd sit on the sofa, waiting for Benji to wake up, *Book of Common Prayer* in my lap.

"It's just You and me, Lord," I whispered. "Thank You."

Today, I will spend time alone with You, God.
—JIM HINCH

Digging Deeper: MK 1:35; JAS 4:8

August

Thu 14

For many years you were patient with them....
—Nehemiah 9:30 (NIV)

I tried everything: deep breathing, tea, taking breaks to go on walks. Nothing seemed to work.

I spent a couple of hours each day pounding my keyboard to write, and, for some reason, it had been causing me a lot of stress and anxiety recently. My heart raced; my body tensed; my adrenaline flowed. However, my search for a remedy had, so far, come up short.

One night, at a neighborhood joint, I ordered the grilled asparagus, marinated in balsamic vinegar and sprinkled with Parmesan cheese to go. When the chef handed me my meal, I thanked him.

"Take it slow," he said.

What a bizarre farewell, I thought to myself. *Take it slow.* The words felt unnatural to me, not only because I'd never heard anyone use them in that context before, but also because they were the exact opposite of the way I approach my work. I take it fast. I put my fingers on fully automatic and unleash a torrent of words as if my life depended on the volume of my output.

The next day when I sat down to write, I took it slow. I tried to work as carefully and deliberately as possible. And you know what? It worked. It wasn't easy. It felt inefficient and tedious, like signing my name with my left hand, but it worked. I'm calmer, more relaxed, more still before the Lord.

Lord, please help me to take it slow.
—Joshua Sundquist

Digging Deeper: Ps 46

Fri 15

If I speak in the tongues of men or of angels, but do not have love, I am only a resounding gong or a clanging cymbal.
—1 CORINTHIANS 13:1 (NIV)

I was mad. Seething, really. My friend had posted a comment on Facebook that really stung. I was ready to put on my boxing gloves.

I typed a sarcastic response and quickly hit Post. There! At least I had stuck up for what was right.

Five minutes later, I got a phone call. It was my friend in tears, explaining to me that she had never intended her original comment to come across the way it had. She had been in the middle of dealing with sick kids and a pushy boss and had typed words that she never meant to say. And I had responded like a sixth grader on the playground. Oh, the power of social media!

Making amends with my friend was the easy part. But the angry words that I had so publicly aired were harder to take back, clashing against the truthful and loving words that I should've said in the first place—words that would've promoted peace and love instead of discord.

Lord, please sprinkle my words with salt and light, and eliminate hurtful or angry words from my vocabulary so that I can speak Your truth and love to my friends.
—ERIN MACPHERSON

Digging Deeper: JAS 3

LIFE LESSONS FROM THOSE I'VE MET

Sat 16

"A man's life does not consist in the abundance of his possessions." —Luke 12:15 (RSV)

MALCOLM MUGGERIDGE, BRITISH AUTHOR

John concentrated on driving on the left, while I fretted about clothes. We'd been in England long enough to know that a luncheon invitation meant—dress up! We were on our way to interview the eminent British author Malcolm Muggeridge; John in a suit; I in my black dress, with white gloves bought for the occasion.

We carried a photo of the Muggeridges' mansion, but we drove twice through the little village of Robertsbridge without spotting it. Stopping a postman on a bicycle, we were directed to a brick cottage where a ruddy-faced, white-haired man was weeding turnips.

"Come on in!" he called. "Kitty's got the soup on!"

In the kitchen, a handsome woman, gray hair pulled back in a bun, was stirring a pot on the stove. "Will you slice the bread?" she asked.

I took off my gloves and cut into a loaf still warm from the oven. We ate at the kitchen table: soup, bread, cheese, honey from their hives. "We have the same lunch every day," Kitty Muggeridge said. "Saves planning and fuss."

The big house we'd looked for? "We sold it. We can care for this place in a quarter of the time at a quarter of the cost." Smaller car. Smaller wardrobes. A well-to-do couple "living simply so others can simply live."

Yes, giving to others was their initial motivation for paring down, they said—we'd read about their many charities. "But so much else has followed!" For the first time in their busy professional lives, they had *time*. Time to read, to pray, to garden, to invite strangers to lunch.

Show me those possessions, Father, that stand between me and Your abundant life. —Elizabeth Sherrill

Digging Deeper: Mt 6:19–21, 19:16–30

Sun 17

There are different kinds of service, but the same Lord.
—1 Corinthians 12:5 (NIV)

The Sunday morning after the mission team returned from Honduras, I was feeling down. *Will I ever be able to make as big a difference in someone's life as I did in Honduras two years ago?* I wondered. There, I'd taught Bible school to hundreds of children.

I listened wistfully as a Sunday school class member chatted about the huge effect they'd had on a family's life when the team put a metal stovepipe in a clay oven inside their adobe home, so the three young children wouldn't constantly suffer from respiratory problems.

Then someone tapped me on the shoulder. It was Dave, the mission team leader. "I have something for you," he said. He handed me a small pale-blue envelope with my name on it. It was a little battered and smudged with dirt. "I'm delivering this to you late. Last time you went to Honduras with us, someone from our class gave me a note to give to you. It got misplaced in my suitcase, and it's traveled all over the country with me since then. I just found it this week."

I opened the envelope and pulled out a note card that read, "Karen, begin to weave and God will give you thread (a German proverb). What an opportunity for you to put His word into action. You have made a difference already through your prayer study. You are a remarkable woman, and I am very proud of you. I continue to pray for you. Love and blessings, Claudia."

I smiled. Even though the letter was two years old, it had been delivered right on time.

Dear Lord Jesus, thank You that anything I do in Your kingdom will have a lasting impact on people's lives. Open my eyes to the possibilities right outside my door today. Amen.

—Karen Barber

Digging Deeper: Is 55:11; 1 Cor 15:58

Mon 18

And he said to them, "Go into all the world and proclaim the good news to the whole creation." —MARK 16:15 (NRSV)

The other evening, a supermarket checker concluded my transaction with "Have a blessed night."

I babbled some response while processing the lovely surprise of a stranger's speaking blessings upon me.

At a discussion the previous evening of Mischa Berlinski's novel *Fieldwork*, a friend had commented that she always avoided saying anything religious around potential nonbelievers, and I recognized that I do the same thing.

In Berlinski's book, a journalist in Thailand researches an anthropologist's murder of a missionary. When the journalist, a nonbeliever, starts getting to know the missionary's family, he's surprised that, though they talk about Jesus a lot, they never try to evangelize. In another scene, the anthropologist, also a nonbeliever, asks the mother of the missionary family to explain salvation and the older woman refuses.

Despite these scenes and Berlinski's secular Jewish heritage, the novel is refreshingly congenial toward the missionaries and Christianity.

It struck me that maybe evangelism—literally, telling the good news—isn't just about telling people how to be saved. It's about telling all the other good news about God. That He made us, pays attention to us, suffers pain when we reject Him. That God is determined to win our love. Evangelism is telling the *gospel*—another word for good news—present in *all* of Scripture, not just in Jesus' death and Resurrection.

Heavenly Father, thank You for the good news of Your love and many mercies to us, Your children. Motivate us to share it with everyone we encounter, wherever we are.

—PATTY KIRK

Digging Deeper: PS 23:6; 1 JN 3:1

Tue 19

Then Philip opened his mouth, and . . . preached Jesus to him.
—ACTS 8:35 (NAS)

Eight-year-old Stephen is excited about being a Cub Scout. He loves being part of the pack, having a place in a group of guys; he loves making things and camping and the other activities; he loves the uniform and the special salute and reciting the Cub Scout Promise and the Law of the Pack.

At last week's meeting, each Scout was given a box of fifty candy bars. Selling candy is the way Stephen's pack raises money, and each Scout who sells a box receives a kit to make a car for the upcoming Pinewood Derby.

His ten-year-old sister Maggie volunteered to help Stephen sell chocolate bars in our building. They rang a few doorbells and staked out the lobby and made seven sales. *At this rate,* I thought, *they've got a week's worth of selling to do.* But I hadn't counted on Maggie's marketing prowess. The next afternoon she decked Stephen out in his uniform and hit the pavement.

After a half-hour, an excited Stephen and Maggie burst into the apartment. "We sold out!" Maggie shouted.

At this week's meeting, Stephen got his Pinewood Derby kit—and another box of candy. "I can get credit for summer camp," he told me. I'm sure Stephen and Maggie can sell this one out too. They make a great team.

Lord, I'm naturally shy, and talking from my heart about my faith has been particularly difficult. When the opportunity arises, help me to share the Good News with Maggie's skill and Stephen's enthusiasm.
—ANDREW ATTAWAY

Digging Deeper: ROM 10:15

Wed 20

Value others above yourselves, not looking to your own interests but each of you to the interests of the others.
—Philippians 2:3–4 (NIV)

As I pulled into the parking spot, Sunrise, my golden retriever, stuck her head between the seats of my station wagon, begging for a scratch. I ruffled her silky fur and said, "I've got a busy afternoon catching up on e-mails." Several were from a group of professionals who contributed wonderful tips. I groaned. *And I'm the professional lurker.* I felt like they all knew more than I did, so I never contributed anything.

I popped some candy pieces into my mouth, stuffed the half-eaten package between the seats, and raced into the store to buy some milk. When I returned, I noticed that Sunrise was in the front seat with the candy package dangling between her teeth.

Fumbling in my pocket for the keys, I banged on the door and yelled, "Drop it!" But instead, she gulped like a bird swallowing a fish. By the time I unlocked the door and pried apart her jaws, the candy was gone. "You hog! You wanted to make sure that you ate every last one because you didn't want to share."

What about you? I heard. I grimaced. I'd been skimming advice from the group but hadn't done anything to share. The rest of the afternoon I read e-mails and returned the best I had: words of encouragement.

Lord, reveal to me ideas of how I can contribute.
—Rebecca Ondov

Digging Deeper: Pss 32:8, 46:1–3; Gal 6:2

A NEW WAY TO SERVE

Thu 21

The Lord said to Abram, "Go from your country and your kindred and your father's house to the land that I will show you." —Genesis 12:1 (NRSV)

JUDGE NOT

I'd met Say at the St. James Shelter years ago. He was a refugee of the USA's military actions in Indonesia. His father had fought with us and had been abandoned to the communist regime when we left. Say does not like to talk about his early life; members of his family were tortured, lost, killed. Say's struggle to survive and make progress is courageous and gut-wrenching.

Just when I thought there was nothing left to know about Say, I was sitting in a coffee shop with a friend. Say seems to live off of coffee, especially after he's added five scoops of sugar, so it was no surprise to see him there. He did not meet my eyes; he knew I was frustrated and impatient with him for being irresponsible with his paycheck and his excuses. I introduced my friend, but Say wandered off.

Soon we heard the most beautiful melody. Say was playing classical music at the coffee shop's piano. Lifting his head for a moment to meet my astonished gaze, he grinned as if to say, "Don't close the book on me yet."

Jesus, remind me not to judge a book by its cover, or even its contents, because it may not be finished.
—Marci Alborghetti

Digging Deeper: Rom 2:1; Jas 4:11–12

August

Fri 22

Consider it pure joy, my brothers and sisters, whenever you face trials of many kinds. —JAMES 1:2 (NIV)

After a bad storm unexpectedly blew through Mandeville, Louisiana, I went outside to survey the neighborhood. A couple of tall pine trees were split in half, and debris was everywhere.

"Looks like a small twister went through here!" I called out to my neighbor who was walking her dog.

"Sure looks like it," she said. "How'd you make out?"

"Awful!" I said. "The wind ripped off some siding from the back of the house and put some deep scratches into the bedroom windows. A bunch of fencing is down in the backyard, and my purple martin birdhouse is knocked down. I'm sure my birds are gone for the season. The storm uprooted my tall Queen Anne palm by the pond too. It survived so many hard freezes over the years, and now a storm uproots it. It's just terrible." I sighed, shaking my head. "How'd you do?"

"A big tree fell through my roof and crashed into my kitchen," she said. "I've got lots of water and structural damage."

"Oh no," I said. "I'm so sorry."

"It's okay," she said. "I've been praying about whether or not to remodel my kitchen." She smiled. "Looks like I got my answer."

"Wow," I said, "you sure have a great attitude about it."

"I'm not going to let anything—even a pine tree in my kitchen—get in the way of my faith," she replied with a smile. "I'm keeping in mind the quote that I hung in my kitchen: 'I got this one, okay? Love, God.'"

She tugged at her dog's leash to coax him on. "Thank goodness that quote survived the storm. We will too."

Next time, God, I want to respond to calamity with a graciousness that reflects my faith in You.

—MELODY BONNETTE SWANG

Digging Deeper: GN 50:20; PS 56:3–4

Sat 23

"The Lord bless you and keep you; the Lord make his face shine on you and be gracious to you; the Lord turn his face toward you and give you peace." —NUMBERS 6:24–26 (NIV)

The restaurant was filled with family and friends anticipating the arrival of the birthday girl, my brother's mother-in-law, a beloved member of our extended family. We were all excited about celebrating Madeline's surprise ninetieth.

Her daughter Margherita had asked me to offer a prayer of blessing. In preparation, I reflected upon Madeline's life and the many ways she blesses those near and far. In a world of e-mails and text messages, Madeline still mails out cards with personal handwritten messages.

I searched the Bible for stories where a prayer of blessing was offered. Jacob blessed his sons and grandchildren, and before his death Moses blessed the people. I learned that a blessing is a prayer for a blessing to come. I thought about those giants of the faith—Jacob, Moses—and asked myself, *Who am I to say this prayer? What kind of blessing can I offer?*

When it was my turn at the party, I stood behind Madeline, laid my hands upon her shoulders, and prayed, "Lord, thank You for Madeline, for her love of the family, her faith, and her zeal for life. Bless her with strength and health so that we may gather again to celebrate her one-hundredth birthday."

It has been a few years since the party, but the spiritual lesson continues to guide me. In spite of my imperfections, God blesses others through me, not because of any merit of my own.

Lord, help me bless my family and friends by praying for them in their different seasons of life.

—PABLO DIAZ

Digging Deeper: JN 14:22; PHIL 2:12–13

August

Sun 24

Let your eyes look straight ahead; fix your gaze directly before you. —Proverbs 4:25 (NIV)

Oh, let me just text him back real quick," my friend said to me. Then, "I've got to take this call. I've been trying to reach her for days. Hang on a sec, okay?"

I would have been upset by this display of divided attention, except that not too long ago the dividing offender was me.

Months ago, I was listening to a podcast of a sermon—while also holding a baby, putting on makeup, eating breakfast, folding laundry, dusting bookshelves, and returning sixteen e-mails—when I heard the pastor say: "If you are the type of person who reads five books at a time instead of finishing one and then actually reflecting on it before moving on to the next, you might need to rethink your ways." *Gulp.* His point was that Jesus never modeled this sort of multitasking efficiency. Therefore, neither should we.

The insight changed me. With uncharacteristic myopia, I began forcing myself to stop typing when my husband walked into the room to talk. I stashed my cell phone when my daughter dragged her little bowling pins out to play. When it was time for work, I parked myself at my desk instead of straightening lampshades and sweeping the floor.

And, you know, that pastor was right. Something that feels a lot like Jesus goes on in me when I choose to be in one place at a time.

Father, wherever I choose to be today, help me be fully there.
—Ashley Wiersma

Digging Deeper: Ps 1:1–2; Eccl 4:6

Mon 25

"For if you forgive men their trespasses, your heavenly Father will also forgive you." —Matthew 6:14 (NKJV)

A nurse who was known to say the first thing that entered her mind made the most cutting remark: "I met your mother yesterday, and she walked like this." She then proceeded to imitate my mother who was horribly crippled with osteoporosis. The shame and humiliation I felt were so great, it made me nauseated.

For two long decades, I harbored a grudge. Every time I saw this woman, I told myself, I will never forget what she did to me. That hurt so bad.

Today, I was teaching a class at the hospital when that same nurse, a student in my class, admired the earrings I was wearing. "Would you mind telling me where you purchased them?" she asked. "I would just love to have a pair."

I'd bought the heart earrings at a resale shop some time back, so the likelihood of her finding another pair was slim to none. They cost only a couple of dollars, but they were one of my favorites.

When I returned to my office, I couldn't stop thinking about that nurse. *Give those earrings to her as a gift of love and forgiveness*, an inner voice nudged. I cleansed the earrings with an alcohol towelette. Forgiveness followed the act of giving—joyful, freeing forgiveness.

When I don't feel like forgiving, Father, help me to do it anyway.
—Roberta Messner

Digging Deeper: Mt 18:21–35

August

Tue 26

And he said, The things which are impossible with men are possible with God. —LUKE 18:27 (KJV)

One of the scariest times for my family was awaiting the birth of my niece Kenedy. As it became clear that the pregnancy was incredibly dangerous for both mother and daughter, fear crept in. I would worry while I crocheted her blanket; I called every available minute for updates (even when I knew there were none); I stressed out every time I lost cell service underground on the subway.

I received some particularly bad news in a phone conversation with my brother. "The doctors said that there's very little chance the baby will survive, but it's not up to them. It's up to God."

This jolted me. I'd been stressing about something I couldn't control instead of talking with God about what He could do. I began to focus on prayers instead of worry, and claim the victory instead of assuming the worst. I silenced my doubting Thomas and worked on strengthening my faith. I prayed earnestly and directly to God. I was able to release the knot that had developed in my shoulders and then provide real support to my brother.

Before her birth, Kenedy was already giving me one of the greatest lessons I've ever been taught.

Help me, Lord, to continue to see Your lessons in my life, regardless of the source.
—NATALIE PERKINS

Digging Deeper: MK 9:24; JN 20:27–31

Wed 27

"Even to your old age... I will carry you...."
—Isaiah 46:4 (NAS)

My experiences with elder care, while serious, have had their lighter moments. My one-hundred-year-old aunt in Pasadena, California, who from excellent long-term memory loved to say, "The Lord's been good to me," had trouble with short-term memory. Each time she watched *National Velvet*'s horse-racing scene, she saw it happening at nearby Santa Anita racetrack. She'd exclaim, "Just think! A girl won—right over there! I'm so proud!"

Staying with two sisters in Minnesota, one recovering from major spinal surgery at eighty-nine and the other with early-stage Alzheimer's at eighty, I learned how the younger sister had already purchased a marker, engraved with name and birth date, set in a family cemetery plot in another state. However, she now planned to be buried locally. Her older sister quipped of the other marker, "They'll think she never died!"

In Washington State, I lived with an eighty-two-year-old recovering from cancer who had an afternoon medical appointment. The receptionist jabbered on about a dental ordeal in hyperdetail while this woman sat in her chair. I hid a grin behind my book as the old woman kept a determined patience and exhibited a dignity I won't soon forget.

I look to the courageous lives of these women to learn how to grow old. James 1:27 calls it "pure religion" to "visit orphans and widows in their distress." God's heart is very near the ones who can't do for themselves. Caring for them is a holy act—one, I have found, that anoints in both directions.

Jesus, had You grown old on this earth, I'd like to think someone would have visited You with gentle care.
—Carol Knapp

Digging Deeper: Ps 71:17–18; Prv 15:30

Thu 28

The Lord is good, a strong hold in the day of trouble; and he knoweth them that trust in him. —Nahum 1:7 (KJV)

Every so often I watch the video of me on YouTube and I still can't quite believe my eyes. Carol recorded it on her phone and posted it, calling the grainy thirty seconds "Rick Gets Caught."

Our friend Stacy had invited us to her birthday party, which involved a small group of couples gathering at a tent on the edge of town to go trapezing. That's right. A bunch of middle-aged adults flying through the air with the greatest of ease like some circus performers . . . or not.

I took one look at the ladder that went up to the platform twenty-three feet above ground and said, "No way am I going up there."

"Try it just once," Stacy urged. "You can just hang from the bar and swing." Maybe just once, but I wasn't about to let my hands off the bar.

Let me assure you, there was a capacious net under the swinging trapeze and professional instructors attaching harnesses to us. We couldn't really fall. But that was hard to remember when I mounted the ladder, grabbed the bar and pushed off. I swung back and forth and dropped into the net.

"Do it again, so you can learn how to be caught," Stacy insisted.

"I don't know . . . "

"Just try." I went up that ladder three more times to get the shot Carol filmed. There I am, swinging out over the net, flipping to my knees, then reaching out and getting caught by a pro. The part that's most instructive is how hesitant I am to let go. The pro has me in his grip, but I don't want to unhook my legs from the bar. It looks like he had to pull me off.

One of the benefits of having that thirty-second clip is I can look at it when I'm in a risk-averse mood, like when I need to make a difficult phone call or reach out to someone who might not welcome it.

The thing is, when you leap forward into the unknown and let yourself fly free, things always seem to work out. You just have to let go.

Give me the courage, Lord, to let go and fly. —Rick Hamlin

Digging Deeper: 1 Chr 28:20; Is 41:13

Fri 29

Holy, holy, holy . . . the whole earth is full of his glory.
—Isaiah 6:3 (KJV)

Someday, we're going to build a cabin on a lake," Daddy was saying as we drove through the night. The scenario was typical for our family trips. My brother and mother would fall asleep, and my daddy and I would sing and tell tall tales and spin wild dreams as we traveled toward our destination. He often talked about this cabin, always adding, "But I can't build it until I find the perfect place."

"What's a perfect place like, Daddy?"

"Well, our front yard will be a lake, and we'll be able to see mountains in the distance. But here's the important part: Our cabin will have a perfect sunset."

Daddy had a sure way of turning dreams into reality, and one day, there we stood on the shore of a lake, looking across at a mountain chain. "This is it, Pam-bo. I'll build our cabin on the hill." He did, and somehow as the years passed, our cabin sunsets seemed to become more glorious.

After Daddy died, my mother divided some of her assets with my brother and me; my husband and I inherited the cabin. The years were lean and holding on to that house was difficult, but it was a legacy far more valuable than anything material and we made sacrifices to keep it.

Now, a third generation skips rocks across the lake. They swim and fish and fly high on the swing set of my youth. But when the day nears its end, something happens as the sun edges the mountain and splashes its outlandish colors across the sky. As heaven and earth touch, the golden hour descends and we inherit the riches of my father's estate once again. Daddy chose this place for the sunset because even then, he had a way of knowing the kind of gold that lasts.

Father, in every sunset, every fall leaf, and every spring shower, You give us the kind of gold that lasts. Thank You, Father, for this, our inheritance.
—Pam Kidd

Digging Deeper: Ps 37:29; Acts 20:32; Eph 1:11–14

Sat 30

But Mary treasured up all these things and pondered them in her heart. —LUKE 2:19 (NIV)

Make sure you pack warm pajamas for the boys," my friend Laura said. "It might get cold at night in the tent."

Laura couldn't wait for us to join her family at the campground, but the thought of huddling in a freezing tent with my two- and four-year-olds suddenly made it sound a little less exciting. "Oh, and there's a slight chance of rain," she added. "But let's just think sunny thoughts and maybe it won't!"

The sunniest thought I could think of at that moment was staying home and sleeping in my nice, warm bed. Suddenly, I agreed with my sister who said I was crazy to take my boys camping. But they were already testing out their sleeping bags in the living room and looking forward to seeing their friends.

I wrestled with my doubts, but in the end my desire for the boys to enjoy this experience won out.

The cab and long bus ride to the campsite was a hassle, but watching my kids laugh and bounce around our little tent was wonderful. Our trips to the Porta-Potty were a nightmare, but seeing the boys' smiles as they toasted marshmallows on a campfire was amazing! It did rain, but my kids saw their very first rainbow.

I filled my camera with incredible moments and memories, which will remind me to be crazy and make the most of this wonderful life and these beautiful children I've been given.

Thank You, Lord, for those moments in life that create lasting memories.
—KAREN VALENTIN

Digging Deeper: Pss 4:7, 16:9, 90:14

Sun 31

Though the Lord is exalted, he looks kindly on the lowly; though lofty, he sees them from afar. —PSALM 138:6 (NIV)

When I was living in Austin, Texas, my parents came to visit. They wanted to see the sights and eat the Mexican food I'd been raving about, but what I most wanted to show them was my church.

I took them to Austin Central Church and happily introduced them to some of the friends I'd made. The church had copastors whom I'd come to appreciate and who always had moving sermons. This time, however, an assistant pastor gave the sermon. She focused on a particular theological doctrine that I didn't agree with, and it didn't fit with the spirit of the congregation and wasn't meaningful to me.

I was upset and embarrassed. When we left, I apologized to my parents and tried to explain that it was usually better.

"I just loved being in a place you love so much," my dad said.

Here I was trying to impress my parents with how great my church was, but not allowing the service to help me grow closer to God. If I didn't agree with a sermon, it was a chance to reexamine my beliefs, not to get angry and defensive. No apologies necessary.

Thank You, Lord, for reminding me that it's You,
not the appreciation of others, that I seek.
—SAM ADRIANCE

Digging Deeper: 1 CHR 16:10; PSS 9:10, 27:8

DAILY MERCIES

1 ______________________________

2 ______________________________

3 ______________________________

4 ______________________________

5 ______________________________

6 ______________________________

7 ______________________________

8 ______________________________

9 ______________________________

10 ______________________________

11 ______________________________

12 ______________________________

13 ______________________________

14 ______________________________

15 ______________________________

16 ____________________

17 ____________________

18 ____________________

19 ____________________

20 ____________________

21 ____________________

22 ____________________

23 ____________________

24 ____________________

25 ____________________

26 ____________________

27 ____________________

28 ____________________

29 ____________________

30 ____________________

31 ____________________

SEPTEMBER

O give thanks unto the Lord; for he is good; for his mercy endureth for ever.

—1 CHRONICLES 16:34 (KJV)

Mon 1

"Observe my Sabbaths and have reverence for my sanctuary. I am the Lord."—LEVITICUS 26:2 (NIV)

We all need rest. Our bodies and minds need it. While scientists still don't fully understand the mechanisms of sleep, they have proved that when we're well rested, we think better, we learn better, and we work better.

So one of the things that delighted me when I arrived at the magazine where I currently work was an unusual line in the employee manual: The company "encourages every employee to take a minimum of three weeks' paid vacation." A minimum—not a maximum. It was such a neat variation on the message that you usually hear.

Our spiritual lives are no different from our professional lives—and in some ways, it's even more crucial that we think of minimums, not maximums. In the Bible—the employee manual that God drafted for us—God lays down the minimum, setting aside the Sabbath, which even He took, according to the creation story. And yet we often fail to abide by that thoughtful recommendation, seeing rest as a luxury, not a necessity.

In God's instructions for healthy living—and in His example—God has given us clear signals: We shouldn't be taking as little time off as we can. We should be taking at least as much time off as we need. Who else would know better than the One Who made us?

Lord, help me to follow Your holy employee manual, knowing when to work and when to rest.

—JEFF CHU

Digging Deeper: HEB 4:9–10

September

Tue 2

If God didn't hesitate to put everything on the line for us, embracing our condition and exposing himself to the worst by sending his own Son, is there anything else he wouldn't gladly and freely do for us? —ROMANS 8:32 (MSG)

I lay Prisca in her crib for her afternoon nap and sit down at my desk, eager to dive into the work I need to complete. I exhale the concerns of the morning, scoot up to my keyboard . . . and then my daughter cries.

In response, I do exactly nothing. *Maybe she's just getting settled. Surely the whimpers will fade.*

And then Prisca cries some more. This goes on for twenty minutes before I realize I have no recourse but to rescue my unhappy child.

I sense my internal protesters raising their picket signs: *But this is our only block of dedicated work time! When else are we supposed to work?* I turn the knob and enter her room. "It's okay, baby girl," I tell her. "Let's see if you can get settled with Mommy holding you in your rocker."

And so we sit . . . for two full hours, the only "me" time of my entire day. But as I watch her sleep, I think: *I know You're here with me, Father, and that You're well aware of the deadline I need to hit. Instead of stress, I choose contentment.*

Prisca and I both rested well that afternoon. She, because she was weary, and I, because I found abundance hiding where it always hides: behind awareness that God sees and provides.

Lord, make me aware, moment by moment,
of Your nearness, Your enoughness, Your grace.
—ASHLEY WIERSMA

Digging Deeper: PS 73:28; ROM 8:31–39

Wed 3

My spirit abides among you; do not fear.
—HAGGAI 2:5 (NRSV)

I don't like my big-boy bed." Benji lay still under the covers and stared up at me.

The day before, I'd taken down his crib and rebuilt the toddler bed, which had sat disassembled in the closet ever since we'd bought a twin bed for Frances. At two, it was Benji's turn to leave behind a major prop of babyhood.

"I'm scared," Benji whispered. He missed the security of the crib. I missed the crib too. One of my favorite bedtime rituals was holding Benji during goodnight prayers. Now we said prayers with him in bed.

Why was I in such a rush anyway? Yes, caring for a baby can be exhausting, and the glimpses we'd had of life with two kids instead of babies—hiking trips, playground games, days ungoverned by nap schedules—were tantalizing. But every milestone of life is like a little death. The past is unrecoverable. Why not try to slow things down?

"Want me to pick you up to say prayers?" I asked. Benji nodded. I picked him up and held him like always. His head burrowed into my neck. We said our thanks, our blessings. I laid him down and pulled up the covers. "Goodnight, little guy. I love you."

I paused at the door. Some things were different; some things were the same. All we could do was trust God to guide us through the changes.

The world changes, but You remain ever faithful, Lord.
—JIM HINCH

Digging Deeper: HEB 13:8; JAS 1:17

Thu 4

Lord, make me to know . . . the measure of my days. . . .
—Psalm 39:4 (KJV)

More than twenty-two years ago, my oldest son Drew tagged along with me to an antique sale in Charleston, South Carolina. Drew was an energetic eight-year-old with no interest in antiques but glad to be with Dad for an afternoon. As we gazed across a panorama of mahogany, walnut, and cherry furniture, we were drawn to an eighteenth-century grandfather clock. The clock's face depicted an oil painting of a farmer sowing seeds in a plowed field. We fell in love with this venerable timekeeper, and after much haggling, I bought the clock.

At first, I could not get used to the loud clanging of its bell as it rang out every hour throughout the night. But now, I sleep soundly through its faithful watch. Each Saturday night I take the clock's key and carefully wind the archaic mechanism to allow another week of measuring time. I think of my three children scattered across the country and the wonderful years that this old clock has lived in our midst, faithfully counting the days until Thanksgiving and Christmas arrive and the family gathers again.

Gazing at the clock's face, I give thanks for another week of life. I meditate on the farmer sowing seeds in his field and I affirm once again that the purpose of life is to sow seeds of love, encouragement, wisdom, forgiveness, and the good news of the Gospel.

Lord, help me to recall my father's favorite motto: "Only one life will soon be past, only what's done for Christ will last. For me to live is Christ."

—Scott Walker

Digging Deeper: Phil 1:21

Fri 5 *For this child I prayed....* —1 Samuel 1:27 (KJV)

Years ago, Mother tried to tell me how fast my children would grow up. "When they're grown, you'll dream they're young again," she said. The thought was unsettling, but she was right. Now that Jamie, Katie, and Thomas are adults, I long to go back for a day or two to mother them.

How could I show my love to them now? I was still their mama.

One day I found several notations in my Bible, certain verses I'd specifically prayed for each child when they were little. Back then, I wrote a prayer and a Scripture verse and tucked love notes in their lunch boxes. I'd prayed for everyday things like math tests, softball games, friendship problems, and cheerleading tryouts.

What if I started praying with the same intensity as I did when they were younger?

I wasn't sure how my grown-up children would respond to my idea, but I bought three prayer journals—one pink, one yellow, and one blue. When I asked if I could pray about anything in particular, they shared prayer requests without hesitating. Katie wanted prayer at one o'clock the following day while she took an insurance test. Thomas needed prayer for his philosophy course. Jamie wanted to make a wise decision about buying her first home.

That night I found an amazing verse in my Bible: "For the Lord gives wisdom, from his mouth come knowledge and understanding" (Proverbs 2:6). I texted the verse to them along with "I'm praying for you. I love you, Mom."

Now, every week I text or e-mail them: "How can I pray for you?" They always have new prayer requests, and God provides just the right verses for their needs.

Father, what a joy to keep praying for my grown-up children!
It never grows old. —Julie Garmon

Digging Deeper: Ps 127:3; Is 54:13; 1 Cor 1:4

Sat 6

The Lord is your keeper.... —Psalm 121:5 (NAS)

I failed guard duty... twice. The first time our one-year-old grandson Ian fell from the kitchen counter, thumping the floor with his head. I'd let go "just for a second" to prepare a 5:30 AM bottle. Another time he managed to pull a heavy wooden TV tray on top of himself, leaving three purple welts on his forehead. My back was turned "just for a second" to place the safety gate across the stairs.

Jesus is actively on guard according to the Apostle Paul in his letter to Timothy, a young pastor in the early Christian church. He writes, "I know whom I have believed and I am convinced that He is able to *guard* what I have entrusted to Him until that day" (2 Timothy 1:12). Jesus is "Shepherd and Guardian" of my soul (1 Peter 2:25).

A surprising second reference to guarding appears in 2 Timothy 1:14, where Paul counsels, "*Guard*, through the Holy Spirit who dwells in us, the treasure which has been entrusted to you." I have a charge to guard the words of life and truth God has made known to me in Jesus Christ, to see they are not diminished or neglected in how I live.

Sometimes I've blown this trust—because I "let go" or "turned my back." But Jesus' faithfulness is unchanging. He is keeper of my soul and protector of my faith. The Guard I can absolutely count on.

Shepherd Savior, You watch over my soul with Your very life.
My heart longs to treasure Your truth.

—Carol Knapp

Digging Deeper: Ps 23

Sun 7

I am reminded of your sincere faith, which first lived in your grandmother Lois and in your mother Eunice and, I am persuaded, now lives in you also. —2 TIMOTHY 1:5 (NIV)

When I was growing up in New York City, our Spanish Pentecostal congregation purchased the building adjacent to the church to expand its ministry. We were in the middle of the construction project to connect both buildings when they collapsed. Thankfully, no one was hurt.

As the news spread, newspapers, TV reporters, strangers, and our church family gathered in front of the rubble. It looked like a scene from a movie. Debris and mangled iron were everywhere, and dust rose up from where the buildings once stood. "What do you think is going to happen to our church?" my cousin Felix asked me.

His mother, Maria Antonia, cried, asking, "Will we be able to rebuild?"

Just when it seemed like a wave of sadness and fear was overtaking us, Pastor Pedro stood up. "I know that we are saddened by the collapse of our buildings and it may seem like our dream is shattered, but God is with our congregation. Our faith will see us through. Our prayers will keep us going."

That event took place more than forty years ago, but it is etched in my mind and heart. When I face challenges, and obstacles seem impossible to overcome, I remember the courage and resilience of those who stood on that city sidewalk—and I am encouraged to press on.

Lord, thank You for the faith passed on to me by my church family.
—PABLO DIAZ

Digging Deeper: 1 COR 12; COL 1:17–20; 1 PT 2:9–10

September

Mon 8

And Jesus answered and said to her, "Martha, Martha, you are worried and troubled about many things. But one thing is needed, and Mary has chosen that good part, which will not be taken away from her." —LUKE 10:41–42 (NKJV)

I was excited to discover a host of online Bible reading plans, which promised an orderly way to finish the Bible in one year—a goal I value. My perfectionist tendencies can sometimes push me too hard with this, a little voice tells me I can't skip a day, can't fall behind in my reading. That voice sucks all the joy out of simply resting my heart in God's beautiful love letter.

After three weeks of daily readings, I logged into my plan and was surprised to find this message: "No reading is scheduled for today. Use today to take a break or to catch up on readings you missed."

For a moment, I didn't know what to do. My inner Martha jumped to high alert. *What do you mean, no reading today? I have to read! There are chapters to finish, verses to master, stories to study!*

Suddenly, a sense of peace washed over me. I took a deep breath and smiled. *It's okay, Martha. It's okay to rest. You don't have to work so hard, even for God. Take a break. Jesus is still with you.*

I set aside my laptop to play with my son. I had a wrestling match in my soul, but in the end, like Mary, I chose the good part.

Lord, slow me down enough to be good company for You.
—BILL GIOVANNETTI

Digging Deeper: MT 11:28–30; LK 10:38–42

Tue 9

When my spirit was overwhelmed within me, Then You knew my path. . . . —Psalm 142:3 (NKJV)

On her eighth birthday, my neighbor girl with special needs invited me to her family's celebration: cake, soda, and balloons. Five adults gathered around the table, sang the traditional song, and urged her to blow out the candles—eight thin stubs encircling a fat figure eight. With big brown eyes, she stared, silent as breath. Her mother, grandmother, and I coaxed. We modeled technique, blowing out one candle at a time. She laughed when her grandmother ran a finger through the icing and slathered it across her cheek. Still, the girl watched the burning candles, speechless, until finally an adult blew out the last flame. After lots of clapping, everyone ate big pieces of cake. A nice little party.

Or so I thought. Fifteen minutes later, she and I sat out on our shared front stoop. "That was a great birthday, wasn't it?"

"Yes," she stammered, "but I didn't get to blow out my candles."

"Were you afraid?" I asked.

"Yes. Too many people."

"Well, let's try again," I suggested.

Days later it was my turn to feel unnerved; the week's demands overwhelmed me. When I heard the school bus brakes and watched my friend trudge into her day, I remembered our workable solution to her birthday dilemma of too many people, too much pressure. Identify the problem and bring a fearsome obstacle down to a manageable size. As I scaled back my to-do list, I made room for God's peace.

Lord, when my loved ones and I feel overwhelmed, help me see options that point us away from fear and toward peace.

—Evelyn Bence

Digging Deeper: Ps 4:8; Phil 4:7; Jas 3:18

Wed 10

Dear children, let us not love with words or speech but with actions and in truth. —1 JOHN 3:18 (NIV)

I gave my students an assignment to explain a major challenge facing people of faith today, in thirty seconds or less, and to be creative!

The first two students stood up, and, after briefly naming some challenges that parents face today (peer pressure, cultural differences, obesity, depression, school issues), they put their arms around each other and said nothing. For twenty seconds, there was simply silence. Finally, one of them said, "One of the big challenges for people of faith is answering too fast and loving too slow."

As a teacher, I've committed my life to helping students know and care about right answers. But there are days when I'm reminded again that the right answer sometimes isn't in the words that we speak, but in just being there for people, caring for them, loving them.

That's the professor's lesson for today—one he learned from his students. Class dismissed.

Help me know what to say to a friend in need, God, and to know when just being present is enough.

—JEFF JAPINGA

Digging Deeper: EPH 4:29; JAS 1:19

Thu 11

"For where two or three gather in my name, there am I with them."—MATTHEW 18:20 (NIV)

The elevator stopped at the twenty-second floor and I got off, just as I did every weekday. "Hey," Elizabeth said, "I heard there's been a plane crash somewhere downtown." We had no information and no idea yet of the enormity of what was happening on that September day in 2001.

We all crowded together with questions that had no answers. There was a portable TV in the conference room, so we strained to make sense of the blurry images of what was happening only a mile and a half from our office. We were transfixed and horrified. As the truth of the disaster became clearer, those with family and friends in the financial district tried to make contact. We held hands with those who could get no response, while the sounds of police cars and fire trucks became one high-pitched wail.

As information trickled in, we began to feel panicked, helpless, unable to function. I felt a kind of unimaginably heavy responsibility because I was the boss. "Let's go to my apartment," I said. It was within walking distance, and we could stay together and find out more about what was happening. Ten of us came together there and prayed. Some prayers were simple: "Help us." Others were the same prayer that was being said all over the city: "I am safe. Are you safe? I love you."

As we prayed for all those who would never say those words, and for those whose lives were forever changed, we were grateful for the hands we held and the comfort we shared.

Lord, comfort those who will never forget, and bring Your peace to the nations of the world.

—BRIGITTE WEEKS

Digging Deeper: IS 26:3; EPH 2:14

Fri 12

Pray for each other so that you can live together whole and healed. —James 5:16 (MSG)

A few months ago, I got word that my friend's daughter Sarah had hemorrhaged during her sixth month of pregnancy and delivered her two-pound son by emergency C-section. I was asked to pray for Boden in his critical fight for life. Eagerly I did, becoming part of a circle of pray-ers that surrounded this family as they began their long journey, filled with uncertainties.

Daily, I scanned my e-mails for updates about Boden and prayed specifically for his brain scans, blood transfusions, heart valves, and weight gain. These prayers infused new vitality into my own prayer life that had recently grown stale and robotic, focusing more on me than others, more on disappointments than gratitude. I'd been invited into this family's story where I joined Sarah and her husband Hank in praising God for His blessings. The updates were tender, sometimes profound, and always totally honest.

Exactly 103 days after Boden entered the NICU, Sarah sent a picture of an adorable, chubby-cheeked baby with the news they were finally headed home. I taped the picture of Boden in my journal to remind me to keep praying for this family, a privilege that refocuses my conversations with God.

Father, the nudge to pray for others comes from You, maybe because You know our shared prayers multiply the blessings.
—Carol Kuykendall

Digging Deeper: Gal 6:2; 1 Tm 2:1

Sat 13

My heart says of you, "Seek his face!" Your face, Lord, I will seek. —PSALM 27:8 (NIV)

Of all things to be pondering while I was running, I was asking myself what it meant to seek the Lord's face. The phrase pops up all over Scripture, "to seek the Lord's face," but how do you seek the face of someone you can't see?

"Good morning," I called to a neighbor. "Keep it up." She used to be a walker and now was jogging. Pretty impressive. She deserved all the encouragement I could muster.

"You too," she called back to me.

I turned the corner and spotted a barefoot man with a dog picking mulberries off the tree and eating them. "Taste good?" I asked as I huffed and puffed. He nodded and smiled.

Going up the hill, I caught the glorious scent of cut grass, the blades brushing against my shoes. "Morning," I said to the man I see every morning when I jog. Same spot, same time. Today he was wearing a T-shirt with Martin Luther King Jr.'s portrait on it. "Nice shirt," I said. He waved.

Out of the park, heading back, I saw my neighbor Michael running toward me. His wife had a very scary cancer diagnosis three months ago. I've been praying for her and for him. What a roller coaster. I reversed my steps and ran with him for a block. "How's she doing?" I asked.

"She got her first treatment this week," he said. "It's just a pill. They don't have to do it intravenously, so she can go to work afterward. They're going to try it for three weeks."

"I will keep hoping," I said. "And praying."

Had I seen the Lord's face? Not exactly. But in seeking it, I had seen His presence in mulberries, joggers, T-shirts, cut grass, and the care of doctors treating a friend.

One thing I ask of You, Lord, one thing I seek: to know Your presence day by day. —RICK HAMLIN

Digging Deeper: 1 CHR 16:10; PS 27

September

Sun 14

"I will rescue my flock. . . ."—Ezekiel 34:10 (NIV)

I met Pastor John in 1994. We had both joined Animas Fire Department, so I knew him as a friend before I began attending his church. One of our first calls was a mobile home on fire. When we arrived at the scene, there was some residual smoke but no flames. The fire started near a gas hot-water heater and melted a copper fitting on one of the water pipes. The resulting leak put out the fire.

Several veteran firefighters clapped me on the back and said, "Don't worry, Tim. You can put out the next one." It felt good to belong, to be with my new friends. We rolled up the hose lines and put away our air packs.

Most men, full of unspent adrenaline and gathered around a fire truck, do not readily take notice of other people. But John is not like most men. He had taken off his helmet and was talking to a young child. "Were you scared?" he asked the little boy. The child didn't say anything, but he buried his head in John's gear and cried.

I never forgot that lesson. A church is not that different from a fire department. It's easy to fall into conversation with friends and ignore those people who aren't familiar, but now I do my best to seek out and comfort those who might be lonely or hurting or scared.

Thank You, God, for giving me a pastor and a friend to light my way.

—Tim Williams

Digging Deeper: Jn 13:34–35; Rom 12:10; Gal 6:2

THE PATH TO ADOPTION

Mon 15

All the days ordained for me were written in your book before one of them came to be. —PSALM 139:16 (NIV)

GOD'S GOT THIS

We said yes to adoption, and God was providing in miraculous ways. I was eager to start checking tasks off our huge to-do list.

But we couldn't do much until we completed our home study, which is the first step in every adoption. It's a weeding process that ends, we hope, with a stamp of approval. So when our first interview approached, I made sure everything was arranged. My dad would watch our son, so we could make the two-hour drive. My husband went into work on Sunday, so he could leave work early on Tuesday. And on Monday, I e-mailed Robin, our social worker, to make sure we were good to go. She quickly e-mailed back. Our interview wasn't Tuesday; it was today.

I was scrambling to make it work, until our son started throwing up and we were forced to reschedule.

Robin said she was free the following Monday. I checked with my husband, and my dad, and I circled the date in our calendars. It wasn't until the day of our appointment that I realized I'd never confirmed with Robin. I called her office, but she was out for the day. I'd messed up twice in a row. I prayed the third time would be a charm, but Robin got sick and we had to reschedule yet again.

How would this adoption happen if we couldn't even get started with our home study? In tears, I called one of my friends. "God's got this, Katie," she reminded me. "He knows exactly who your child will be. Canceled appointments aren't going to change that."

Thank You, Lord, that nothing will thwart Your plans—not sick tummies and not my mistakes. —KATIE GANSHERT

Digging Deeper: EX 4:11; JOB 31:4, 42:2

Tue 16

Seekest thou great things for thyself? seek them not....
—JEREMIAH 45:5 (KJV)

Pam," my friend said, "be at my house next Friday at noon. We're going to have a luncheon to celebrate your camp."

Oh wow, I thought as I hung up, *my friends are recognizing my efforts!*

It had started on a whim, sitting out in the church garden, watching the children play on eighteen acres of beautiful land with a spacious playground, fields of green grass for running and rolling, and dozens of trees for climbing. *The children in the downtown projects have never experienced anything like this,* I thought. *Why not organize a summer camp and invite them here each day to play with our children?* Soon, an entire team was on board. There were volunteers to do nature classes and hikes in the woods, craft sessions, sports, even birdhouse building. Others offered to provide lunches and snacks.

Now the summer was over and, expecting fanfare, I was a bit nervous arriving for the luncheon. But no sooner was the iced tea poured than the young woman across the table took the conversation in an unanticipated direction. There were "so many ways the camp could have been better," she announced, pointing out flaws, mistakes, and things she would have done had she been in charge.

My heart felt like a deflated balloon. I glanced around for a shred of support. There were stunned looks on everyone's faces. Silence. Later, at home, I was working past embarrassment to a place of mortification when my husband tossed a paper on the table. "Found this in the car," he said.

I unfolded the paper and saw written in a child's hand: "Miss Pam, you are nice. I climed *[sic]* a tree. Love, Sheldon."

There were no framed certificates that summer; just a note from God, via Sheldon, reminding me why I had been chosen to do His work.

Father, help me to always look past myself and see my importance in what I can do for You. —PAM KIDD

Digging Deeper: PHIL 2:13; COL 3:23–24

Wed 17

You shall not wrong or oppress a resident alien, for you were aliens in the land of Egypt. —EXODUS 22:21 (NRSV)

We all sit in the same places at the same time with the same people every week in church. Each person, couple, and family stakes out territory at a careful distance from the rest.

One Sunday, five minutes late, a young couple with a baby walked in. It was like an alarm had gone off: stranger alert! While our pastor graciously welcomed them, I rolled my eyes, silently ticking off their transgressions: late; disruptive; the baby was already crying; and they sat right next to our oldest member, crawling over her when she refused to surrender her aisle seat.

Then I saw the hurt and embarrassment on the wife's face as she glanced at her husband. *Why did we come here?* she seemed to ask. I felt my own face flush with hurt and embarrassment. But not for them.

Jesus, forgive me when I am unwelcoming.
Teach me compassion and hospitality.
—MARCI ALBORGHETTI

Digging Deeper: ACTS 28:2; ROM 12:13; 1 PT 4:9

September

Thu 18

You are the God who performs miracles. . . .
—PSALM 77:14 (NIV)

In the last few years I have been graced by a correspondence with a man who is in prison until the day he dies. "I deserve to be here," he says, "and all I ask is the chance after I die to apologize to God face to face for wasting His gifts. But maybe I would never have seen those gifts so clear if I wasn't here."

I go back through his letters, noting all the things he has written, painstakingly, in blue ink on loose-leaf paper, about gifts that are new every morning.

"Good old rain. Crawdads, woodpeckers, church choirs. The way people line up for things like buses and voting and never jostle. Dragonflies over ponds. Sandwiches made by someone who likes you. Good old towels. Toast with jam not from a factory. Toasters. Fried trout in butter. Teachers. Mud with a point to it, like in gardens and farms. Animals. Big birds that are not scared of you, like hawks. Jars on shelves. Berries on bushes. People talking to you who don't want anything from you. Folks making music with real instruments somewhere close, but you can't see them, only hear them faintly. *That's* a great sound, that is.

"I used to think that the thing I missed the most was pets. I sure wanted a dog around; dogs are just the best. But now the thing I miss the most is kids around. I'll just never have kids around underfoot, laughing and yelling and arguing and falling asleep in half a second right wherever they landed last. If ever I do get to see God face to face and can ask one favor, I'd ask for kids around again. That's what heaven is, seems to me."

Dear Lord, there are no little things, are there? I mean, You know that, but we forget. Nothing's little. Everything's huge and holy and so stuffed with miracle, the miracles leak out, laughing. Thanks. And, Lord, hey, a little favor? Can You salt our awful jails with a little extra hope today?
—BRIAN DOYLE

Digging Deeper: JAS 1:17

Fri 19

Let the morning bring me word of your unfailing love, for I have put my trust in you. Show me the way I should go, for to you I entrust my life. —PSALM 143:8 (NIV)

The plan was simple. I'd go to Birmingham, Alabama, for a three-day weekend to look at a dozen or so houses. Then my husband and I would go back a few weeks later to see the ones that passed the first round. Maybe, afterward, we'd put in an offer.

Instead, after thirty-six hours of looking, I'd found a house, put in an offer, and gone under contract, all without Brian having seen it.

"It's perfect!" I told him, and it was. It had everything on our lists, which we'd created as we diligently did our homework.

Brian packed a bag and told his boss, "I sent Ashley to look at houses, and it seems she's purchased one."

To his credit, the boss replied, "Well, Brian, sounds like you better go see it!"

"Didn't you guys just test-drive cars for a year before buying?" his coworkers asked.

"I did," Brian replied as he rushed out of the office, "but this time I sent Ashley!"

There are times I try to make life more complicated. *If I do all these steps,* I think, *then surely that is God's path.* I'm ever thankful when God, Who knows my love of planning and order, thrusts me out of my comfort zone with a situation only He could align and whispers, "Go forward. Keep walking. Trust me."

God, thank You for reminding me that Your time is the only time that matters.

—ASHLEY KAPPEL

Digging Deeper: PS 32:8; PRV 3:5–6; JER 29:11

September

Sat 20

For the Lord will be at your side and will keep your foot from being snared. —PROVERBS 3:26 (NIV)

The place I find it hardest to act like a good person of faith is at the Laundromat. I visit once a year during spring cleaning at our beach rental house. I come in staggering under enough bedspreads, mattress covers, and blankets to do eleven loads in the biggest super-duper washers they have.

I realized I had a serious problem the year I pushed my cart over to the dryer and came back and found a retired couple using my yellow bottle of detergent that I'd left on top of the washer. Of course I said something to them, and they had the audacity to act like it was theirs! Five minutes later, I discovered *my* bottle of detergent hidden under dirty blankets in my cart. I apologized but felt like dirty clothes inside.

After that, I started praying in advance of my Laundromat trip. And I'm always glad because my character is usually tested in some new way. One year it was a stranger who told me she wanted to get out of an abusive relationship when the man she was arguing with left to get change. I wasn't sure if she was sincere or conning me to get a handout, but I prayed with her and got the number of a local abuse hotline to slip to her before the guy came back.

This year I was sorely tested by a woman who let her two girls chase each other around the table where I was trying to fold queen-size spreads. I learned that it's good to remember my past mistakes when I'm in a place where my worst side usually comes out.

Dear Father, here's the specific place and situation that always brings out the worst in me. I need Your help, so I can give it my best shot to be a good person even when I'm there. Amen. —KAREN BARBER

Digging Deeper: IS 64:6; ROM 7:15–25; 1 JN 1:7–9

Sun 21

"Behold, I will do a new thing. . . ."
—Isaiah 43:19 (NKJV)

I have lost more than ninety pounds. One unexpected downside is getting rid of my "heavy" wardrobe. I invested considerable time and money putting those outfits together and even had costume jewelry to coordinate with each one.

There is the black twill blazer with the gold and red crest on the pocket. I wore it with a crisp pair of black slacks and a wide gold necklace, which I found deeply discounted at an outlet.

Then there is the light-blue denim pantsuit. The collar is studded with rhinestones, and I accented it with a large rhinestone cross and wore it with a shimmering silver shell. I found it all in a charming little Texas town when I was vacationing there.

Memories, all. It was as much fun acquiring those clothes as it was wearing them. And now they are five sizes too large.

Today, in church, the pastor spoke about how the Lord is doing a brand-new thing in each of our lives and how it should fill our hearts to overflowing. So I found an organization that provides appropriate clothing for women who are going on job interviews. Suddenly, the thought of someone wearing my clothes to have a better life fills me with amazing joy.

Everything I have, God, really belongs to You. Help me
to release it today with a heart full of joy.
—Roberta Messner

Digging Deeper: Lk 6:38; 2 Cor 5:17, 9:7

Mon 22

"Whatever you ask the Father in my name, he may give it to you."—John 15:16 (RSV)

I was called in at the very last minute to substitute in a very lively class of fourth graders. Feeling disorganized and unprepared, I felt even worse when I searched the desk and couldn't find the lesson plan the principal had mentioned. *God, help me get through this day. Or if You are really busy, at least this morning.*

I did find the roll book, though, and just as I was about to call names, a boy sidled up to my desk and whispered among the roar, "Miss, when you call the roll, can you please do it by first names, not by last?"

Mystified, I murmured, "Sure," and he looked relieved. As I scanned the list, I saw his reason; his last name was Looney. I could just imagine the catcalls and teasing he got when his name was mentioned.

The best thing was, it gave me a good idea for the impromptu lesson: "What does it mean to have a good name?" As the kids came up with answers—good reputation, no lying, no cheating, no stealing—a nice little discussion followed.

As I dismissed them for lunch, another kid sidled up to my desk. "Uh, teacher?"

"Yes?"

"Um, some kids and I thought it'd be funny to put your lesson plan up there." He pointed to the top of a very tall cabinet.

I opened my mouth to scold him but then stopped. "Thank you for being honest," I said.

He grinned. "I have my good name to think about!"

Lord, let me be honest and kind today. In all I do,
let me try to keep my good name.
—Linda Neukrug

Digging Deeper: Prv 12:22; 2 Cor 8:21

Tue 23

Be still, and know that I am God. . . .
—Psalm 46:10 (KJV)

I spoke to a friend about my struggles to pray, and she shared with me an experience she had when her mother was in the hospital, fighting cancer. Molly told me that every day she would go to the chapel in the hospital. When she got there, however, she found herself too afraid to pray. She couldn't find the words. She didn't even want to say, "Thy will be done."

"What if God's will was to take my mother?" she said to me. "I couldn't pray for that." Molly would sit there, with her hands folded tightly in front of her face and her eyes pressed shut, afraid to have a complete thought pass through her mind.

Then one day, she noticed an inscription in the chapel: "Be still, and know that I am God."

"This," Molly said, "was something I could pray. I would just repeat those words over and over."

Hearing my friend's story gave me fresh meaning for that Scripture and a new outlook on praying. I was trying to force a connection with God through a series of words.

My pastor says, "Prayer is the soul's sincere desire to commune with God." Since my soul desires, I only need to be still and allow the opportunity.

Lord, thank You for continuing to provide me with guidance that draws me nearer to You.
—Natalie Perkins

Digging Deeper: Ps 46; Mt 6:9–10

Wed 24

I trust in your unfailing love; my heart rejoices in your salvation. I will sing the Lord's praise, for he has been good to me. —PSALM 13:5–6 (NIV)

In a feat only a mom could pull off, I managed to wrangle three kids through bath time and into their pajamas, through story time and bedtime prayers, and get them all tucked into their beds before eight o'clock. All with my husband out of town on business, thank you very much.

My reward? A big bowl of mint chip ice cream and an evening on the couch watching TV. Or so I thought.

Joey came trudging into the living room with big eyes and a quivery smile. I could just tell that this wasn't going to be one of those *give-me-a-hug-then-get-back-to-bed-this-instant* nights. I pulled him onto my lap and asked him what he was thinking about. He told me he couldn't sleep, wasn't sure why, and then his voice cracked. A tear streamed down his face. "Mommy, I miss Daddy!"

I sat there rubbing his back and told him about Christ's unfailing love—a love that always comes back to us, no matter what; a love that always comforts, protects, hopes, perseveres. Joey's tears dried. His heartbeat slowed. And, eventually, he drifted off to sleep.

I had looked forward to some quiet time and, instead, God rewarded me with something bigger: time to share His joy, hope, and love with my precious son.

Lord, give me opportunities to tell my kids how big, how deep,
how wide, and how great Your love is.
—ERIN MACPHERSON

Digging Deeper: EPH 3:14–19

Thu 25

*Your robes are all fragrant with myrrh and aloes and cassia.
From ivory palaces stringed instruments make you glad.*
—Psalm 45:8 (ESV)

My son Solomon doesn't care about the clothes he wears. No matter the occasion, he puts on whatever is on top in his dresser drawer. A few times a year, he happens to get dressed in his younger brother's clothes that were put in his dresser by mistake. There's a four-year gap between them, so when Solomon comes from his room, wearing Henry's very small clothes, it's an obvious error.

"Wrong pants, Sol," I say. "Those are Henry's."

"They were in my dresser," he says. "How was I supposed to know they weren't mine?"

So today when Solomon put on his shirt and smelled his arm, I was more than a little surprised by his reaction. "*Mmm,*" he said, holding the crook of his elbow to his nose. "This smells so good! Mom, smell this."

He held out his arm and walked toward me. As I leaned in and took a whiff, Solomon said, "How'd you make it smell so good? How did you make it smell like Cape Cod?"

"It's from being on the clothesline," I said. "Yesterday was like spring, so I hung the clothes on the line outside."

Solomon smelled his arm again. "It's unbelievable," he said. "It's just like being on vacation. Dad, come here. You won't believe this. Smell. My shirt smells just like the ocean."

Dear Lord, thank You for the gift of a spring day that commands our attention and makes us say, "Mmm."
—Sabra Ciancanelli

Digging Deeper: Lk 11:13; Jas 1:17

September

Fri 26

But you—who are you to judge your neighbor?
—James 4:12 (NIV)

My first year out of college, I worked as a math tutor at a charter school in Rhode Island. I loved that I got to be the primary math instructor to several students, often in very small group settings.

One day, as I explained linear equations, I felt like I was hitting a brick wall. Two students, Solomon and Roberto, wouldn't stop talking to each other about the basketball game that was happening later and even talked over me when I asked them to stop. Another student, Cesar, just kept staring at his paper and wouldn't even give it a try, no matter how much I encouraged him. I was their teacher, so I had to hold it together, but inside I wanted to scream.

After class was over, I had lunch with my fellow tutors, Patrick and Doug, who were both in their early forties.

"I just can't get them to work," I whined. "It's like they don't care about the future. I can't get them to grow up."

"You've got to try to make it real somehow," Patrick said. "Back when I was applying to MBA programs, I wrote my essays and filled out all the applications at school, so they could see what it took. I think that helped a little."

"I try to talk to them about what it's like being in the business world," Doug chimed in. "Practical stuff seems to help."

Patrick worked two jobs and was getting his MBA in his free time, and Doug had been a CFO before becoming a teacher. I was just starting out and here I was complaining to them about how my kids wouldn't make life easy for me. My students weren't the only ones who needed to grow up.

Thank You, God, for always reminding me I have more work to do.
—Sam Adriance

Digging Deeper: 1 Cor 13:11; Eph 4:14–15

HOPE IN HOSPICE

Sat 27 *Praise be to the God and Father of our Lord Jesus Christ, the Father of compassion and the God of all comfort.*
—2 Corinthians 1:3 (NIV)

WALLY, THE GOOD DOG

Wally is a medium-size dog with a woolly brown coat and a pair of the warmest, sweetest eyes imaginable. He wears a colored scarf around his neck, identifying him as a "Good Dog" who has been trained and licensed by the Good Dog Foundation to interact with the sick. His handler Irene has also taken the eleven weeks of training that assures each Good Dog has a special way of engaging with strangers in an unfamiliar environment.

Wally is amazing. I watch with fascination as he trots to the bedside of a frail and barely conscious hospice patient named Anne. She reaches out her open hand, and Wally lifts up his front paw, puts it into her hand, and moves his head to be stroked.

All over the country there are more than one thousand Good Dogs doing good work for the lonely and the sick. The sight of Wally as he wags his tail and enters another room immediately reminds me of the hymn: "All creatures great and small, All things wise and wonderful: The Lord God made them all."

God definitely had a hand in creating Wally, the Good Dog.

Let us give thanks and praise, God, for all our animal friends and the solace they bring.
—Brigitte Weeks

Digging Deeper: Pss 145:9, 150:6

September

Sun 28

We are surrounded by such a great cloud of witnesses....
—Hebrews 12:1 (NIV)

I have long been drawn to old roads. I look at well-worn tracks in the forest or up the mountain and wonder who walked them for the first time and what the land looked like then. Sometimes I imagine deer or moose trekking along a ridge down from the mountain to a stream, and eventually men following until a path is formed and then a road is built in its place.

Walking these roads every day, I am sometimes reminded of other important "roads" in my life.

Traveling along the road of faith, I am never alone. My great-grandmother used to challenge me as a boy. She told me to learn the Bible, inspiring me to follow her example by reading it every day and memorizing many verses. Then my grandparents asked me to love the Lord and, more importantly, showed me how to do it in the hands-on ways that their compassion went out to the elderly, whom they served every week in nursing homes.

My parents, too, shined a light down that path of faith that can sometimes be dark and tough to follow. Also, aunts and uncles, friends and mentors have walked the path before me. I am able to follow their well-worn treads. Because of them all, I know which way to go.

I will follow You today, Lord.
—Jon Sweeney

Digging Deeper: Heb 12:1–17

Mon 29

The Lord watches over the strangers....
—Psalm 146:9 (NKJV)

I glanced at my to-do list. "Call Cindie" glared back at me. I sighed. A couple of years ago I'd met Cindie at a friend's wedding. At that time Cindie was living in another state. When she and her husband retired, they moved to Montana and bought a home a few miles down the road from me. We hit it off, except for one thing: She was retired and I was working, so I didn't have much time to spend with her.

Suddenly, a horse's shrill whinny pierced the afternoon. I looked out the window. The neighbors across the road had put a horse in their pasture. The poor herd animal was alone and screaming for company. Suddenly, thundering hooves rocked the ground as my horses ran full blast around the corner of the house. Sliding to a stop at the fence, they lined up, smelling the new horse. I listened as they nickered greetings, and all afternoon my horses stood bunched in the corner near her.

The next evening, when I drove home from work, I noticed that the horses still stood in the corner by their new friend. *That's so nice to welcome a stranger. Even though you can't be in the field together, you can keep her company. It's too bad more people aren't that way.*

With that thought, I inhaled. I'd put off calling Cindie because I couldn't squeeze in enough time with her. But I could call for a few minutes to let her know that she was not alone.

Lord, help me to be sensitive to newcomers.
—Rebecca Ondov

Digging Deeper: Ps 146; Rom 12:13; 1 Pt 4:9

Tue 30

Then, because so many people were coming and going that they did not even have a chance to eat, he said to them, "Come with me by yourselves to a quiet place and get some rest."
—MARK 6:31 (NIV)

What did you do for your kids-free weekend?" my friend asked.

"I cleaned," I said flatly. "What I always do for my kids-free weekends."

Laundry, scattered toys, and dishes will pile up as I work full days. Mommy-guilt sets in on my days off, and I prefer to spend time doing fun things with the boys instead of chores, errands, and appointments. That leaves my kids-free weekend to get it all done.

"You're going to burn yourself out," my friend said. "What you need is a Sabbath!" She ordered me to take the next kids-free weekend to do absolutely nothing. I agreed.

When it arrived, I woke up at 10:00 AM. I stayed in bed for an hour more, just relaxing. I strolled into the kitchen and poured a bowl of cereal and plopped on the couch with the remote control. Later, I walked past a huge bag of dirty clothes and resisted the temptation to do laundry.

I read; I napped; I strolled in the park; I ate lunch at an outdoor café. My body had to settle into the slowness of the day. The next day looked the same; my friend even came by to make sure I wasn't scrubbing floors.

By the end of the weekend my house wasn't sparkling, but I was rested and rejuvenated. Of all the responsibilities I needed to do, taking care of myself was the most important one.

Lord, thank You for giving me not only the permission
but the command to rest.
—KAREN VALENTIN

Digging Deeper: Ex 20:8–11; Mk 6:45–46; Lk 5:16

DAILY MERCIES

1 ______________________________

2 ______________________________

3 ______________________________

4 ______________________________

5 ______________________________

6 ______________________________

7 ______________________________

8 ______________________________

9 ______________________________

10 ______________________________

11 ______________________________

12 ______________________________

13 ______________________________

14 ______________________________

15 ______________________________

September

16 ______________________________

17 ______________________________

18 ______________________________

19 ______________________________

20 ______________________________

21 ______________________________

22 ______________________________

23 ______________________________

24 ______________________________

25 ______________________________

26 ______________________________

27 ______________________________

28 ______________________________

29 ______________________________

30 ______________________________

October

For as the heaven is high above the earth, so great is his mercy toward them that fear him.

—Psalm 103:11 (KJV)

Wed 1

"See, darkness covers the earth and thick darkness is over the peoples, but the Lord rises upon you. . . ."
—Isaiah 60:2 (NIV)

The golden glow of dawn crowned the mountain. I drummed my fingers on the steering wheel of the pickup. A cloud of dust swirled behind the horse trailer as I barreled down the dirt road to the trailhead. It'd been a long week at work. My income from my commission-sales job had plummeted because of the downturn in the economy. All the joy had drained out of me, and I viewed myself as a failure. I couldn't wait to unload my horse for an all-day trail ride.

The road meandered through a gully. The truck chugged through the curve and up a steep hill. Suddenly, the sun popped over the mountain. It reflected off the dust on the windshield and blinded me with seven thousand pounds of horse trailer pushing me. Frantically, I grasped the steering wheel and floored the brakes. The truck and trailer skidded to a stop.

I leaned my head backward against the window. My heart pounded. For that fraction of a second I was blinded to the world. All I could see and think about was the light.

I sighed. *That's what I need to do. God is the Light. Quit feeding on thoughts of failure and focus on His Word.*

I had lost my peace because I'd concentrated on the darkness of failure. But I hadn't failed because I hadn't quit. After my horseback ride, I found encouraging verses in the Bible and meditated on them daily. At work, I expanded in new directions. It wasn't long before I was wrapped in God's peace once again.

Lord, thank You for showing me how to persevere by reflecting on You.
—Rebecca Ondov

Digging Deeper: Jn 8:12

Thu 2

Whatever is true, whatever is noble, whatever is right, whatever is pure, whatever is lovely, whatever is admirable—if anything is excellent or praiseworthy—think about such things. —PHILIPPIANS 4:8 (NIV)

My husband and I had been counting the days until the debut of a new TV drama that promised great things. The producer was world renowned. The lead female was immensely likable. The premise intrigued us both. And so, with sky-high expectations, we set our DVR to record the program and were childishly giddy the night we actually got to pile into bed, a giant bowl of popcorn between us, and hit Play.

The first half hour had us hooked. But then came episode two. Within fifteen minutes, I knew my husband and I weren't long for this particular path. As the characters' stories unfolded, so did vast amounts of selfishness, scheming, and smut. "No," I screamed at the TV, "the teasers looked so good!"

My husband laughed as he flipped channels to find something else, and a verse I'd known since I was a kid eased its way through: "Whatever is *true, noble, right, pure, lovely, admirable, excellent, praiseworthy,* think about such things."

Avoiding a not-so-pure TV show is admittedly a very small step in what is the vast universe of God-honoring activity in this life. But it was a small step toward the God I adore.

Thanks, Father, for even small victories that lead to big transformations in my life.
—ASHLEY WIERSMA

Digging Deeper: ROM 12:1–2; 2 COR 4:16; 1 PT 1:13

Fri 3 *"Sit in silence. . . ."*—Isaiah 47:5 (NIV)

This year I attended a leadership conference. Sessions were broadcast live around the world and my church was one of the remote sites. Mama Maggie Gobran, founder of Stephen's Children, an organization that feeds the hungry in Egypt, began to speak. In a hushed voice, she talked about the importance of spending quiet time alone with God: "For it is in silence that you leave the many to be with the One."

After she finished, I turned to my friend Debbie who was sitting next to me. "Finding time to be quiet with the Lord is definitely a challenge for me," I said ruefully. "I think I've been *talking* to God a lot more than *listening* to Him."

Debbie took my hand. "Let's pray," she said. "Lord, thanks for reminding us that sometimes we need to just listen. Show us ways to sit in silence with You."

I didn't have to wait long. At work the next day, I saw my colleague John and walked over to him. "Eating alone?" I asked.

He nodded. "Sometimes I need to sit quietly." He thought for a moment. "You know, that's really when I hear the voice of God most clearly."

Just then my cell phone rang. It was a friend inviting me to lunch. "No thanks," I said. "I think I'll pick up a sandwich and sit on the bench under the oak tree here at work."

"Really?" my friend asked curiously. "By yourself? I mean, who will you to talk to?"

"No one," I said, laughing. "I'll just be listening."

In this world of incessant chatter, Lord, teach me to listen.
I want to hear all You have to say to me.
—Melody Bonnette Swang

Digging Deeper: Prv 2:1–5; Jn 10:27

Sat 4

You made me; you created me. Now give me the sense to follow your commands. —PSALM 119:73 (NLT)

Ain't got the good sense God gave ya!" my mother would sometimes say to my brother and me after some incredibly foolish act on our parts. This same statement fell from my grandmother's tongue, so I know my mom got it honest. And now I find myself muttering this same expression under my breath or, depending on the company, saying it right out loud to the foolish party: the woman on the bus who gets into an argument every day with the bus driver about not having the correct fare; the man who throws his garbage onto the subway tracks when the trash can is literally ten steps away; the delivery guy on his bike who speeds out in front of oncoming traffic.

But as I sit back in judgment, I can't help but feel a little guilty. I admit there are times when I don't follow the rules. And I know there are times when I'm acting outside the will of God. Once God gives me the understanding, it's my job to know what to do with it.

So even though it's New York City, I should probably bother to look up at the crosswalk sign instead of the oncoming traffic to judge if I should cross the street or not. And even though I study God's Word, I should probably spend more time applying it in my daily life. What recourse do I have but to get back up, dust myself off, and try to hold on to the good sense that God gave me?

I will find the strength and courage, Lord, to live outright through You.
—NATALIE PERKINS

Digging Deeper: MT 7:1–5; JAS 2:13

Sun 5

A wife of noble character . . . is worth far more than rubies.
—Proverbs 31:10 (NIV)

Our pastor and his wife are leaving soon. John and Diane were married in our church about fifteen years ago. I am grateful for what John has done for me and our entire congregation during those years. He comforted me when my mom died and again when my dad died five years later. He visited me in the hospital when I broke my collarbone and when I needed a stent. Those times and so many more, I thanked him for what he did.

I never thought to thank Diane, though. Diane has shared John with our church and the entire community throughout their marriage. John is a firefighter and an EMT, so he responds to physical and spiritual emergencies.

Whenever we invited our pastor to our home, we always invited John and Diane. *So why was it such a breach of etiquette to exclude someone's spouse from my home but not from my heart?* I asked myself. Only on the last week did I thank Diane for her generosity and vigilant behind-the-scenes prayer each time I saw her. I don't know why I was so slow to catch on.

Dear God, help me always to thank both the husband and the wife as one.
—Tim Williams

Digging Deeper: Gn 2:24; Mk 10:7–9

Mon 6

May your fountain be blessed, and may you rejoice in the wife of your youth. —PROVERBS 5:18 (NIV)

"So what did you do this weekend, Dad?" Timothy asked me on the phone. (It's always flattering when your twenty-year-old wants to know how you spent your weekend when it can hardly compare with the campus delights of his life.)

"Not much." I paused, trying to remember. "Your mom and I celebrated our wedding anniversary."

"That's great," he said, a little breathless. He was walking to the campus cafeteria. "How did you celebrate?"

"Went to Jim and Kate's for dinner."

"Was this your twenty-sixth?"

"Our twenty-seventh."

"Wow," he said. There was some clatter in the background. He was going through the cafeteria line. A brief pause as he said, "Yo" to a friend. "That means you've passed the mark."

"What mark?"

"You've spent more years married than apart."

"Oh," I said, roughly calculating. "That's right." Now it was my turn to say, "Wow. How did you remember that?"

"Will and I figured it out. We wondered what it would be like to be married for more years than not being married."

"It feels pretty good," I had to admit. Our twenty-seventh didn't seem like something that called for much celebrating. I was wrong.

"Okay, Dad," he said. "Gotta go."

"I love you," I said.

"Love you too," he said. Twenty-seven years ago, I would never have expected to have such a bright, perceptive son. But then I wouldn't have expected half of the good things that have happened to me since. You say "I do," put it in God's hands, and the rest is a wonder.

Thank You, God, for the blessings of a family. —RICK HAMLIN

Digging Deeper: GN 33:5; SG 8:6–7

Tue 7

Wait for the Lord; be strong, and let your heart take courage. . . .
—Psalm 27:14 (ESV)

My friend Rick and I jogged through the park near his New York City apartment. Kate and I were staying with him on an East Coast trip. The kids were back home in California with my mom.

Maybe it was all the grown-up time we'd had on this trip. Maybe it was seeing old friends. Whatever it was, Kate and I ached for the city, where we'd lived for nearly six years. "Even Kate wonders whether we should have moved," I said to Rick, who didn't say anything. It wasn't the first time I'd voiced this complaint.

I was about to launch into yet another complaint about the lack of good museums in Silicon Valley, when suddenly a memory struck me. Shortly after we moved to New York City during a torrid summer, Kate and I had taken the subway uptown to the Cloisters. My main memory of that visit was not the art but my dismay upon learning that the Cloisters was not air-conditioned. The humidity was killing me. I'd wondered what on earth we'd been thinking when we decided to move to New York, and yet God had met us there, giving us a rich and full life.

"It'll take time for you guys to settle in," said Rick as the Cloisters disappeared behind us.

I glanced over my shoulder. I knew exactly what he meant.

I will wait upon You patiently, Lord.
—Jim Hinch

Digging Deeper: Col 1:11–12; Heb 6:11–12

Wed 8 *Harden not your heart*. . . . —Psalm 95:8 (KJV)

I was sick and tired of certain e-mails that made their way into my in-box. The one before me now was a blistering untruth about a public figure who had spent much of her life advocating for the poor, especially women in need. But now she was running for office, and her opponents were intent on destroying her good name.

Who in the world had the nerve to send this to me? I checked the Sender box and found the name Martha. *I don't even know a Martha. The very nerve!* Without thinking, I dashed out a reply and hit Send. "Are you crazy?" I wrote. "I don't know you and I don't appreciate your sending me such a terrible e-mail."

I can't find words that come close to describing the humiliation I felt the next morning when I found Martha's reply on my computer screen. "It's me, Martha. You wrote to me after I sent the money for your project in Africa. I'm sorry if I upset you."

Oh, dear God, I was half-thinking, half-praying. *I remember now*... Martha was a poor elderly woman living in government housing and barely surviving on Social Security! She had sent me a crumpled five-dollar bill some months before "to help with the poor children."

For the rest of the day, Martha sat heavy in my heart. She probably thought she was being helpful, sending the e-mail to me! My response had been hateful. All I wanted now was a second chance to be decent.

First, I e-mailed a request for forgiveness. Martha didn't hesitate in her response, and soon we were exchanging notes as if we were best friends. She shared stories of her Italian heritage and sent me recipes. I was able to reciprocate with shipments of fresh fruit and a warm shawl.

I didn't try to fix Martha's habit of forwarding awful e-mails; I just didn't open them. Instead, I spent my second chance filling her in-box with love.

Father, soften my heart so that I might counter hatred with love.
—Pam Kidd

Digging Deeper: Prv 28:13–14; Ez 36:26

Thu 9

And all thy children shall be taught of the Lord; and great shall be the peace of thy children. —Isaiah 54:13 (KJV)

I watch my son rushing to check his luggage. Chase will soon board a plane for Oman after singing at a prayer breakfast at the United Nations and performing in Cooperstown, New York.

It is exciting and a joy to watch and listen to him, but it was not always so. Once upon a time, he was unhappy, his grades were slipping, he didn't want to talk. We had survived the death of his father in a motorcycle accident when Chase was five, but I suspected the loss was now haunting him. "I don't know how to help him become a man, God. Please help us."

The most unlikely idea came to me: Share the story of King David. So we sat next to each other on the sofa, evening after evening, sharing the story of David's life—from lonely shepherd boy to warrior to singer, poet, dancer, husband, father, and king. We talked about manhood and God.

Though Chase still had some challenges, he seemed to relax into becoming. Now, he spreads encouragement to others, flying all over the world to sing for God.

Thank You, Lord, for my son and for his peace.
I pray for peace for all of Your children.
—Sharon Foster

Digging Deeper: 1 Sm 16–17; Ps 23

Fri 10

Ye have heard that it hath been said, An eye for an eye, and a tooth for a tooth: But I say unto you, That ye resist not evil: but whosoever shall smite thee on thy right cheek, turn to him the other also. —Matthew 5:38–39 (KJV)

I have been witnessing a lot of arguments lately—on the streets, in cars, even between friends—and I find myself frozen, unsure what to do. Then, the other day, I suddenly remembered an instance from my childhood.

The playground in elementary school was a safe and fun place, but by junior high, relationships between boys had become more complicated and dangerous. Just as my memories of elementary days usually center on sunshine and climbing on the jungle gym, my memories of junior high are equally dark. There were fights almost every day.

The violence of other boys scared me. I knew that a Christian was supposed to be different, but I had no idea how to accomplish anything but fear.

One afternoon when school was over, two boys began to argue and push each other. I was standing next to a friend of mine who was also a Christian. I thought that he, too, was frightened. And maybe he was, but he surprised me by what he did. Just as the boys went from pushing to punching each other, my friend ran to them. "Don't! Don't! Don't!" he yelled, hiding his face as he waved his arms in front of them. The commotion that my friend caused made the boys stop. One of them ran away. The other began to cry. It was the most courageous act that I ever saw.

Holy One, give me courage to be a peacemaker today.
—Jon Sweeney

Digging Deeper: 1 Chr 28:20; Mt 5:9

Sat 11

Seek the Lord while he may be found; call on him while he is near. —Isaiah 55:6 (NIV)

Waiting in an airport—on a long immigration line after an overnight flight—was one of those chaotic places where it didn't seem remotely possible to start my day with God, as I try to do back home. My legs and back ached, and my eyes burned from a sleepless night in a tiny airline seat. Now I was trapped in a mob of people chattering in foreign languages.

At least I'm not traveling with a baby and a toddler like that young couple over there, I thought, glancing at folks I guessed to be Hasidic Jews. The mother inched a child in a stroller over to the wall to wait as the father stationed himself on the customs line, grasping four passports in one hand and dragging two suitcases in the other.

The baby was positioned upright in a carrier facing his father's chest, and there was just enough give in the carrier so the baby could hold up his small head and look up into his father's face. It was mesmerizing to see his wide-eyed adoration in the middle of all of the confusion and noise. Even though the father was concentrating on his responsibilities, he seemed to feel the baby's sweet, silent gaze. The father instinctively placed a gentle kiss on top of the baby's head.

That tender kiss made me realize that there's never a time or place where it's impossible to start my day with God—even from the immigration line.

Father, forgive me for starting too many days without leaning back and looking up into Your beautiful, loving face. Amen.

—Karen Barber

Digging Deeper: 1 Chr 16:9; Pss 5:7, 34:3

Sun 12

The Lord blessed the latter part of Job's life more than the former part. . . . —JOB 42:12 (NIV)

I was invited to give the homecoming address at an old country church where I had taught Sunday school many years before. Alas, it was discouraging when I saw how much my friends had aged. I hardly recognized them, nor did they know who I was. Even the building had deteriorated. The old wooden pew sagged deeply when I sat down in the back row, and I could see the same ancient piano on the stage, with crackled varnish and chipped keys.

"They need to tear this building down and build a new one," I whispered to my wife, Sharon.

"Now, now, don't be hasty. I love this old building. It still has much to offer."

The service began with one of my former Sunday school students playing a medley of hymns. Mike is an award-winning high-school music teacher and the only one of us who has not visibly aged. Thirty years ago he was our substitute pianist, a beginner struggling to find the right keys. Mike played softly at first and then moved into a crescendo of hymns that made us swoon. I saw tears of pride in members' eyes. When he was done, he received thunderous applause.

When, at last, I stood up to speak, I was flooded with emotions and began with an apology. "When I arrived this morning, I felt discouraged by how much we have all aged, but Mike has shown me that even older folks can still make music. We may be wrinkled and worn, but we still have something to say to the world."

Lord, You are the Master Musician. Touch the keys of our hearts and draw out a melody that will make the world around us rejoice to be alive. And may the latter end of our lives be even better than the beginning.

—DANIEL SCHANTZ

Digging Deeper: PRV 20:29; 2 COR 4:16

October

Mon 13

A good name is more desirable than great riches....
—PROVERBS 22:1 (NIV)

My friend Kathy called early one morning because she knows I am a dog person. "I heard about a boy at Children's Hospital who's dying of cancer, and all he wants is a little yellow puppy," she told me.

With that, we were off and running to fulfill this little boy's wish. We found a breeder who offered us a sweet eight-week-old golden retriever puppy she couldn't sell because she had "cloudy eyes," which would diminish her vision all her life.

The next day, Kathy and I went to the hospital and a nurse wheeled this young boy out the front doors and into the sunshine where we placed the puppy on his lap. The boy smiled and stroked the puppy. "Chocolate," he said. "Her name is Chocolate."

We didn't stay long. The boy tired easily. But we've been repeating these visits to the hospital regularly for several weeks. Sometimes the boy has the energy to enjoy the little yellow puppy. Other times he's too uncomfortable. As playful as the puppy is, she seems to sense when to settle down and snuggle up with the boy.

We know these visits won't last. Meanwhile, my family has also fallen in love with this little yellow puppy. The breeder called her Lucy. The little boy called her Chocolate, and then a few visits later he changed her name to Butterfly.

My daughter Kendall is giving the puppy a home and now we call her Roi, which in Hebrew means "God sees," because this little puppy with vision problems seems to be guided by God to places where she can bring comfort and love.

Lord, I'm grateful that You see and creatively meet
our needs for comfort and love.
—CAROL KUYKENDALL

Digging Deeper: PS 33:13; PHIL 4:19

Tue 14

Do not be overcome by evil, but overcome evil with good.
—Romans 12:21 (NIV)

Since I am a professor, today's devotional begins with a quiz, and it's a tough one: Do we live in a world that is mostly bad or mostly good?

That's quite a question with which to begin your day—or end it, depending on when you read this. It's one that has been debated for centuries, is both difficult and complex, and has no easy answers. But how you think about it is important, and here's why—because you may have to answer it many times over today, or help someone else answer it.

Consider these three examples I read in the newspaper, all in one day: A star high-school basketball player is in a plane crash that kills his father and sister—a decade after another crash took his mother's life; a church pastor is shot and killed by a person who couldn't get food at the church's food pantry because he'd already received some; a mother of four is diagnosed with an aggressive form of breast cancer.

You can probably add to my list many crucial challenges of life that you or people you know are facing. Illness. Family problems. Loss of a job. There are days when it can all feel overwhelming.

But in each of the newspaper stories I read, the writer went on to explain how these difficult situations had rallied the generosity of people of faith. Each time, the people involved summoned the power of good to eventually overcome the bad.

I think that's right. And that's why I always leave a blank column on the right side of my prayer book, a place where I can go back and record how good was eventually found. Because finally, I believe the answer to today's quiz is: This is God's world. And God is good.

Today and every day, God, show me how might my words and actions reveal You as a good and generous God Who loves this world.

—Jeff Japinga

Digging Deeper: Gn 50:1–20

Wed 15

He refreshes my soul. He guides me along the right paths for his name's sake. —PSALM 23:3 (NIV)

They lost," I moaned. "I can't believe it."

"Can we talk?" my wife said.

"Sure," I answered glumly, not that I was in the mood. I had another game coming up in a few minutes. This one had better not end so badly.

"I know you love your teams, honey, but sometimes when one loses you sink into a real funk."

"But they blew it!" I protested. "They're going to miss the playoffs!"

"I know, but you can't let it ruin your day . . . our day."

Our day. Now I felt guilty. Because I knew I didn't always get over it, not quickly, at least. I could mope and carry on, that was for sure.

"Jules," I said, "I'm sorry. I guess I know what you mean. It's just that I care about the teams and the players. It kills me when we lose."

"We?" Julee said. "You don't lose. You just watch."

Julee was absolutely right. I took my teams' losses personally and that was dumb. That took all the fun out of being a fan . . . and out of being around me.

"Why don't you change clothes and we'll go out for dinner," I said.

"Someplace with no TV?"

"I promise."

Dear God: please help me stay focused on the things that really matter and the people who make them matter.

—EDWARD GRINNAN

Digging Deeper: Pss 25:5, 143:10

LIFE LESSONS FROM THOSE I'VE MET

Thu 16 *For freedom Christ has set us free. . . .*
—Galatians 5:1 (RSV)

DICK RILEY, ACCOUNTANT

It was twelve-year-old Liz's turn to go with me on an interview. But, oh dear, I thought as we set out in the car for Pennsylvania, how would she react when she saw Dick Riley?

Sixteen years earlier, an ambitious young man with a wife and a baby on the way, Dick had fallen from a ladder. Paralyzed except for partial use of one arm, his legs had been amputated so he could turn himself in bed.

"You mustn't cry," I coached Liz. "You mustn't act sorry for him."

Dick's wife led me to the room where he sat in a motorized bed surrounded by the files of his accounting business. I wrenched my eyes from the sheet—too flat where his body ended at the hips—and met a pair of smiling eyes. "I didn't used to smile," he told me. "All I cared about was getting rich fast." Too fast to follow tedious safety rules for ladder use. As for smiling: "Only at someone who could help me get ahead."

After the interview, Dick turned to Liz. Who was her best friend? What was her hardest class? "I'll pray at exam time." When teenage Dicky came home, his father asked after an ailing schoolmate. A client phoned. "I won't charge him," Dick said afterward. "He's struggling to keep his kid in college."

And that self-absorbed young man he used to be? "He was a lot more handicapped than I am. Sure, I'm trapped in this useless body, but when you're wrapped up in yourself, that's the real prison."

Grant me the true liberty, Father, of self-forgetfulness.
—Elizabeth Sherrill

Digging Deeper: Rom 6:17–18

A NEW WAY TO SERVE

Fri 17 *You shall live in booths for seven days . . . so that your generations may know that I made the people of Israel live in booths. . . .* —Leviticus 23:42–43 (NRSV)

ONE SMALL THING

It all started one night when I was passing out sandwiches and fruit at the homeless shelter. There was talk of some city councilors who opposed the shelter, dismissing those who needed it. Rich, a Vietnam vet whose life had never been the same since he'd fought the Tet Offensive, looked at me with anguish. "What does *homeless* mean? Do they know that we're parents and laid-off workers and vets? That some of us are really sick or addicted?"

I merely nodded in sympathy, not knowing what to say. I'm not a great talker, but the one thing I knew I could do was to write about homelessness. I hesitated though. Many people weren't happy about the shelter; the local newspaper wasn't supportive. But I also knew God had given me one gift and that He'd put Rich in my path to make me use it.

The next night at the shelter, after the article about Rich and homelessness appeared in our Sunday paper, he hugged me. "Marci, I can't believe you wrote about me—about all of us! It will change how people look at us."

It was like I'd given him an unimaginable gift. Yet all I'd done was the one small thing I could. I started to wonder what else was possible.

Generous God, help me to remember that doing Your work may not be as hard as I think.

—Marci Alborghetti

Digging Deeper: Phil 2:13; Col 3:23

Sat 18

My little children, these things I write to you, so that you may not sin. And if anyone sins, we have an Advocate with the Father, Jesus Christ the righteous. —1 JOHN 2:1 (NKJV)

Firewood normally sold for over two hundred dollars per cord, but my neighbor was offering it at thirty dollars. "Come and get it," he said. I'd use our newly acquired pickup truck to haul the firewood. The truck was old, but it was clean and dent-free—something my wife appreciated.

When I arrived at John's wooded eight-acre spread, he directed me to back up a narrow path to the top of a hill. We filled the truck bed, and I made my first delivery without incident. When I returned for the second load, I backed up the hill again, only to hear a grinding noise against the driver's door. I mistook it for a branch scraping the door, so I pressed on. The grinding got louder. I adjusted my direction and finished backing up the hill. When I exited the truck, my heart sank.

I had smashed in the driver's door and put a hefty scrape in the paint.

John arrived moments later to help with the final load. I hoped he didn't notice the door. We chatted, but all I could think about was how to tell my wife. Maybe I could hide it and get it fixed. Or I could wait till the next day. Or . . .

Minutes later, I was home. I chose a direct approach. "Honey, I just put a big dent in the truck door."

Her head snapped in my direction. "How bad?"

"Pretty bad."

She smiled and shrugged. "Well, it is our utility vehicle, right?"

"That's why I love you," I said.

We saved hundreds of dollars in heating costs, but my wife's mercy that day was the greatest treasure of all.

Thank You, Lord, for the grace that forgives my dumbest mistakes.
—BILL GIOVANNETTI

Digging Deeper: Ps 55:22; PRV 11:2; PHIL 3:13

Sun 19

And ye shall seek me, and find me, when ye shall search for me with all your heart. —JEREMIAH 29:13 (KJV)

"One, two, three . . . " I continued my search through my bookshelves. "You're kidding!" I said out loud. "Eight Bibles? Do I really own *eight* versions of God's Word?"

I hadn't realized the depth of my passion for God's holy Word until that moment. Often I pore over several Bibles when I want to discover deeper meanings in my readings. It's like a treasure hunt. I have the New Living Translation and Today's English Version for clarity. I adore the King James Version for the sheer poetry of the verse. I like the Geneva edition so I can see what infuriated King James, inspiring him to refute that translation.

I scanned the other books in my collection. Scores of classics, dog-eared childhood stories, novels, nonfiction, and poetry. For all of these favorites, I never once considered reading, much less owning, any other versions.

And yet with the Bible, the more translations I read, the closer I feel to understanding God's meanings and desires for me. It truly is a *living* Word! It takes on many shapes and sizes . . . God isn't confined in the least! He keeps growing. He threads Himself through each and every one. I love seeking—and finding—Him in so many unique ways.

Dear Lord, You are not curbed and typecast. You speak in myriad ways.
Teach me Your meanings, and may I keep seeking until
I find Your will for me.
—ERIKA BENTSEN

Digging Deeper: PS 119:50, 105; 2 TM 3:16–17; HEB 4:12

Mon 20

Your path led through the sea, your way through the mighty waters, though your footprints were not seen.
—Psalm 77:19 (NIV)

I went camping with seventeen Cub Scouts last weekend. It was an experience that required a go-with-the-flow mentality, not just because of the kids, but because the person in charge approaches life very differently than I do.

Fortunately, I'd been warned in advance. So when we arrived a couple of hours late and hiked a mile through freezing woods by moonlight, that was fine. When we started cooking supper at 9:30 PM, I raised my eyebrows but shrugged my shoulders. And when the boys didn't get to bed until midnight, I figured at least they'd sleep soundly. It wasn't the way I'd have done it, but no one was dying, so I guess it worked.

On the second day, I had a great talk with a Jamaican dad about his ADHD son, which probably wouldn't have happened if I'd been grousing about disorganization. I laughed for hours with two moms, entirely in Spanish, instead of being grumpy about the timing of meals. I learned about Peruvian fruit punch and where to find the best Portuguese food, when I could have been cranky about how long it took to prepare supper.

Yes, the boys were blue with cold and black with dirt. They were never tired and constantly hungry. But on Sunday morning when Stephen said, "Mom, this was better than I could have imagined!" I knew he was right.

Lord, teach me to let go of my way. Teach me to follow Yours.
—Julia Attaway

Digging Deeper: Ps 77:13–20

October

Tue 21

That you may become blameless and harmless, children of God without fault in the midst of a crooked and perverse generation, among whom you shine as lights in the world.
—PHILIPPIANS 2:15 (NKJV)

As a teacher in a Christian college, my life has been lived in a somewhat protected culture, but my son-in-law, who is also named Dan, lets his light shine in the often brutal world of business.

Dan is a gifted manager of some six hundred large vehicles for a utility company. He works with vendors, goes to meetings, inspects vehicles . . . and he is guided by his faith in all he does. For example, he maintains his vehicles scrupulously because he knows that the safety of his workers depends on attention to such details as worn tires and brakes or burned-out headlights.

He treats his staff with respect. If he has to correct a worker, he goes in person, face-to-face, the way the Bible says to do. "I was told that you are using a company vehicle for personal trips. Is this true or just a rumor?"

When he fills out performance reviews, he tells the truth, neither all-nice nor all-negative. "I really appreciate your hard work, but your mileage records need a bit of work."

It's a large company, but when there is a death in a worker's family, Dan goes to the funeral to show support. "I'm sorry about your great loss. I will be praying for you."

Little wonder that Dan is highly respected and appreciated.

I have learned that everything I do has a spiritual dimension, and not just Bible reading or church attendance. Whether I am shopping for clothes, fixing a flat tire, or just driving down the freeway, my spiritual light is on and the meter is running.

The world is a dark place, Lord. Help me to keep
my light shining at all times.
—DANIEL SCHANTZ

Digging Deeper: MT 5:13–16

HOPE IN HOSPICE

Wed 22 *"Whoever hears my word and believes him who sent me has eternal life and will not be judged but has crossed over from death to life."*—John 5:24 (NIV)

A SOOTHING PRESENCE

Marilyn was nonresponsive when I visited with her in hospice. She seemed peaceful, her hands resting quietly on the blanket. The idea of launching a conversation without knowing if she could hear me was difficult. I simply didn't know what to say. But that's the wonderful thing about books: They can bring comfort in challenging situations.

So I visited the book cart and found a small volume of *Best Loved Poetry*. For about twenty minutes, I read poems by William Shakespeare, William Cullen Bryant, John Donne, and Helen Steiner Rice to Marilyn. I enjoyed the flow of words and hoped she might too.

Then I switched to something that sounds easier, but is, in fact, quite difficult—at least at first. That's being a "soothing presence." Hospice visitors, families, caregivers, and volunteers do a lot of this. Part of the hospice commitment is that no one should die alone. Whenever possible, the support team of family and hospice workers are there at the end of life. This is, for everyone, a moment of sadness, relief, amazing quiet.

As I continue my work in hospice, I see over and over that we are never alone. I feel the presence of the Lord right there. I can almost touch Him.

I trust that You are always with us, God, in times of hope and fear.
—Brigitte Weeks

Digging Deeper: Pss 16:11, 139:7, 140:13

October

Thu 23

Then they sat on the ground with him for seven days and seven nights. No one said a word to him, because they saw how great his suffering was. —JOB 2:13 (NIV)

My grandfather passed away this morning.

I was able to see him a few weeks ago. He was thin and frail—words I never would have associated with the man I knew growing up, a former bodybuilder and gymnast. We sat around a table and ate dinner—Papa, Granny, my girlfriend, and me.

Throughout the meal, Papa kept asking me questions about my job, my church, my life. He wanted to hear the story again of how my girlfriend and I met. But the conversation was strained. He had a difficult time staying alert, and his hearing was poor. Sometimes he would trail off midsentence. Then he'd apologize.

After the dishes were cleared, my girlfriend sat down beside Papa and held one of his hands and smiled at him. He smiled back. Following her lead, I reached out and held his other hand. We sat like that for a long time. Few words were uttered, but more was communicated in those silent moments than in all the words spoken at dinner.

That night I learned conversation isn't our only means of communication, either with each other or with God. The deepest communion we can experience takes place in silence.

Lord, allow me to find Your voice in the stillness and to connect with others in the silence.

—JOSHUA SUNDQUIST

Digging Deeper: PSS 46:10, 62:5; LAM 3:26

Fri 24

We take captive every thought to make it obedient to Christ.
—2 Corinthians 10:5 (NIV)

My job of selling lumber had become extremely intense with the volatile housing market. During the weeks when my sales slowed, thoughts of being a failure swirled through my mind. This was one of those weeks.

After cleaning up the dishes, I decided to throw rocks into the hole that my golden retriever had dug. When I stepped out the door, Sunrise stopped and grinned at me like she had a mouth full of marbles. Then she walked to the other side of the yard. *Strange*, I thought.

As I tossed rocks, I noticed her nose something in the grass, scoop it up in her mouth, and lay down for a couple of minutes. Then she opened her mouth. I saw a flutter. It was a baby bird!

I vaulted across the yard, tackled the dog, and pried open her mouth. I snatched the shivering bird off Sunrise's tongue. My emotions swung between feeling sorry for the bird and laughing as I remembered cartoons of Tweety Bird looking at Sylvester's tonsils. How many times had this poor bird stared at Sunrise's tonsils?

Slowly it dawned on me as I cradled the bird in my hands. I was the one in the mouth of the beast. I had been allowing thoughts of failure to swallow me over and over again.

It's time to give yourself the gift of mercy, I heard in my spirit. I lifted the bird into the air. It flew away—free—and so did I.

Lord, thank You for showing me how to give myself mercy.
—Rebecca Ondov

Digging Deeper: Pss 86:5, 145:9; Lk 6:36

Sat 25

Let us run with patience the particular race that God has set before us. —HEBREWS 12:1 (TLB)

It's hard to admit, but getting older means I'm slower and most tasks take longer than they once did. At thirty, I could clean my house in four hours, tops! Today that job takes twice as long. But I wasn't as disturbed by my physical slowdown as I was by the snail's pace of my spiritual journey. My prayer life was more rote and routine than praise and petition. I wasn't consistently becoming kinder, more generous, or less critical. I was going nowhere.

Then one afternoon I watched my grandson Caleb compete in a cross-country meet. He was in the first group to finish, and I headed to the medal presentation when an official shouted, "Wait! There's still a runner on the course." So we waited and watched.

Finally, a full six minutes after everyone else, we cheered as an exhausted young man stumbled across the finish line with an exultant grin. "I did it! I finished the race!" he said.

This young man's goal wasn't about having the fastest time or getting a medal, but about completing the race. And that, I decided, was a worthy goal for me as well.

There are still moments when I see no signs that I'm growing in God's grace or going on to perfection in Christ. But when those times occur, the runner's triumphant words echo in my mind: "I finished the race!"

Lord, guide my feet as I run the course at the speed
that You deem best. Amen.
—PENNEY SCHWAB

Digging Deeper: HEB 12:1–3

Sun 26

You have searched me, Lord, and you know me.
—Psalm 139:1 (NIV)

The moment I opened my eyes I was in a frenzy. I woke up late, had to pack overnight bags for my sons, feed them, dress them, and wait for my ex-husband to pick them up. When they finally left, I wanted to collapse back into bed, but missing church was not an option. Sundays are part of my workweek, and I had to do nursery. I ran out the door, looking as tired and panicked as I felt.

After my subway rides, I jogged the rest of the way to church, wanting to cry, hating myself for always forgetting things, pitying my life as a single mother. Every negative thought of my disappointments and failures wrapped around me till I could barely breathe.

I arrived in the middle of praise and worship. Babies and toddlers go downstairs after the music, but so far I didn't see one child under four years old. I sat down, caught my breath, and then quietly sang praises to God. I kept looking at the back door, waiting for kids who never came.

Before he preached, the pastor started talking about my after-school program and all the "great work Karen is doing there." Then he put on a video I had made about the kids, one that always makes me smile and cry as I watch their little faces and listen to the inspiring music. The tears came, but they were about more than just the video. God was reminding me of what I was doing right.

Lord, thank You for giving me exactly what I need,
when I need it the most.
—Karen Valentin

Digging Deeper: Ps 111:5; Mt 6:33; Phil 4:19

Mon 27

"But the seed on good soil stands for those with a noble and good heart, who hear the word, retain it, and by persevering produce a crop." —LUKE 8:15 (NIV)

I was playing Boggle with a friend. I'm good at finding real words in the jumble of letters on the game board, but after I'd outscored her three rounds in a row, she interrupted me as I was reading my list of words. "Do you even know what that means?" she asked.

"No," I replied, "but I know it's a word!"

She looked at me skeptically and said it was ridiculous to use words that I didn't know.

We played on, but later this gnawed at me, and I went to the dictionary. One way the dictionary defines *word* is as a sound or a series of letters that "symbolizes and communicates a meaning." My friend was right. Without meaning, a word is merely lines and squiggles.

This is as true of *the* Word as a word. While reading Scripture, I may gloss over it—reading without really absorbing or understanding or even trying to understand, my eyes glancing over a string of words without comprehending what makes them words and how together they form the Word.

In Boggle, I can get away with not knowing the meaning of a word. I might even win. But in life and in faith, the rules are different. Allow myself a blithe and careless attitude toward the Word and, ultimately, I'm the one who will come out a l-o-s-e-r.

Lord, give me a deeper understanding of Scripture and
a stronger desire to hear Your Word.

—JEFF CHU

Digging Deeper: JN 1:1–5

Tue 28

Even though I walk through the darkest valley, I will fear no evil, for you are with me; your rod and your staff, they comfort me. —PSALM 23:4 (NIV)

The power went out about an hour ago, right after I got a robocall followed by a text message warning about severe weather and a tornado watch. I made sure all of my devices were fully charged and that the flashlights were working. They were, thanks to my wife Julee's persistent reminders to replace the batteries and my foot-dragging compliance.

Millie, our golden retriever, is curled up on the couch in the flickering glow of a candle. She seems glad not to be alone and close to her humans.

Big storms have struck terror into the hearts of man and beast alike since the beginning of time. Last year, when I visited Israel, I rode on the Sea of Galilee in a replica fishing boat circa AD 33. I remember our guide's vivid retelling of the storm that terrified the apostles and how, to their relief and astonishment, Jesus stood at the prow and calmed the seas and sky. A memorable biblical miracle, certainly, but a perfect metaphor as well. Today, Doppler radar would have kept the boat at dock. Yet Christ still calms the storms we all face, those roiling seas upon which our lives are often tossed.

Maybe that's why I feel strangely comfortable right now. This is a reminder of the source of my true spiritual strength, my true refuge in a storm. The crack of thunder, the platinum flashes of lightning, the pounding rain are a kind of reassurance.

Lord, Your love is our ultimate protection on earth,
a power no storm can disrupt.
—EDWARD GRINNAN

Digging Deeper: MK 4:35–41

Wed 29

May God's grace and blessing be upon all who sincerely love our Lord Jesus Christ. —EPHESIANS 6:24 (TLB)

When my friend Dolores's husband, Milt, died, I wanted to do something special for her. But what? Flowers? Casserole? I knew she'd get plenty of those. A plant? No, she lives in Florida but spends the summers in New York and shouldn't have to worry about houseplants.

I went to the supermarket, wandering around the aisles tormented. *What can I get her? I should be home baking something from scratch*, I thought. I wheeled my grocery cart up and down the aisles. *What?* Finally, I grabbed a box of big fresh strawberries. Next, I tossed my two favorite kinds of chocolate candies into the cart. In the bakery, I thought about comfort foods and selected a long loaf of whole grain bread.

At home, I put the chocolates into two jars I'd hand-painted, arranged everything in a big bag, and wrote her a note. When I arrived at her house, I placed the bag on the kitchen counter as I was ushered into the living room.

After a few tearful moments of talking about Milt's death after a long struggle with kidney disease, Dolores started telling heartfelt stories about him that included quite a few good laughs. Later, after good-bye hugs, I saw the bag on the kitchen counter, unopened, as I walked out the door.

I shouldn't have worried about what to bring to my friend. My presence with Dolores and letting her share stories of her beloved husband meant much more to her than anything I could have put in that bag.

Father, help me to remember that comforting friends is more than giving them things. It's giving them me.

—PATRICIA LORENZ

Digging Deeper: LK 6:31; 2 COR 1:3–5

Thu 30

You will surely forget your trouble, recalling it only as waters gone by. Life will be brighter than noonday, and darkness will become like morning. —JOB 11:16–17 (NIV)

I wake at six, same as usual. Wake up snarling Son One, same as usual, to get ready for Boring Old School, same as usual. Do not, this morning, wake up Son Two. This is *not* usual.

Son Two, who is a roaring, vulgar, growling, rude, selfish, disrespectful *pain* to wake up on school mornings, had his heart architecture rearranged yesterday, and today he gets to sleep in, all day, no school, by direct command of his surgeon. The surgeon spent two hours poking around our son's heart, and he made some adjustments, and closed off two new tiny curling veins, and told me afterward, cheerfully, that Son Two did swimmingly and should be good to go for another five years.

I stand in the kitchen weeping into the coffee beans because my son didn't die on the surgery table, and my son didn't die last night when his mom tucked him in tight along the sides like she did when he was a fat smiling baby. When I look in on him this morning, he is snoring like a sea lion with a sinus condition, which means he *still* isn't dead, and he could so easily *be* dead, and he isn't.

I dry the coffee beans with a dish towel and make the coffee, and my lovely bride osmoses into the kitchen with that effortless grace like she weighs zero pounds and is made of grinning and light. We embrace, and there is nothing to say that comes anywhere close to the words you would need to have in order to say our second son isn't dead, and he could so easily be, and he isn't.

Dear Lord, yes, that kid is a sneery kid and, yes, that surly tone makes me want to shriek and, yes, he is a grump and, no, he didn't do his homework. But, Lord, thank You thank You thank You for that kid, alive and well and sneery. Thank You.

—BRIAN DOYLE

Digging Deeper: PRV 17:6; MK 10:14

Fri 31

One gives freely, yet grows all the richer. . . .
—PROVERBS 11:24 (ESV)

Can we go there first?" Henry points down the road with his black-gloved finger. The feathers of his big black wings stretch over his older brother, Solomon, who is dressed as his favorite *Star Wars* character. "Can we, Mom? Can we just go there first?" Henry asks again.

"I don't know," I say. This year there are fewer porch lights lit, fewer people giving out candy.

"It must be the economy," my husband says. "People can't afford to give out candy." We pass other trick-or-treaters along the way.

"I can hear the music," Henry says.

"Me too!" Solomon shouts.

"Listen, that house might not be giving out big candy bars this year," I say, preparing them. "Maybe they're giving out regular ones. Okay? I don't want you to be disappointed." We follow the sound of the organ to the doorstep. A woman dressed as a queen, complete with a crown, plays spooky music on a keyboard on her front porch.

The boys climb the steps. They marvel at the table covered with rows and rows of king-size candy bars. "Help yourself," the woman says sweetly.

"Just one," I remind them.

Henry's and Solomon's eyes grow wide as they make their selection. Their smiles are huge. The woman keeps playing the organ, but I see her looking at the boys, watching their expressions. She smiles.

"Thanks," I say. "It means a lot to them."

"Pleasure's all mine," she answers.

As we walk to the next house, Solomon looks down at his huge candy bar. "I know why they call them king-size," he says. "'Cause when you get one, you feel like a king, right?"

Dear Lord, thank You for the generosity of others that makes us feel special, that makes us feel loved. —SABRA CIANCANELLI

Digging Deeper: MT 10:42; LK 6:38; 2 COR 9:6

DAILY MERCIES

1 ______________________________

2 ______________________________

3 ______________________________

4 ______________________________

5 ______________________________

6 ______________________________

7 ______________________________

8 ______________________________

9 ______________________________

10 ______________________________

11 ______________________________

12 ______________________________

13 ______________________________

14 ______________________________

15 ______________________________

October

16 ____________________

17 ____________________

18 ____________________

19 ____________________

20 ____________________

21 ____________________

22 ____________________

23 ____________________

24 ____________________

25 ____________________

26 ____________________

27 ____________________

28 ____________________

29 ____________________

30 ____________________

31 ____________________

NOVEMBER

So let us confidently approach the throne of grace to receive mercy and favor and find help in time of need.

—HEBREWS 4:16 (TIB)

Sat 1

My times are in your hands. . . . —PSALM 31:15 (NIV)

Our three oldest granddaughters, ages nine, seven, and six, came to our house for a Saturday sleepover the night we set our clocks back one hour, ending daylight saving time. The girls were in their pajamas, nearing bedtime. "I have an idea," I told them. "Let's set our clocks back right now and spend our extra hour doing something fun before we go to bed."

"Yes!" they agreed. So 9:00 PM became 8:00 PM, and we had the gift of one hour still ahead of us. "What should we do?" was the next question.

"Let's go to the store and get a new game!" I suggested.

"In our jammies?" they chorused, wide-eyed.

"Why not? Just put on a jacket and shoes."

A short time later, we entered a mostly deserted store. We found the games section, easily agreed on one, and headed to the checkout stand, picking up a box of ice-cream treats on the way. We were back home with almost a half-a-gift-hour to spend, playing our new game and eating ice cream. When we rereached 9:00 PM, the girls brushed their teeth and climbed into the big bed where all three slept together.

As I tucked them in, I placed a clock with the new time beside their bed. "You can't get up until at least seven o'clock," I told them. Since I'd already used up my extra hour, I now needed the gift of a full night's sleep.

Lord, teach me to savor Your gift of every hour, every day.

—CAROL KUYKENDALL

Digging Deeper: Pss 96:1–2, 118:24

Sun 2

"Give, and it will be given to you. A good measure, pressed down, shaken together and running over, will be poured into your lap. For with the measure you use, it will be measured to you."—LUKE 6:38 (NIV)

I received a letter from an organization called Jobs for America's Graduates (JAG, for short). JAG works with students who are at risk of dropping out of school to help them earn a high school diploma and assists the students in job placement after graduation. The letter said that JAG students had an opportunity to attend a national convention not too far away where they would participate in workshops and interact with other students across the state. Funding, though, had been cut. The letter asked for a twenty-dollar donation to sponsor a student to attend the conference. I immediately pulled out my checkbook, wrote a twenty-dollar check, and placed it in the mail.

The following Sunday in church, I sat alongside my daughter Misty and her three boys. Before the service began, her oldest son whispered, "Hey, Mom, can we get donuts after church?"

"No, honey," she replied quietly. "It's not in our budget this week."

I felt a twinge of remorse. I thought about the donation I'd made just a few days ago. *It's sure hard to give to others when I see those closest to me needing help too*, I thought. I bowed my head. "Lord," I prayed, "give me faith big enough to know that You are taking care of it all, from my own kids on tight budgets to needy students whom I may never know."

At the end of the service, a woman seated behind us leaned over the pew and said to Misty, "I watched your boys all through church. They were so well-mannered! Here," she said with a smile, handing Misty a twenty-dollar bill. "Please take your boys out for a treat after church."

Lord, I want a faith as big as Your generosity.
—MELODY BONNETTE SWANG

Digging Deeper: MT 17:14–20

Mon 3

"As long as I am in the world, I am the light of the world."
—John 9:5 (ESV)

Yesterday, as I went around the house changing clocks for daylight saving time, I explained to my youngest, Henry, the story behind why we do it, how it began. "We lost an hour as we slept," I said.

Henry watched as I clicked the digits on the oven and microwave, moved the hour hand on the wall clock in the mudroom. He followed me upstairs as I changed the alarm clocks in the bedrooms.

"But, Mom, what time is it really?" Henry asked. "What do you mean we lost an hour? Where does it go?"

I tried to explain the history of daylight saving and how it makes the most of natural light. "By changing the clocks, we use less electricity."

"You just delete an hour?" Henry looked at me with a mixture of disbelief and intrigue as if I'd told him I made the sun rise.

"Well, we lose an hour on the clock, but we gain an hour of daylight," I said.

"Oh, Mom, I think I understand. It's so we get more light. Why didn't you say so in the first place?"

So we get more light, I said to myself. It's no wonder *light* appears more than two hundred times in the Bible. Light represents the presence of God. Light gives us comfort and understanding. We strive to walk in God's light. Wouldn't it be great if each of us would use each day to set our spirit for more light?

Dear Lord, thank You for being the Source that brightens my life and the lives of those around me.
—Sabra Ciancanelli

Digging Deeper: Pss 4:6, 89:15; Is 42:16

Tue 4

To every thing there is a season, and a time to every purpose under the heaven: A time to be born, and a time to die; a time to plant.... —ECCLESIASTES 3:1–2 (KJV)

Let your light shine!" I say to Bishop Oby, echoing back to him the words he has spoken to me countless times, over the twenty something years I have know him. Words he has spoken to countless others.

When I was a discouraged, unemployed—despite my qualifications—single parent barely scraping by, he and his wife came to my family's rescue. She sewed clothes for me so I would be presentable. He personally baked chickens and cakes to feed us. His countenance and voice were reassuring. "All right, daughter. Keep your head up!" What they did for my family, they did for many others in the rural North Carolina area where we lived.

When I finally found employment, they babysat my son so that I could work. Years later, Bishop Oby and his wife moved to Rhode Island. Less than a year ago, his wife passed away. Bishop Oby is now in a Providence rehabilitation center and I know that he misses her. His strong body seems to be failing him. Now, I pray for him and it is my turn to give back what he gave to me. "The people in the rehab center need to see the light that you showed me; don't be discouraged," I say quietly.

"You are right, daughter." I hear hope creep back into his voice.

Lord, help me to share the fruit and seeds of love and joy
that have been planted in me.
—SHARON FOSTER

Digging Deeper: Pss 31:24, 39:7, 43:5

November

Wed 5

"Peace I leave with you; my peace I give you. I do not give to you as the world gives. Do not let your hearts be troubled and do not be afraid." —JOHN 14:27 (NIV)

I'd decided I wanted to go to law school. That meant getting together professors' recommendations, writing a personal statement, and taking the law school admission test.

I read books to develop the skills I needed and took tons of practice tests. I re-created the test-day conditions, so I wouldn't be surprised. I especially needed to get used to the timing. The only way to know how much time was remaining in each section was by using your own watch. I prepared as best as I knew how and by test day I was ready.

I was taken to my seat and given a test booklet. I was nervous and started fiddling with my watch as I listened to the instructions. *Snap*. I'd torn the dial out of my watch! The proctor called for us to start.

I was breathing too quickly and shallowly and didn't know what to do. My heart was beating wildly, but I didn't have time to think. I started reading and answering the questions. By the time I finished the first page, I wasn't scared anymore. I didn't have my watch, but I could feel that the timing was right.

A voice inside me said, *You've done this a hundred times. You're prepared.* I kept my head down and kept working. The voice was right. I finished every section with time to spare.

Thank You, Lord, for Your always-calming voice.
—SAM ADRIANCE

Digging Deeper: PHIL 4:6–7; 2 THES 3:16

Thu 6

"I called you so often, but you wouldn't come. I reached out to you, but you paid no attention."—PROVERBS 1:24 (NLT)

At first I ignored it, but the strange noise didn't go away. I sat in my office, hunkered down to prepare a sermon. My son and his friends attended our church's kids' club. Since I chauffeured them to and from church, I used this night for much-needed prep time.

I'd been so busy lately. God's presence felt crowded out by the relentless demands of work, family, ministry, home, and a thousand other priorities. I needed these extra hours for work, but the noise distracted me.

Two full minutes passed before recognition dawned, and my eyes grew wide. Fire alarm!

I raced toward the multipurpose room. The kids' club had not yet started, and hundreds of children were running around. Their noise drowned out the clanging of the alarm.

As I helped to get the kids out of the building, another children's leader told us it was a false alarm, triggered by a mischievous child.

Alarms are good. They save lives. We had procedures in place. We knew how to respond to the fire alarm. But nobody heard it.

As I returned to my office, God whispered, *Bill, I've been sounding a spiritual alarm and you haven't heard it. What if your life is just too loud?*

I set aside my work, prayed, and read Scriptures. I spent time with God. I rested. Nothing extravagant, just a heartfelt recalibration toward what matters most and a determination to heed His gracious alarms.

Compassionate Father, keep me attuned to Your loving call and grant enough quiet to always hear Your alarms.
—BILL GIOVANNETTI

Digging Deeper: IS 55:6; JAS 4:8

LIFE LESSONS FROM THOSE I'VE MET

Fri 7 *For my thoughts are not your thoughts. . . .*
—Isaiah 55:8 (KJV)

THOR HEYERDAHL, NORWEGIAN ETHNOGRAPHER/ ADVENTURER

Thor Heyerdahl's home was high on a cliff on the northwest coast of Italy. John and I had come to interview him about the epic journey of the Kon Tiki, six men traveling five thousand miles across the Pacific Ocean on a balsa wood raft.

Preparing for the interview, we'd sketched out potential story themes. How had they handled isolation? Monotony? Personality conflicts in that confined space? Eagerly we scribbled his answers to our questions.

Satisfied with the interview, we followed him onto the balcony overlooking the Tyrrhenian Sea. "How you must enjoy this view," I said, "loving water as you do."

"Loving it?" Heyerdahl said. "I've always been terrified of water!"

Isolation. Monotony. Conflict. I foresaw our piles of notes on these subjects tossed into a wastebasket. Nothing in our research had hinted at the story he told us now. Twice as a child he'd come so near drowning that the mere sight of an expanse of water would make him physically ill. Then his lifework brought him face-to-face with the thing he dreaded—here was the best theme for our story yet!

Oh, I still prepare questions before an interview, but I hold them loosely. Planning for a story, a day, or a life is important, but God may have something different in mind.

Don't let me stick so rigidly to my own agenda, Father,
that I miss the better things You have in store.
—Elizabeth Sherrill

Digging Deeper: Pss 32:8, 118:8

Sat 8

Having been firmly rooted and now being built up in Him. . . .
—Colossians 2:7 (NAS)

Lately I've been interested in the Bible's references to *roots.* Isaiah says of the coming of Christ, "He grew up before Him . . . like a *root* out of parched ground" (Isaiah 53:2). Jesus tells a parable of those who hear the Word of God but fall away because "they have no firm *root* in themselves" (Mark 4:17). The New Testament letters teach "being *rooted* and grounded in love" (Ephesians 3:17), and warn against a "*root* of bitterness springing up" to cause trouble (Hebrews 12:15).

Anyone who has ever tried to pull a stubborn weed knows how hard it is. It takes some digging. From an early age, one of my children had an attitude toward me. It isn't that we didn't get along, but our connection didn't flow smoothly. There was an unnamed something separating us.

One time, trying to yank at the problem, I blurted, "I don't want you to have a wasted mother experience." Then came the moment my daughter, now in her late thirties, asked me to come quickly in a time of need. I did.

During those days we were able to open a compassionate conversation. We discovered that the reason for the root of bitterness was really unknown. I asked forgiveness for anything I might have done, confessing that I had perhaps been an attention-grabber or steamrolled over her more private personality.

The root of whatever it was snapped that afternoon. God dug it out. He reset us in His sincere and lasting love—and that's some fertile ground.

Jesus, how deep-down good Your root of reconciliation is!
—Carol Knapp

Digging Deeper: Rom 14:19; 1 Thes 5:14–15

A NEW WAY TO SERVE

Sun 9 *"If you love those who love you, what credit is that to you?. . ."*
—Luke 6:32 (NRSV)

PASSING ON THE THRILL OF SHARING

I don't mind sharing my things, but my thoughts and heart . . . not so much! However, I've learned that when you're really into something, you end up sharing without even knowing it.

Everyone who knows my husband, Charlie, and me learns of our involvement at the St. James Shelter and the St. James Literary Society. No one invites us out on Monday nights because they know where we'll be. When others are asked about jobs, families, or the weather, we're asked about our friends at the shelter. Gradually, it's become more than just talk.

A friend who owns a restaurant started sending leftover muffins for shelter guests. People with holiday party leftovers call us to find out who needs the food. My parents collect canned goods and snacks. My sister and brother-in-law donate clothes. Charlie's siblings contribute to a fund that runs the shelter. Elected officials and judicial court staff who know Charlie from his years in government have become advocates for better housing and criminal-justice programs. Some members of our church wrap packages of new socks every year, so all of the residents will have something to open on Christmas Day.

We started out sharing our things and time with the homeless but ended up sharing and passing along the thrill of sharing.

Lord, let my work reflect Yours.
—Marci Alborghetti

Digging Deeper: Lk 6:27–36; 1 Tm 6:18; Heb 13:16

Mon 10

"For where your treasure is, there your heart will be also."
—LUKE 12:34 (NKJV)

It had been one of those weeks at the Veterans Affairs Medical Center where I work; I'd had trouble remembering the Lord's blessings. Amid all the confusion, my boss reminded me that I was to work at the ambassador's desk, our welcoming place where patients and family members stop to ask for information or directions.

I hadn't been at my post long when a young girl came up to me, pushing a wheelchair. An elderly gentleman with a crop of snowy-white hair was seated in it. He wore cotton periwinkle-blue pajamas that still held creases like they might have been in a gift box. "Would you mind watching Grandpa while I get the car?" Then she added, "I need to let you know. He doesn't talk or anything and has Alzheimer's disease."

As the girl left, I wrapped an arm around the veteran's shoulders. "You're with me for a little while," I said into glassy green eyes and gave his shoulders a squeeze.

Then the most unbelievable thing happened. The gentleman gazed into my eyes and marveled, "We've got a treasure here, don't we?"

"You're the treasure," I answered.

"World War II, army," he continued. Then utter silence ensued until his granddaughter returned.

As the periwinkle pajamas disappeared through the exit, I thought of how I needed that reminder in the worst way.

Yes, Lord, these dear veterans, this job of mine, it's all a treasure.
I forgot for a little while. Thank You.
—ROBERTA MESSNER

Digging Deeper: LK 12:22–34

November

Tue 11

When you lie down, you will not be afraid; when you lie down, your sleep will be sweet. —PROVERBS 3:24 (NIV)

I watch the red numbers on the clock turn to two o'clock. My husband sleeps beside me. His breathing is calm and even. I get up and check on the boys and find them asleep and fine. I go back to bed and look out the sheer curtain into the darkness. Our cat Frank settles at my feet.

My eyes fall on the streetlight down the road, but my mind is on my worries. Nothing big, just the usual everyday struggles: My son has a problem on the school bus; our tax bill will be due in a week or two. I went over a work e-mail I wish I'd written differently. Little problems have a way of snowballing in the night.

The wind howls, and the window shutters rattle. The pine tree down the road bends to and fro, and as the gusts change direction, the light of the streetlight pulses bright to dark.

I watch the blinking light and say the Lord's Prayer. The wind settles and the bright stream of the streetlight does too, almost on cue. My eyes are tired, and just as I'm feeling relaxed, the gusts begin again, the windows shudder, and the boughs shift just enough to block the light. I focus on the words of the prayer, imagining the light in my mind's eye until I find rest.

Dear Lord, help me silence the chatter of my worries and focus on You.
—SABRA CIANCANELLI

Digging Deeper: MT 6:9–13

Wed 12

By faith we understand that the universe was formed at God's command, so that what is seen was not made out of what was visible. —HEBREWS 11:3 (NIV)

A few days ago there was a massive jackpot that had folks going crazy buying tickets. My friend Jaseem, whose father owns our little neighborhood newsstand and who is studying psychology in college, tells me, "Buying a ticket is hope-affirming. It makes people think that they could wake up in the morning to find their lives completely changed."

Except aren't we already supposed to be doing what we really want with our lives? I have nothing at all against people playing lotto. I caught my mother at it once, which, if you knew my mother, would have surprised you too. When I teasingly confronted her, she said that if she won the jackpot she would give it all to her church for programs to help the poor. That was Mom.

For me, at least, hope is the product of faith. I pray that I wake up every morning, thinking that my life could be changed not by a random number or lucky hunch but by the grace of God.

Father, with You nothing is a gamble; nothing happens to us by chance. Faith is the surest bet I know. Please help me live fully the life You have planned for me.

—EDWARD GRINNAN

Digging Deeper: ROM 5:2–5, 12:12

Thu 13

When my soul fainted within me I remembered the Lord. . . .
—JONAH 2:7 (KJV)

I woke up with a shudder as a feeling of impending doom settled around me. The bad dream that had jolted me awake was receding, but it had clouded my usual optimism. Lying there in the dark, I was an easy target for the demons of worry and pessimism and hopelessness.

My mother is getting older . . . what will life be like without her? How much longer can I manage to raise all the money we need for Zimbabwe? Our house needs so many repairs we can't afford. What if something bad happens to my children? What if I end up alone without David or too sick or too poor to care for myself? What if . . . ? The longer I lay there, the worse the what-ifs became.

There was only one thing left to do, which I knew from experience could save me. I slipped out of bed and tiptoed out of the room, so I wouldn't wake my husband. I walked through the dark house and peered out the living room window. Ah, there it was. The moon. The night was chilly as I stepped out onto the deck, but the air made me feel real. I looked up at the sky and began to talk to God.

"Okay, I had a bad dream and I'm afraid. So many awful things can happen, things that I don't know how to handle. Are You here, God?" I waited. The moonlight shimmered through the trees. I kept waiting. A breeze, ever so slight, brushed against my face. I caught sight of one star and then another.

All is well, God seemed to say.

I enjoyed the night for a few minutes more and then went back inside and snuggled into the warm bed. "All is well," I whispered to the now familiar darkness. And I closed my eyes and went to sleep.

Father, even in the darkest night, let me remember You.
—PAM KIDD

Digging Deeper: LK 17:5; EPH 2:8–9

Fri 14

And now, behold, we are in thine hand. . . .
—Joshua 9:25 (KJV)

"Take your time, ma'am," the EMT urged. "No need to rush. She's in good hands." And even though my ninety-three-year-old mother writhed in pain on the gurney, straining the straps as he rolled her toward the flashing red lights of the ambulance, I knew he was right.

After more than a dozen wee-hour episodes like this, I also knew the routine: Call my brother, dress, find my purse and keys, and grab my knitting. I had arrived from Europe the day before, so I was groggy from jet lag, and my hope was at low ebb.

Hadn't my friends thought I was crazy to cut my sabbatical short and leave France a month early? Yesterday, Mom glowed with frail health and happiness. Now, a few hours later, she was deathly ill.

In the emergency room, Mom woke from her medication-induced peace, blinked, and clutched one of my hands. For several hours, all I could do was balance on a stool and hold that dearly familiar hand, now so thin her diamond ring hung upside down against her palm. Was this why I felt compelled to return home ahead of schedule? Just to hold Mom's hand? What divine hand guided *me*? Mom had lived alone for ten years, yet tonight she hadn't remembered to push her Medic Alert button to call the ambulance. I had done that.

Instead of knitting tonight, I hold Mom's hand—and God holds me just as firmly.

Lord, You hold me gently, securely, in Your almighty palm. I have no fear.
—Gail Thorell Schilling

Digging Deeper: Is 49:16; Jn 10:27–30

Sat 15

Outdo one another in showing honor.
—Romans 12:10 (ESV)

When our son Chris was scheduled to return home from a fifteen-month deployment to Iraq, only our immediate family was able to travel to North Carolina to welcome him, so we decided to record video greetings from people back home. When I was recording a neighbor, she mentioned that a group was carrying on a tradition at Chris's old high school that he and his buddies had started. I remembered the autumn night seven years earlier when my husband, Gordon, and I were at a football game and we saw a group of shirtless guys, painted totally red, who must have been freezing to death. When they broke out onto the field after a touchdown to run a victory lap, carrying a flag, we realized that one of the guys was our son!

Today, the group was an official high school pep squad called the Bravehearts. I told my neighbor, "It would mean so much if they'd let me record a greeting for him."

My neighbor told me to come by the school when the Bravehearts would be painted up in their "uniforms." I met them in a gym hallway, and they enthusiastically hammed up a greeting to Chris for the camera. At the pep rally, the announcer boomed, "Let's give a cheer for alumnus Chris Barber who's returning from Iraq!" I was totally blown away when the gymnasium erupted in loud cheers and applause. To think they were honoring our son who had once painted himself red! Not only had he accomplished something good for our country, but he was recognized for it by thousands of students who didn't even know him.

Father, help me honor the many unsung heroes and helpers in my life who serve with little recognition. Amen.

—Karen Barber

Digging Deeper: Rom 13:1; 1 Cor 10:31; 1 Pt 4:10

Sun 16

Now there are varieties of gifts, but the same Spirit; and there are varieties of service, but the same Lord.
— 1 CORINTHIANS 12:4–5 (RSV)

That Sunday morning, I could have used some healing. For weeks I'd been fighting an infection. Not that I was terribly sick, but I was weary of trips to the doctor's office with no specific answer. That day, sitting in the choir loft during worship, I looked over and saw my friend Roberta.

Roberta is a healer, both professionally and spiritually. She's an RN with an advanced degree. Yet she also has spiritual gifts, and I've known her to pray for people who need healing. It seemed a lot to ask, and I didn't quite know how to bring it up. She'd probably need to rush off after church . . . and besides, what would she actually say?

The choir room was clearing out at the end of the service. Our fellow choristers had put away their robes; kids had gone off to Sunday school; people were trooping downstairs to coffee hour. "Roberta," I said, "I've had this infection for a while . . . "

"Shall I pray for you?" she asked.

We found a quiet corner in the back of the hall and talked. Then we closed our eyes, and she prayed for my healing. I prayed too—for myself and for Roberta—that her daughter would find her way in life.

"Amen," she said. I opened my eyes. I didn't know about the mysterious infection, but I certainly felt better. A little less inclined to obsess about it, a little more hopeful that it would finally go away.

"I hope you feel better," I told her.

"I always do," she said. "That's one of the things that comes with healing. I get more back than I could possibly give."

I had been hesitant to ask, but what a gift she had shared.

Lord, may I never be too timid to share my gifts or ask people to share theirs. —RICK HAMLIN

Digging Deeper: 1 COR 12

November

Mon 17

And I will say to them which were not my people, Thou art my people. . . . —Hosea 2:23 (KJV)

Many of my favorite foods are dishes that I first found revolting. My first taste of pizza made me gag. Now I crave it. When I took my first sip of coffee, I felt I had been poisoned. Now it's ambrosia. I puckered up at my first cranberries. Now my wife makes a cranberry-orange relish that is the first dish to run out at Thanksgiving.

First impressions are often faulty. The first pizza I tasted was made from a box, with "cardboard" dough and powdered cheese. *Ugh.* The first coffee I sipped was loaded with cream and sugar. Give me black! My first cranberries were from a can, unsweetened. Add some chopped oranges and a little bit of sugar, and it's a treat!

What is true of food is often true of people. First impressions can be oh-so-wrong.

"Remember that student you couldn't stand at first," my wife reminds me. "That country girl from the Ozarks?"

"Oh yes, how can I forget her? She turned out to be a dream student and a great friend."

I'm glad when people don't judge me by first impressions. I'm quiet and sometimes come across as aloof or disinterested. Without the patience of others, I might be a very lonely man.

I need to give other people the same chance. Maybe they just need a bit of sugar to bring out the goodness in them: a little bit of praise, a little bit of attention, a little bit of time spent getting to know them better. They may never become my favorites, but at least we can be friends.

Help me to be more like You, God—ready to claim everyone as my kind of people.

—Daniel Schantz

Digging Deeper: Rom 15:7; Jas 2:8

Tue 18

"Greater love has no one than this: to lay down one's life for one's friends."—John 15:13 (NIV)

My father was a soldier who fought in World War II. He survived, but many of his friends did not. The "greater love" of Christ was more than just a concept to my father; it was part of his daily life for more than two years.

Ten years after the war, Dad taught me to play baseball, but my friends and I preferred playing army. We killed one another with imaginary guns and then went home and ate supper. Can you learn anything about ultimate sacrifice or the price of liberty by playing army? I don't think so. Fortunately, the young people in our lives can teach us about our parents' sacrifices long after they are gone.

Antony, who is an exchange student from Taiwan, stayed with friends of mine for a year. He was so intrigued by American freedom that he decided to return the next year. Antony enrolled in the local college's semester abroad program this spring and is studying in France. He sent a postcard to my friends of the thousands of white crosses at the Cimetière Américain overlooking Omaha Beach. On the other side Antony wrote, "You won't actually understand the real meaning of liberty and how pricey it is until you stand in front of this cemetery."

I suspect Antony, like my father, has gained a deeper understanding of the greater love of Christ.

Dear God, thank You for people who teach us to fully appreciate what Your Son did for us.
—Tim Williams

Digging Deeper: Lk 22:42; Jn 3:16

Wed 19

I remember my affliction and my wandering. . . . I well remember them, and my soul is downcast within me.
—LAMENTATIONS 3:19–20 (NIV)

Today, I'm plowing through the stack of books perched on my desk, searching for kernels to inform a new project I've just accepted. I pick one up, *Story: Recapture the Mystery* by Steven James, and find these words: *God loves stories. He loves the people whose stories are being told moment by moment across the globe. And I'm amazed that the story of my choices, mistakes, regrets—the story of my life—actually matters to God.*

Choices, mistakes, regrets—these are the three words that get me, that thrust me back in time. The banner that flew high over my life years ago quite aptly featured those words. I said too much, drank too much, promoted myself too much, pushed nearly every limit I could find. I loved God but refused His input, intent on my will, my wants, my way.

In the book of Lamentations, the prophet Jeremiah mourns the destruction of his beloved city Jerusalem, which had been handpicked by God but then insisted on going its own way. He recounts Jerusalem's demise, saying, "I remember my affliction and my wandering, the bitterness and the gall . . . and my soul is downcast within me." But then he offers these words: "Yet this I call to mind and therefore I have hope: Because of the Lord's great love we are not consumed, for his compassions never fail. They are new every morning; great is your faithfulness" (Lamentations 3:19–23).

I read these words with grateful eyes. My afflictions were painful, my wandering near-fatal and, yes, "downcast" described my soul. But because of the Lord's great love for me, by His grace, I was not consumed.

Father, please let every hard remembrance of where I've been and what I've done serve only to point me toward You.
—ASHLEY WIERSMA

Digging Deeper: LAM 3

Thu 20

"Your words were found, and I ate them, And Your word was to me the joy and rejoicing of my heart; For I am called by Your name, O Lord God of hosts."
—JEREMIAH 15:16 (NKJV)

Jon, a young man excited about his newfound faith, approached me with a major frustration. He had a consistent devotional life, but his Bible reading felt cold. He said he forgot what he was reading as fast as he read it. He knew what book of the Bible he was in, but to repeat the content or even the main idea was a hopeless task. Tempted to throw in the towel, he decided to talk it over with me first.

I had been in his shoes and experienced the same frustration. I remembered back to the tiny Chicago church that reared me. One of the sweetest women I knew, Aunt Izzy, had a warm heart for the motley assortment of kids who ran around the church.

"Aunt Izzy," I said, "I don't see what good it's doing me to read the Bible. I can't remember anything I read."

Aunt Izzy's eyes sparkled as she gave a knowing nod. "Bill, tell me what you ate for dinner the last few days."

I thought hard but could only remember yesterday's dinner. "Last night, pork chops," I said. "I don't remember much before that."

"Does that mean those meals did you no good?"

I shook my head.

"So it is with God's Word. It's like a feast. You just keep on digging in." Aunt Izzy smiled. "Don't worry about what you forget. Be faithful, and you'll have all the spiritual muscle you need before you know it."

I put my hand on Jon's shoulder and smiled. "Jon, tell me what you ate for dinner the last few days . . . "

Lord, let Your Word be to me as daily bread and strengthen me by it as You fill my heart with truth.
—BILL GIOVANNETTI

Digging Deeper: MT 4:4; JN 6:25–58

November

Fri 21

"Anyone who loves their life will lose it, while anyone who hates their life in this world will keep it for eternal life."
—JOHN 12:25 (NIV)

I've long searched for a great home. Once, I thought the Brooklyn apartment that I moved into two years ago would be it. But the real estate listing never said anything about the kids downstairs who ran laps around their apartment so enthusiastically that the silverware would rattle on my dining table.

Nor did it mention the woman across the street who, when my car was broken down one day, yelled at me for being in everyone's way.

When, I thought, *am I ever going to find a place that feels like home?*

Really, the feeling wasn't much different from what I felt at high school dances (I was a wallflower) and what I feel at work-related cocktail parties (I'm still a wallflower). It's a sense that I just don't fit in, that I'm not at home.

Then I remembered some counsel that a wise friend gave me during college. "Jeff, I think you'll never feel quite at home," she said. "But you shouldn't."

What? I thought. *Is this some cruel joke?* But, actually, it was a profound spiritual lesson. My friend was reminding me that I should be focused less on the comforts of four walls and furniture and more on this truth: A home on this earth is just temporary. It's the home that money can't buy that I ought to be looking for.

Lord, help me to remember that my true home is wherever You are.
—JEFF CHU

Digging Deeper: 1 COR 2:7–9; 2 COR 5:8; PHIL 3:20–21

Sat 22

Be of good cheer; I have overcome the world.
—John 16:33 (KJV)

The sun was setting as I drove through one of the poorest areas in Nashville, Tennessee. I saw a child sitting alone on a dirty porch, just staring ahead. "God, Thanksgiving's coming. Where's the hope?" I was startled to hear myself say out loud.

Within minutes I arrived at the Martha O'Bryan Center, the oldest intercity mission. I had committed to chairing the board, and I was doing my best to keep up with the unrelenting needs of the people we were serving. "God," I breathed in, "am I a fool to think I can change the world?"

I found the center's director, Marsha, in her office.

"Have I got a story for you, Brock," she said without a pause. "Yesterday we had our annual turkey sharing, distributing over three hundred turkeys to the community. This morning these two boys show up, asking if there are any leftovers. I had remembered seeing them, their smiles wide as they set off for home with their bag. 'Now, boys,' I began.

"'We know, Miss Marsha, we already got a turkey. And it's all right.' The older boy grabbed his brother's hand and lowered his head to go.

"Then the younger brother spoke up, 'We couldn't help it, Miss Marsha. Poor old Mrs. Thompson next door was too sick to come get a turkey, so me and my brother decided to give her ours.'

"'Momma said she was real proud of us, but we could tell she was sad,' the older brother added. 'So we was just seeing if there was any more.'"

A huge lump was forming in my throat as I waited for Marsha to finish. "Don't worry, Brock." She laughed, sensing my distress and pointing heavenward. "We found the boys another turkey!"

I smiled then, breathing a prayer of renewed hope for all humankind.

One turkey at a time, God. That's how we overcome the world!
Just one turkey at a time! —Brock Kidd

Digging Deeper: Mk 5:35–36; Heb 11:1

Sun 23

The Lord is nigh unto all them that call upon him, to all that call upon him in truth. —Psalm 145:18 (KJV)

My place of worship is sometimes the front seat of the ranch pickup. Sometimes it's my kitchen table. It can be a mossy boulder of basalt lava, shaded by a sweet-smelling ponderosa pine tree. Or it can be on a stack of baled hay in the barn with an unseen batch of kittens mewing somewhere nearby. Here, it's easy to sit right next to God.

As a child, my family and I were members of a small Lutheran church. I miss it now that I've made my way as a rancher. It is a downside to living so far from town and working seven days a week. I miss the old hymns sung off-key. I miss Pastor Bob and his broad smile of genuine welcome. I miss the potlucks with the inevitable *lutefisk* and the Scandinavian dishes. I miss catechism class, all three of us.

Although I sincerely long for the companionship and fellowship of a church congregation, every day can be Sunday if I work it right. God is everywhere . . . all I have to do is look.

Dear Lord, give me comfort when I miss Your people.
My heart belongs to You, and that's the important part.
—Erika Bentsen

Digging Deeper: Pss 5:7, 99:5; Eph 5:19–20

Mon 24

The words of a gossip are like choice morsels; they go down to a man's inmost parts. —Proverbs 18:8 (NIV)

Work had been horrendous. Today my phone wouldn't work; other days it was the Internet or computer. I was in commission-only sales, so it was affecting my paycheck.

I'd tried to explain to tech support. They didn't have any solutions, so I carried my complaints up the corporate ladder. When nothing got done, I resorted to "blowing off steam" with other employees.

Once home, I grabbed a couple of pickles—comfort food for me—and headed out to feed Dazzle, my black mare. Her nostrils flared, and she licked her lips. "What's that about?" Her eyes locked on my pickle, and she batted her long lashes. I shook my head and pulled away the pickle. "Pickles aren't good for horses." She craned her neck. I giggled. "Okay, but you won't like it."

I pinched off a small piece and set it on the palm of my hand. Quickly, Dazzle snatched it. She squinted. Her eyes watered; then she spit it out. I broke out laughing. "See, I told you it wasn't good for you."

At that moment I heard, *And gossip isn't good for you.* I took a deep breath. My blowing off steam had blossomed into nonproductive talk that only served to rehash problems. Instead of feeling better from venting, I was becoming embittered.

I had a choice to make: Either get another job or make the best of it where I was.

Lord, when I'm tempted to gossip, please convict me.
—Rebecca Ondov

Digging Deeper: Prv 21:23; Jas 3:5–12

November

Tue 25

God saw everything that He had made, and indeed it was very good. . . . —GENESIS 1:31 (NKJV)

I've dreamed for years of writing books for children. This book, my first, seemed like a daily rebuke to that dream. I couldn't get it right, no matter how hard I tried. Now the workday was over, the kids were in bed, the dishes done. I saw the computer on my desk. I knew I should go back at it.

Instead, I walked outside to the driveway. Deep twilight. The Santa Cruz Mountains, normally visible to the west, were smothered in a blanket of fog. The fog piled up against the peaks, reaching for the sky and sending pearly rivulets down ravines.

A little to the north, the fog trailed into streamers silhouetted against the last of the sunset. Bands of yellow and orange hugged the horizon, backlighting the trees on our block. Birds sang. The air filled with that strange, heavy luminescence that always precedes the moment just before dark.

I had spent all day laboring to find a few perfect words, and here was God throwing off a composition of stunning beauty like an afterthought. His art was impermanent, meant to be given away.

"Am I trying too hard, God?" I asked. Maybe that's the problem with perfectionism. Not once during my frustrating workday had I offered the work to God.

I waited until the last of the light was gone and then went back inside. Tomorrow, I vowed, would be different. I would start the workday with prayer. I would let God be the artist.

All that I do, make it Yours, Lord.
—JIM HINCH

Digging Deeper: PRV 16:3; COL 3:23

Wed 26 *O give thanks to the Lord. . . .* —Psalm 105:1 (RSV)

I have always felt it is my mission in life to get people to say thank you when they are complimented. It seems demeaning to the compliment-giver to hear that the pretty blouse you admired cost $1.98 at Goodwill or demeaning to God that another person hates the freckles that He put there and that you think are adorable. I speak my piece when the opportunity occurs though I always wonder if my message gets across.

So I was surprised one day at a coffee shop I rarely go to, when the girl behind the counter said, "I have to thank you so much for something you did for me!"

"Me?" I looked around the counter to see who she was talking to.

She nodded, shaking her red curls vigorously. "Yes, you said you like my auburn hair color and—"

It was coming back to me, so I replied, "And you said, 'It's really dirty today. I have to wash it.' Then you pointed out a speck of hot chocolate on it, which nobody would have noticed without a magnifying glass."

"Yes, and you forced me to just say thank you. You said that if someone says something nice and you shrug it off, it's almost like disparaging God's handiwork." She poured my coffee. "You know, I've thought about that a dozen times and even passed it along to a lady at church. I even prayed that you'd come back so that I could thank you, and here you are!"

"Well, it's not a unique idea," I said. "I'm sure others have said it better than I could." Then I saw the look on her face and said—what else but—"Thank you."

Dear God, thank You.
—Linda Neukrug

Digging Deeper: Pss 69:30, 95:2

November

Thu 27

Give thanks in all circumstances....
—1 THESSALONIANS 5:18 (NIV)

For years, our family has gathered at my brother's house for Thanksgiving. Dexter and his wife, Billie, live in a large home in the country that easily absorbs three generations. "The more the merrier," Billie assures us when we ask if we can bring others to share in the celebration.

This year Billie's dad is gravely ill, Dexter and Billie are stretched at their businesses, and Billie is facing the prospect of a hip replacement. I proposed that we remove the Thanksgiving responsibility from them, but they wouldn't hear of it. "More than ever, we need the tradition," Billie said.

Through a flurry of e-mails among siblings and cousins, we've come up with ways to simplify the celebration. We're bringing all the plates, napkins, and flowers; each family is contributing a decorative candle for the table; and we'll set the tables when we arrive, with the help of seventeen grandchildren.

When the feast is ready, we'll circle the buffet to bless the food, fill our plates, and find our places around the table. Then Dexter will stand and begin what I call our "popcorn praises." He'll describe something he's thankful for and then name someone to stand next and do the same. Randomly, we'll all have our chance; most of our popcorn praises grow out of the challenges each of us has faced. Those shared thanks fill our hungry souls, and more than ever, we all need that tradition this year.

Lord, the tradition of giving thanks together brings us closer to You and to one another.
—CAROL KUYKENDALL

Digging Deeper: 1 CHR 29:13; PS 100

LIFE LESSONS FROM THOSE I'VE MET

Fri 28 *My cup overflows.* —PSALM 23:5 (RSV)

MOLLY SHELLEY, A JOYFUL MOM

I had misgivings as I drove to Millersville, Pennsylvania.

A *Guideposts* reader had written that someone should interview a "remarkable woman" who at forty-three, with six young children, was dying of cancer. Doubtless, Molly Shelley was faith-filled and brave, as the letter said, but I knew I'd drive away, as always when confronted with untimely death, feeling more grief than inspiration.

I was hailed from the side door of a house with baseball bats and bicycles in the driveway by a far-too-thin woman.

Soon I had my shoes off to enjoy with her "the way the carpet tickles." We counted the shades of green in her yard, smelled the sun-dried clothes we pulled from the line. Her children drifted in from school one by one and joined us in an impromptu game of who-can-hear-the-most-sounds.

When I marveled at the high spirits of children who knew their mother was dying, Molly said, "That's because I'm passing on to them what I learned only after getting sick. I used to thank God just for the big things. Life. Health. Family." Her thank-you list was short "because there aren't that many big things in an ordinary life." It was in the forced inactivity following surgery that God began to show her Himself in the sound of her husband's voice, the warmth of a blanket, the dust motes in a beam of light.

"Why, it will take an eternity to thank Him for all His gifts! And I'll soon be seeing ones, I tell the children, that we can't even imagine now."

As I drove home, I rolled down the window to feel the evening air on my face.

Father, thank You for the inummerable small gifts You lavish on me!

—ELIZABETH SHERRILL

Digging Deeper: 2 SM 22:47; 1 THES 5:16–18; JAS 1:1–17

November

Sat 29

I pray that the God of our Lord Jesus Christ, the Father of glory, may give you a spirit of wisdom and revelation . . . so that, with the eyes of your heart enlightened, you may know what is the hope to which he has called you . . . .
—EPHESIANS 1:17–18 (NRSV)

My daughter Annie and I were at a basketball game when one of the players crumpled to the floor. As the trainers leaped to his aid, a hush fell over the fans. No one around us was speaking.

Except my daughter. In whispered tones, she began describing what the trainers were doing and why. "See the way they're manipulating his leg? That's how you test for a torn anterior cruciate ligament." A slightly different movement: "Now they're testing the MCL. That's the medial collateral ligament."

Annie is an athletic-training major in college, so the details she relayed weren't a surprise. What I noticed more was how her eyes seemed to dance as she did it. She smiled and said simply, "Dad, it's not about just knowing the facts. I have to know how to apply what I know, so I can make a difference for someone."

I've applied that same principle to my faith. It's not enough just to know the words, but I also have to know how to apply them . . . because it can make a difference. Remembering that makes my devotional study more than just about understanding the words. Every day I'm now also asking, *How might I use these words to make this world a better place?* And when I ask that question, my eyes sparkle a bit too!

Give me a new insight, God, into how Your Word might affect my life —and those around me—with the hope You provide.
—JEFF JAPINGA

Digging Deeper: MK 16:15; 2 COR 1:3–7

GIFTS OF MERCY

Sun 30

"To you is born this day in the city of David a Savior, who is the Messiah, the Lord." —LUKE 2:11 (NRSV)

FIRST SUNDAY IN ADVENT: LOVE, GOD'S CHRISTMAS COUPON

I was cleaning out drawers in advance of my daughters' Christmas fly-in from college and came across several homemade coupon books Lulu had given me when she was younger. Each set was handcrafted—one with shiny hearts, another speckled with stars—and her handwriting evolved with the years.

Initially, they were generous: helping me in the garden or setting the table twenty-five times, being nice fifteen times, leaving me alone twelve times. "This card is good for making me ____________," one read. She promised love-feats beyond her talents even today, as a college student: cooking five dinners, for example. Or being nice.

Redeeming the coupons that first year proved burdensome, so the next year she promised less: letting me brush her hair two times, for example. Still, she worried I might overuse the coupons or use one after she'd forgotten her promises. So she set strict expiration dates and issued me a stamp and stamp pad for keeping track.

I never thought to use any except when she was mad at me and thus unlikely to make good on old promises. And really, all I've ever wanted from her is just what God wants from us: love.

One coupon I especially cherish promises just that: "Good for being loved on. No limits! Never expires!"

That's God's Christmas coupon every year.

Father God, thank You for Your merciful love that ignores our faults and promises us delights beyond what we can imagine.

—PATTY KIRK

Digging Deeper: EPH 2:4–9

DAILY MERCIES

1 __________

2 __________

3 __________

4 __________

5 __________

6 __________

7 __________

8 __________

9 __________

10 __________

11 __________

12 __________

13 __________

14 __________

15 __________

16 __________

17 __________

18 __________

19 __________

20 __________

21 __________

22 __________

23 __________

24 __________

25 __________

26 __________

27 __________

28 __________

29 __________

30 __________

DECEMBER

May grace, mercy, and peace be with you in truth and love, from God our Creator and from Jesus Christ, God's Only Begotten.

—2 JOHN 1:3 (TIB)

Mon 1

When you lie down, you will not be afraid; when you lie down, your sleep will be sweet. —Proverbs 3:24 (NIV)

Even before I decided I wanted to be a lawyer, I fell in love with Yale Law School, which is famous for essentially having no grades, a supportive, collegial atmosphere, and letting students follow their own paths. It's no wonder some of the more remarkable graduates work on international human rights or even become president. Yale was truly my dream school.

So you can imagine what a marvelous early Christmas present it was when I got the call from the Yale admissions office offering me a place in the class. But since I'm crazy sometimes and can't just accept the wonder of the life God gave me, my happiness didn't last long. Soon after, another law school offered me a full-tuition scholarship. I'd have to take out many times more money in loans to attend Yale.

Yes, it was a significant and difficult decision to make, but I turned it into an excuse to worry. I talked about it with my fiancée, Emily, and my parents. I woke up nights in a cold sweat, imagining all the money I would lose if I followed my heart and went to Yale.

As I went through the conversation one more time with Emily, she said, "Don't be afraid. You can't go wrong."

Yes, life was incredibly good and there was no wrong choice.

Thank You, my Lord, for this wonderful life and
the wisdom to appreciate it.
—Sam Adriance

Digging Deeper: Ps 51:6; Prv 2:6; Jas 1:5

Tue 2

Praise him, sun and moon; praise him, all you shining stars.
—PSALM 148:3 (NIV)

A portion of my faith comes from looking at the night sky. After a dazzling day, a colorful sunset can be glorious, unpredictable, and brief. However, there is nothing brief about the nightly glories of a desert sky.

For instance, when the new moon hovers near Venus, their dual reflected luminosity is not usually hidden behind clouds. The conspicuous cycle of Venus, called its synodic period, lasts nineteen months. During this time, Venus is the evening star for nine months. The new moon and Venus will flirt in proximity somewhere above the western horizon once every month. The two crescents slowly set together but not until savored minutes have stretched into hours.

Did Sarah stare at a sliver of silver in the west for nine months and know that the God Who placed such a lamp also could place a baby in the womb of an old woman? Did Mary see the light of Venus, brighter than any other star, and hang her faith on the new moon next to it? Couldn't she indeed carry the Light of the World within her because the Creator of life also created the two bright lights hovering over her? Did her faith increase, as mine does today, from seeing a cycle of light that lasts from conception to birth? The same cycle, then as now, for Sarah, for Mary, for me.

Dear God, may we always draw comfort from
Your cycles of light in the night.
—TIM WILLIAMS

Digging Deeper: HEB 13:8; JAS 1:17

Wed 3

We live by faith, not by sight. —2 CORINTHIANS 5:7 (NIV)

I'm an overly cautious person. Unfortunately, that's not a good trait when you're trying to start a new ministry. My journal is crammed with my struggles to take the risks that go along with start-ups. One day I wrote to myself, "I need to pray often because I am always one doubt away from failing to act."

A few days later, the word *faith* popped into my mind during my morning prayer walk. Since I sorely needed faith, I decided to try an experiment. I closed my eyes and attempted to continue walking at my normal pace.

What if I get off the sidewalk and into the road? I worried. One, two, three blind steps. I suddenly knew how Peter felt walking on water. *You're okay for exactly three steps, then you absolutely have to look!*

I didn't open my eyes all the way—just squinted for a second, taking a small peek to make sure I was still on the sidewalk. One, two, three more blind steps and then I had to peek. No matter how much I challenged myself, I couldn't overcome the compulsion to take a small, reassuring peek after three steps.

The Bible says we should walk by faith, not by sight. Easier said than done! Fortunately, if you're a little on the cautious side like me, God knows you'll need to peek sometimes too.

Father, I'm a little afraid to take these steps today. Help me to not waste my time or Yours trying to see every angle before I get going. Amen.

—KAREN BARBER

Digging Deeper: EPH 2:8–9; HEB 11:6

December

Thu 4

While they were there, the time came for the baby to be born, and she gave birth to her firstborn, a son. She wrapped him in cloths and placed him in a manger, because there was no guest room for them. —LUKE 2:6–7 (NIV)

On a cold and rainy day before Christmas, I found myself in a crowded shopping mall filled with last-minute holiday shoppers. I was juggling a heavy coat, an umbrella, and three shopping bags packed with gifts when my purse slipped off my shoulder. My wallet tumbled out, and loose change spilled everywhere. Shoppers ignored my plight and gingerly navigated around me, not bothering to stop.

I knelt down quickly and tried to gather up as much as I could, when a pink knit-gloved hand reached out and put a hand over mine. "Here, honey," I heard someone say, "let me help. Looks like your hands are pretty full already." I looked up to see a gray-haired woman with a matching pink knit cap smiling down on me.

"Thank you so much," I said. "It's really nice of you to help."

"My pleasure," she replied. "I learned a long time ago never to miss an opportunity to do good—especially around this time of year.

"You know that innkeeper that gave Joseph and Mary a stable because there was no room at the inn?" she asked.

"Why, sure," I said. "That was so kind of him."

"Indeed, it was," she said. "But Mary was about to give birth! Why, if no rooms were available at the inn, then what about a room in his own home?" She shook her head gently, stood up to leave, and exclaimed, "Why, he could have hosted the newborn King!"

May I never miss an opportunity to glorify You, Lord.
—MELODY BONNETTE SWANG

Digging Deeper: PS 86:12; LK 2:1–7

Fri 5 *Prepare ye the way of the Lord....* —MARK 1:3 (KJV)

Christmas was coming, but I wasn't feeling it. It was way too early for carols to be pouring out of hidden speakers everywhere: "Away in a manager, no crib for a bed . . . " "Round yon virgin, mother and child . . . ." When I heard Perry Como croon, "Do you hear what I hear?" I felt like snapping, "No, I don't!" Wreaths with bright red bows, evergreens festooned with twinkling lights, jolly department store Santas did nothing for me. Was I turning into some sort of Scrooge?

"You haven't even set candles in the windows," my wife, Carol, said.

I sighed. One more thing to do. Soon the boys would be home from college, and if I didn't get to work, nothing about the house would say, "Christmas is coming! Welcome home!" I found the box with plastic candles at the top of the hall closet. I gathered up extension cords and went outside to clip some evergreens.

"Act as if," Norman Vincent Peale used to say. If you didn't feel positive, if your faith was flagging, act *as if* you believed and belief followed. Okay, I would act as if I was thrilled with Christmas coming. I found an old CD of carols and put it on.

I untangled the cords, tested the bulbs, positioned three candles in the three windows facing the drive in our apartment complex, and put greens around them. I started humming along with the music: "O, little town of Bethlehem . . . " I waved to a neighbor walking by, laden with shopping bags.

I plugged in the lights, then went outside to admire my handiwork. "Come," the candles seemed to say. "Come, Lord, come," my spirit could say. If welcoming God was at the heart of this hectic, crazy, overstuffed season, I was ready. "As if" was turning to "As is."

I went back inside. I had some presents to wrap.

Let me prepare in my heart, Lord, as I prepare my home,
a place for Your coming. —RICK HAMLIN

Digging Deeper: Ps 19:14; Rv 3:20

LIFE LESSONS FROM THOSE I'VE MET

Sat 6 *Father, forgive them; for they know not what they do....*
—LUKE 23:34 (KJV)

MITSUO FUCHIDA, JAPANESE COMMANDER

I flew to Japan in 1974 to meet a man I'd hated for thirty years—the commander who led the infamous attack on Pearl Harbor.

Mitsuo Fuchida, a small, erect man of seventy-two, met me at my hotel in Kyoto. As a translator repeated his words, I saw a boy dreaming of serving his divine emperor by driving Western colonial powers out of Asia. "When we lost the war, most of my officers committed suicide. But I had a wife and children." He moved them to a farm where, as he worked the fields, news of the war crimes trials in Tokyo came over the radio. "It was then I learned about atrocities in our prisoner-of-war camps." In his eyes, I read the horror and disillusionment of this patriotic man.

It was in a train station that someone handed him a leaflet written by an American ex-prisoner of war. "But... the American wrote that he loved us! The Japanese who'd tortured him!" This was because, the leaflet said, Jesus did.

Fuchida recognized that name: Jesus was one of the gods of the enemy. Fuchida purchased a Bible and, alone in the farmhouse, discovered there were not many gods but One, Who loved all people; Who came to earth not as an emperor but a common workingman; Who said as he was tortured and killed, "Father, forgive them, for they know not what they do."

"Why then... this Jesus had prayed for me too!" Tears trembled in his eyes as he said this. By now I was fighting tears too.

To his countrymen, conversion made him a traitor; he and his wife still received death threats. "We do not care. It is better to die and be with Jesus."

Father, forgive my unforgivingness. —ELIZABETH SHERRILL

Digging Deeper: PRV 17:9; MT 6:14–15, 18:21–22

GIFTS OF MERCY

Sun 7 *There remains, then, a Sabbath-rest for the people of God.*
—HEBREWS 4:9 (NIV)

SECOND SUNDAY IN ADVENT: JESUS, OUR SABBATH REST

One of our family's Christmas traditions is napping. Having gotten up uncommonly early to open presents, then eat Mamaw's country breakfast—eggs scrambled with ham, biscuits and gravy, fried potatoes—we all retreat, sluggish and cranky, to our rooms.

First, though, my husband, Kris, gathers up the trash and I sort out the good boxes for next Christmas.

This year one box's top was missing, so I went upstairs to look in the girls' rooms. As soon as I opened Charlotte's door, I realized my mistake.

"What?" she asked, jerking awake.

I might have escaped her wrath even then had I not spied the box lid, holding trinkets from her stocking. As I reached for it, she surged up from the covers. "You came in, when I was sleeping, to get a box lid?"

I slunk out.

After cleaning up from breakfast, I lay down, fretting about Charlotte's fury, replaying it in my head and chiding myself for my thoughtlessness. I prayed she'd sleep it off and not, in the way of teenagers, emerge from her room later, surly and silent. Before I knew it, though, I, too, was asleep.

Later, Charlotte hugged me, her momentary outrage transformed by the great panacea of sleep into a fond story to retell next Christmas.

Sleep, our best Christmas present, transforms us.

Baby Jesus, our Sabbath rest, on this day You slept. Thank You for coming to us and healing us with Your presence, with Your offers of rest.
—PATTY KIRK

Digging Deeper: MT 11:28–30

December

Mon 8

"The people are to go out each day and gather enough for that day. . . ."—Exodus 16:4 (NIV)

I'm looking at high schools for Mary, middle schools for Maggie, and elementary schools for Stephen. In New York City, it's not easy. I plod through the maze of tours and applications and deadlines. We come up with lists, do research online, visit schools, revise plans.

I keep up a decent outer demeanor, but I *so* don't want to do this. I don't want to stop homeschooling, don't think this approach is what's best for my two youngest, don't know what kind of job I'm going to get once they're in school. My desires aren't the main factor here; finances are. So I keep going, until one night I am overwhelmed by the enormity of it all.

I crumple and send up a weary plea: "Lord, show me where You want my kids to go. Show me the job You want me to have." I yearn for the big picture, clarity, faster answers, certainty.

God's reply comes gently: *I have given you something to do. It's right in front of you.* Startled, I look at the next item on my to-do list. I nod, remembering that manna came in small portions. Sometimes the grace to do big things, hard things, comes in just-what-we-can-swallow increments.

Father, grant me the patience to live one day at a time.

—Julia Attaway

Digging Deeper: Eph 2:4–9; 1 Pt 5:10

Tue 9

"And now, when shall I also provide for my own house?"
—GENESIS 30:30 (NKJV)

I saved for retirement from the time I was in my twenties, and as my husband, Keith, neared the end of his career, I felt confident that we had a good nest egg. Then the economy crashed, our savings dropped more than 60 percent, a consulting gig fell away, and the publisher of my new book declared bankruptcy.

Because I've always had fears of penury, I started counting every cent, which drove Keith crazy. "We're not starving," he said. "Relax. Things will turn around."

"I don't see how," I replied.

"Have a little faith," he told me. We would find a way.

Somehow, we did—and continue to.

Help me learn to be like my husband, Lord. He understands Your ways so much more completely than I do.
—RHODA BLECKER

Digging Deeper: PRV 9:10; IS 55:9

THE TRUE GIFTS OF CHRISTMAS

Wed 10 *It is the gift of God.* —Ecclesiastes 3:13 (KJV)

A MOMENT WITH MOTHER

I miss my mother . . . especially at Christmas. She's been dead for thirteen years. Sometimes I relive the things we did together. Mother served delectable ambrosia. I haven't had any since she made it. Not a lot of people make it today. It's simple, but time-consuming. Grated coconut mixed with sections of oranges cut up, orange juice, and perhaps cherries. Mother traditionally served it in small flowered china dishes from the china cabinet. She loved to watch me take the first bite, even as an adult.

My neighbor Bea always bakes something for us at Christmas. She's a gourmet cook and a gracious lady.

This year, her husband, Wayne, came over with a large, white wicker basket filled with goodies. Beautiful handmade kitchen items, homemade Brunswick stew, candies, a miniature fruitcake, jams, and then, tah-dah—a nice-size Mason jar of ambrosia. The jar wore a jaunty Christmas hat. I gasped out loud. "Oh!" My joyful heart raced. I suddenly remembered my mother's Christmas apron, red pleated, tying in the back.

Carrying the precious jar of ambrosia, I went to that same china cabinet my mother first used as a bride in 1931. Carefully, I removed the exact same china bowl in which she'd served me ambrosia for all those years. With my dish filled to the brim, I sat close to the Christmas tree in a rocker from my mother's living room. Dusk was falling and the lights glowed softly. At last, I took that first wondrous bite and experienced Mother's Christmas smile and God's powerful love.

Thank You, Father, for giving me back Mother for a brief moment.
—Marion Bond West

Digging Deeper: 2 Cor 9:15; Jas 1:17

Thu 11

Always keep on praying. No matter what happens, always be thankful, for this is God's will for you who belong to Christ Jesus. —1 THESSALONIANS 5:17–18 (TLB)

I remember feeling waves of despair and depression four times in my life: when my mother died of ALS at age fifty-seven; when my husband left me for another woman; when my nephew Jacob was killed in a plane crash at age eighteen; and when Jack broke up with me.

Recently, my son Michael shared something he'd read about the despair, destruction, and depression that permeated our country after Pearl Harbor in 1941. Admiral Nimitz, after touring Pearl Harbor for the first time after the bombings, told the young helmsman on the tour boat that either the enemy had made three serious mistakes that day or God was protecting the United States in a big way.

First mistake: The attack was on a Sunday morning when nine out of every ten crewmen were ashore on leave. Any other day we would have lost 38,000 men instead of 3,800.

Second mistake: The attackers were so busy sinking our battleships that they forgot to bomb the dry docks. That allowed the American fleet to tow the sunken ships into dry dock and repair them right there, instead of towing them all the way to the mainland, which would have taken months, perhaps years.

Third mistake: Every drop of fuel was in storage tanks five miles away. One attack plane could have destroyed the entire supply, but the tanks were left intact.

When I look back at the tough times in my own life, I see that God got me through the gloom . . . just like He did for America seventy-three years ago. God is truly there orchestrating the aftermath of destruction that sometimes permeates our lives.

Father, Your solution is so simple, yet how many times have
I given in to despair? Nudge me to pray unceasingly.
—PATRICIA LORENZ

Digging Deeper: EPH 6:18

Fri 12

"[Nothing] shall be able to separate us from the love of God which is in Christ Jesus our Lord."—ROMANS 8:39 (NKJV)

I was born in December 1950. A few months prior, the Korean War erupted and young men throughout America were responding to draft boards while veterans of World War II reported for duty once again.

My mother was also having a difficult year. Doctors told her that she would not be able to have children. She grieved only to discover with delight that she was pregnant.

I have seldom been punctual, and my birth was no exception. My mother's labor was long but concluded with the birth of a healthy, red-headed boy. Mom lay back and slept until they brought her baby to be nursed. She looked at the boy in the nurse's arms, saw that he had thick black hair, and blurted, "This is not my child!" The young nurse laughed and said, "Yes, Mrs. Walker, this is your baby and he is hungry!" Mom shot back, "Well, look at the armband and read it to me." The exasperated nurse glanced at the identification band and read the name Wilson instead of Walker; she was mortified!

Years later, there were times when my mother wished she had kept that Wilson baby. And there have been moments when I have wondered what my life would be like if the mistake had not been discovered. However, I have come to understand that God has placed His clear identification band on each of us. We are all His children and nothing can separate us from the love of God.

Dear Father, in the midst of the chaos of life,
may I not forget Whose child I am. Amen.

—SCOTT WALKER

Digging Deeper: JN 1:12; 1 JN 3:1–2

THE TRUE GIFTS OF CHRISTMAS

Sat 13

He shall give thee the desires of thine heart.
—Psalm 37:4 (KJV)

SECOND CHANCES

One week before Christmas, my husband, Gene, and I sat in church. Our congregation is small; not many children. I missed them—especially little girls excited about Christmas. I hadn't been patient with my own two daughters in church so long ago: "Girls, stop talking. Sit up straight, Jennifer. Pull up your socks, Julie, and your sash is untied."

I'd do it differently if I had another chance, I thought as a new family came in and sat right behind us. Gene and I turned around to greet them.

"I'm Julia," the beautiful child told me, holding out her hand.

I took the dainty hand. "Hello, Julia. Welcome."

At the altar, praying with a friend, I imagined asking little Julia to sit with me. But she probably wouldn't want to. However, when I returned to my seat, Julia was sitting next to Gene, smiling. "May I sit with you?" she asked. I nodded, amazed. Her mother and I exchanged smiles.

As though we were old buddies, Julia leaned against me comfortably. I glanced down at her: shiny blonde hair; blue hair band; dark-blue velveteen dress; Mary Jane shoes with lace socks, carefully turned down. Her feet dangled far above the floor, and she swung them slightly. Julia caught me checking out her shoes and volunteered, "These are my new Christmas shoes. I got to wear them early."

Two unexpected, joyful tears plopped onto my Bible. I wiped them away quickly. When we stood for the first hymn, Julia slipped her hand into mine and we swung our hands slightly, back and forth.

"Away in a manger, no crib for His head . . . ," we sang.

What a Christmas Giver You are, Father! —Marion Bond West

Digging Deeper: Mt 19:14

GIFTS OF MERCY

Sun 14

We know that all things work together for good for those who love God, who are called according to his purpose.
—ROMANS 8:28 (NRSV)

THIRD SUNDAY IN ADVENT: GOOD RECLAIMED

When my grandmother died, her living space had shrunk to a bare kitchenette decorated with a few photos. She was ninety-five—a perky woman, well-loved at the school where she'd volunteered before osteoporosis crippled her. Teachers converged on her funeral. One, a young man who'd visited regularly, sobbed. I didn't attend—an act of neglect I still regret.

Here's my rationalization: People should visit the housebound while they're alive; after they die, it's too late.

But I rarely visited her. Rarely phoned. Rarely communicated beyond the Christmas cards I used to make. When my daughters got older and Christmas became more frantic, I stopped even that minimal contact.

After the funeral, my dad sent me the cards I'd mailed her from grad school in New Orleans; from Berlin, Beijing, Hong Kong; from Oklahoma, when my girls were little. When I saw them, I, too, cried.

My most vivid memory of her is that empty room. It looked as though she'd just moved in, so spare were her quarters. No bookshelves. No messy side table or magazine rack. Her life was bed, then chair, then bed. Nevertheless, she carted those old homemade cards around with her from apartment to apartment, Christmas to Christmas, until her death.

Can good be reclaimed from our mistakes? That is my hope—that, opening one of those bright envelopes, my grandmother felt loved.

Creator God, reclaim my self-obsession for Your good ends! This I pray in the name of Your Son, Who promised us Your power and love, despite our failings. —PATTY KIRK

Digging Deeper: ROM 5:1; EPH 1:3–8

Mon 15

"I will lead the blind by ways they have not known, along unfamiliar paths I will guide them; I will turn the darkness into light before them and make the rough places smooth. These are the things I will do; I will not forsake them."
—Isaiah 42:16 (NIV)

Janet Eckles, a fellow Latina and author, invited my family and me to her home. I'd been looking forward to meeting her after hearing about her book *Simply Salsa.* After losing her sight, struggling in her marriage, and grieving the murder of her teenage son, she began writing to encourage others in their own struggles.

She was every bit the radiant and energetic spirit I imagined. Meeting her was inspiring and exciting, but I was mortified when my father spoke about his fear of going blind. He'd had an optical stroke that blinded his left eye and later had cataracts removed in his right one. "I don't know what I'd do if I ever went completely blind," he said. "I don't think I could handle that!"

Janet grabbed his hand and said with a laugh, "Are you kidding me? Going blind is the best thing that ever happened to me! I learned to appreciate things I had taken for granted before. It led me to a new and exciting career, and I discovered things I could do in spite of my blindness and found adventure in that."

Father wasn't trying to offend, and Janet wasn't at all insulted. Instead, she assured my father and reminded all of us that we can find joy and purpose in whatever circumstances come our way.

Help me not to fear the struggles that may lie ahead, Lord, but to anticipate the blessings and joy that await in spite of them.
—Karen Valentin

Digging Deeper: Ps 27:1; Is 41:13

THE TRUE GIFTS OF CHRISTMAS

Tue 16 *I'm singing my heart out to God—what a victory!...*
—Exodus 15:1 (MSG)

O CHRISTMAS TREE

I made a sensible decision as Christmas approached. Because of my lack of energy and enthusiasm (related to three autoimmune diseases), I wouldn't let my son Jeremy erect the tree. Just thinking about decorating it made me tired.

As I enjoyed a manicure with Sandy, who's done my nails for years, I asked for Big Apple Red.

Sandy looked stunned. Red's not my color. "It's for Christmas." I smiled into her eyes. "I'm not going to have a tree." She filed my nails quietly, not looking at me. "Nope. No tree this year," I added for emphasis.

Finally, she met my eyes and said solemnly, "If you don't put up a tree this year, you never will again."

I didn't respond. When I left, she called out, "Merry Christmas, Marion!"

I responded in kind, but felt—well, forlorn. *Never have a tree again?* I saw my neighbors' trees shining brightly, and they tugged at my heart.

When my son Jeremy came to eat supper with us the next night, I asked him to put up the tree. *Go slowly, Marion. No rush.* I hung the bright items at a snail's pace, even took breaks. I finished trimming the tree without aches, pains, or weariness.

When my husband, Gene, plugged in the white lights, my heart sang and rejoiced as Christmas carols played in the background and the spirit of Christmas once again filled our living room. Joy to the world, indeed!

Thank You for volunteering to come to us, Lord Jesus.
—Marion Bond West

Digging Deeper: Is 9:6–7; Lk 1:31

Wed 17

"I came that they may have life, and have it abundantly."
—John 10:10 (NRSV)

There were more Christmas gifts to open, but my wife, Kate, announced, "Okay, everyone, time to get ready." Kate is the rector at our small Episcopal church, and she had to lead a morning service.

I gritted my teeth. *Why*, I wondered, *can't we be like normal families?* Everything is different in a clergy household. Sunday is a workday, holidays are workdays, Fridays are sermon-writing days, and every week seems to bring some fresh reason why the rector needs to be out several evenings in a row. I'm not always good-natured about this rule of life. We got dressed, and our son Benji climbed into his stroller. Walking along the quiet streets, I had to admit it was nice to be outside—cool air, bright sun, hillsides tawny with winter-brown grass. A couple dozen people gathered in the sanctuary. Those wonderful Bible verses were read: "Now the birth of Jesus the Messiah took place in this way." We gathered around the altar for Communion. I looked around at everyone's warm, happy faces. Taking the bread and wine, I felt foolish and glad at the same time: foolish for begrudging this wonderful life at the heart of God's work in the world; glad that my church community, and Kate, loved me anyway.

Teach me to be thankful at all times, Lord.
—Jim Hinch

Digging Deeper: Jn 1:14, 3:16–17

Thu 18

The Lord is good to those whose hope is in him....
—LAMENTATIONS 3:25 (NIV)

It's time for my annual accordion concert," I announced a few days before Christmas. My accordion-saga started when I was eleven and longed to know my daddy loved me. He was a man of few words and had a quick temper. His name was Carroll, and I was named after him.

He was proud of my older sister, who was getting rave reviews in community theater productions. My father feared I might suffer in her shadow, so he suggested I play the accordion. "You'll be invited to all the parties because everyone will want you to bring your accordion and play."

He got me a sparkly gold accordion, and I learned to play a couple of polkas and some Christmas carols. But it didn't take long for me to realize that a fat girl with glasses wasn't going to be invited to parties because she played the accordion. So I quit... and resented my father for suggesting the idea.

After I was grown and my father had died, I found my accordion at my mother's house. Instantly, I was an eleven-year-old girl again, playing the accordion, hoping to make her father proud. The memory was the same, but I was different.

I'd become a mom and learned that, in spite of our best efforts, parents don't always give the kind of love that perfectly meets a child's unique needs. I'd also learned that only God's love perfectly fills those longings and helps me love others, even if they don't love me exactly the way I want. So every Christmas, I take out my accordion and play carols in memory of my father because our name means "song of joy."

Jesus, Your love and grace shapes the way I understand my memories.
—CAROL KUYKENDALL

Digging Deeper: 1 JN 4:7–12

Fri 19

"I was a stranger and you welcomed me . . . sick and you visited me. . . ." —MATTHEW 25:35–36 (ESV)

I hurried home from running errands, dropped my shopping bags, and checked my phone messages. "Hi, you don't know me, but I read *Daily Guideposts*. I need a huge favor, hon. Call me please, and I'll explain."

Her voice sounded friendly but a huge favor? I still had to bake pecan pies, wrap presents, and write a blog post for a ministry site. Sighing, I dialed her number.

She lived in another state and asked me to visit a friend of hers—a ninety-five-year-old woman in a home not far from me. Hospice had been called in. "My friend's a retired marine. She never married . . . such a sweetheart. Wish I could be there. Please wish her a merry Christmas for me, if it suits you to go."

It didn't suit me at all.

Jotting down the address, I promised to visit, but explained it probably wouldn't be today or tomorrow. Graciously, she thanked me. I turned on my computer to sift through the facts for the blog, but all I could think about was the phone call. *Lord, here's a chance to care about someone and I'm too busy writing about ministry.*

I called the home, and the caretaker said to come on over.

The dear woman smiled from her worn recliner—short gray hair, pale-blue eyes, and so tiny. "Hi," she said. "Come in." Stepping inside her warm, cozy room, I bent beside her. She reached for my hand and gave a strong squeeze. "Merry Christmas," she said softly.

As she welcomed me, a stranger, I blinked back tears. I hadn't brought Christmas to her. Just the opposite. Kneeling in that small, quiet room, the gift of Christmas joy was given to me.

Lord, blessings follow obedience. You continually surprise me.
—JULIE GARMON

Digging Deeper: LK 2:9–12; 1 PT 1:8

A NEW WAY TO SERVE

Sat 20

"Do not judge, so that you may not be judged."
—Matthew 7:1 (NRSV)

JUST LIKE ME

When my husband, Charlie, and I decided to volunteer at the shelter, I figured I'd arranged a nice, little controlled situation where we could be together while helping others. My plan, however, unraveled. We found ourselves talking about "our people" over dinners, then planning our time around volunteering, checking in on folks during the week, meeting some of their families and, eventually, making plans with our shelter friends just like we would with real friends. Because that's what they'd become.

We asked two of them to join us for our annual Christmas Eve tradition of early Mass and a car ride to look at Christmas lights. Dan and Jeff met us for church, an infrequent occurrence for them, and then we set out for the drive. We saw brightly lit mangers, spectacular homes draped with colored lights, yards with every imaginable Christmas character, twinkling lights on porches, and glowing orbs in trees so tall they must have been decorated with a crane. Finally, we came to a house decorated with wreaths and spotlights. "That's my favorite," Dan said. "Simple. Just simple. My mother would have liked that house."

I suddenly realized that we weren't providing our friends with joyous new memories; we were merely extending the traditions they'd experienced years ago. They had not always been homeless and alone. They had families just like mine who'd taken Christmas drives and critiqued lights and decorations. It was only one of the ways that they were just like me.

Father, thank You for giving me so many brothers and sisters.
—Marci Alborghetti

Digging Deeper: Mt 2:10; Phil 2:8–10

GIFTS OF MERCY

Sun 21

For God, who said, "Let light shine out of darkness," made his light shine in our hearts to give us the light of the knowledge of God's glory displayed in the face of Christ.
—2 CORINTHIANS 4:6 (NIV)

FOURTH SUNDAY IN ADVENT: LIGHT SHINES OUT OF DARKNESS

My most successful Christmas present this year was a tiny crystal poinsettia for my mother-in-law. Normally I'd be loath to spend money on a knickknack, but I thought it might, to use one of her pet phrases, "catch her eye."

Mamaw, as we call her, has slipped so deep into dementia she's past knowing it's Christmas. Still, I go through the motions of buying gifts *for* and *from* her. It's tradition.

Mamaw's Christmas sweater has poinsettias on it. And she likes red, she told a nurse the other day. It was like a gift, that remark. "Red," she said, as the nurse adjusted the blood pressure cuff on her skinny arm.

"You mean this?" The nurse touched her name tag, which had red letters. I doubted Mamaw, with her failing eyesight, could see them.

"I like red," Mamaw clarified.

After breakfast, I set the poinsettia on its mirror on her kitchen table. It collected the meager illumination in her dark house to create a pond of light, shimmering with red. Mamaw reached out a finger. I could tell she liked it. "The girls got it for you," I lied. She especially prizes gifts from them.

The poinsettia stayed on her table long after Christmas. Every so often, when I'd visit, she'd point to it there, in its pool of light, and say the girls' names. Or pretty. Or red.

Father, thank You for light and beauty and love. Thank You for the gift of Your Son. —PATTY KIRK

Digging Deeper: MT 1:23, 2:11

LIFE LESSONS FROM THOSE I'VE MET

Mon 22 *I was glad when they said to me, "Let us go to the house of the Lord!"* —PSALM 122:1 (RSV)

DR. LI, CHINESE PHYSICIAN

The Christmas Eve service at our church begins at 11:00 PM. But for my husband and me—ever since meeting Dr. Li—it begins at home when we put on our coats to go.

We'd gone to China in 1981 to investigate a rumor that churches were reopening. In Shanghai, sure enough, we attended Sunday service in a redbrick church with a standing-room-only congregation. Afterward, we talked with an elderly physician who'd studied in the United States in the 1930s. For two decades, Dr. Li said, this church had been boarded up. Three months before our visit, it had reopened. "Our first service in twenty-two years."

The first service, that is, inside.... The first Christmas Eve after the church closed in 1959 was just an ordinary night shift at the hospital for Dr. Li. It was cold and drizzly when he returned to his apartment at 10:30. He took off his damp coat—then, suddenly, put it back on. His wife put hers on too, and followed him outside. Through the icy drizzle they walked, left at the corner, across a square, turn right... headed to church. As they drew closer, they became aware of other silent walkers. From every side street they came, alone or in twos or threes, until hundreds were standing shoulder to shoulder before the locked door. For two hours they stood in the rain. No hymns. No sermon. "But it was Communion all the same."

For twenty-two years, this was their Christmas service. No one planned any of it. "Just, that night, year after year, we put on our coats and came."

Remind me this Christmas, Father, that all over the world, millions are joining with us as the angels sing. —ELIZABETH SHERRILL

Digging Deeper: Is 11:1; Lk 2:1–15

THE TRUE GIFTS OF CHRISTMAS

Tue 23 *For he satisfieth the longing soul.* —PSALM 107:9 (KJV)

A FULL SOUL

A certain longing continued to creep up on me. I missed those shy, little soft-haired girls who once rang my doorbell decades ago. "Can Julie and Jennifer come out and play?" the bravest one would inquire.

Why hadn't I marveled over them, bent over, and spoken kindly? Instead, I'd bellowed, "Girls, your friends are at the door!" I hadn't even invited them inside most of the time.

Our doorbell rang Christmas Eve. Somewhat grudgingly, I answered it. As I opened it, dainty, beautiful sounds floated up to my ears . . . and heart. "Silent night, holy night, all is calm, all is bright . . . "

I gazed down at five little girls singing their Christmas gift to me.

Oh, Lord, they've come. You've sent them!

Two new families had moved onto our street. Regrettably, I hadn't yet been to call. The two mothers of the girls stood smiling in the background.

My husband, Gene, joined me, and we stood arm in arm taking it all in. Their fresh, eager faces. Sweet voices. Enthusiasm. The never-changing message in the ancient carols. I bent down. "Oh, please come inside." Their mothers ushered them in. At our tree, I gave them candy, then took them to a bedroom I refer to as "the little girls' room." Of course, we don't have a little girl; the room's just decorated that way.

"Can we touch the dolls?" one child whispered.

"Yes. Touch all of them. The paper dolls and books too."

Finally the children and their mothers said good-bye and strode out into the starry night, leaving behind the almost unbearable tenderness of little girls.

Father, bless You for filling up my soul this Christmas Eve.
—MARION BOND WEST

Digging Deeper: MT 2:2; LK 2:14

GIFTS OF MERCY

Wed 24

On entering the house, they saw the child with Mary his mother; and they knelt down and paid him homage. Then, opening their treasure chests, they offered him gifts of gold, frankincense, and myrrh. —MATTHEW 2:11 (NRSV)

CHRISTMAS EVE: PAYING HOMAGE

Our daughter Lulu's idea of the perfect Christmas is lots of presents—not merely for her, but for the whole family, and more than last year. She likes abundance.

This Christmas should have been a complete failure by Lulu's standards. Charlotte had asked for a contribution toward a plane ticket to meet her Australian boyfriend's family over the holidays. We agreed, and Charlotte, dazed with love, was adamantly content.

No presents for Charlotte under the tree was depressing for the rest of the family though, especially Lulu. Initially, she reveled in her own growing piles compared to the few tights and socks I'd wrapped just to give Charlotte something to open on Christmas morning. But as the day approached, Lulu became increasingly agitated about the disparity. By Christmas Eve, even Charlotte seemed depressed, and I dreaded our ritual, officiated by Lulu, of taking turns opening presents.

The two appeared in our bed at 6:00 AM, as pushy and merry as ever, and somehow, despite Lulu's careful calculations of who should open what, her sister ended up with a little stash of gifts at the end when ours were all opened—a loaves-and-fishes miracle of sisterly love! It was my best present this year, sure to redeem this sad business of presents for years to come.

Good Father, thank You for the enormous mercy with which You meet our smallness. —PATTY KIRK

Digging Deeper: MT 1:18–24: ROM 6:23

GIFTS OF MERCY

Thu 25 *Jesus answered, "The work of God is this: to believe in the one he has sent."* —JOHN 6:29 (NIV)

CHRISTMAS: BELIEVING IN THE ONE GOD SENT

Recently, a student in my Writing from Faith course voiced a revelation. "Until now," she said, "I've always thought 'Be concrete' meant 'Use more adjectives.' Now I see I need to make people see what I saw, hear what I heard, smell what I smelled. Using your senses helps people believe and care about what you're saying."

She was responding to a fellow student's psalm about not being able to afford to go home for Christmas—to Costa Rica, where her family are missionaries. In the poem, the student-psalmist is alone in her room, staring at the computer while, just beyond the thin walls, her dorm-mates chatter excitedly about their holiday plans. She recounts family traditions she'll miss: getting ornaments out of dusty boxes, drinking hot cocoa with her siblings while Dad reads Christmas stories, sharing a festive dinner of *arroz con pollo*. Then, like a good psalmist, she affirms her faith.

We all teared up. Afterward, her classmates raised money for her flight and launched a ministry to do the same for every missionary kid on campus.

It was a big moment for me. Not only had a student's writing spurred others to action, but they'd all finally acknowledged the persuasive power of sensory data, which I'd been trying to convince them of from day one.

Christmas is such a sensory celebration. Carols. Pine smells. Fruitcakes and sugar cookies. Snow. The concreteness of Christmas crystallizes its gospel: that our invisible Creator sent us palpable evidence, in the form of a newborn, so that we might believe and have eternal life.

Beloved Creator, let the sights, sounds, smells, and tastes of Your creation lead us to You. —PATTY KIRK

Digging Deeper: IS 9:6–7; LK 2:1–20; 2 COR 9:15

Fri 26

For He shall give His angels charge over you, to keep you in all your ways. —Psalm 91:11 (NKJV)

Barbara is my earth angel. She is the first person I call when something has gone awry or if I need prayerful support and the hand of a friend. But today her words stopped me short when I called her for prayer for an upcoming inspection at work.

"I don't know what good I can be," she said. "I feel like an angel with only one wing." She gave a little laugh, but I could tell her comment did not come from a funny place. Barbara had recently retired from her job as a secretary in the chaplain's office of our veterans hospital. "I don't feel like I help anyone anymore."

The odd thing was I felt the same way. Life had gotten to be too much; my heart felt tattered by life.

When I discovered a pair of carved wooden angel wings at a gift shop, I knew exactly what I would do with them. I'd give one to Barbara and I'd keep one, with the words of Luciano de Crescenzo close in thought: "We are each of us angels with only one wing, and we can only fly by embracing one another."

Thank You, Lord, for friends with only one wing.
Help me always to embrace them.
—Roberta Messner

Digging Deeper: Prv 12:26, 27:9

Sat 27

Go to the ant, O sluggard; consider her ways, and be wise. Without having any chief, officer or ruler, she prepares her food in summer, and gathers her sustenance in harvest.
—Proverbs 6:6–8 (RSV)

I'm successfully ignoring the stack of dishes by the sink, but it's getting harder to do every day. I hope I break down and wash them before all that's left for my cereal is the colander.

Procrastination is a constant companion of mine. More like an anchor I cling to when I'm in over my head! It's one of those New Year's resolutions I never quite got around to addressing.

When I get busy on our family ranch, which is most of the time, housework takes the hardest hit. There are times when my vinyl flooring looks more like a shag carpet from all the pet hair I neglected to sweep. The firewood bin is almost always empty. If the dust on my furniture gets any deeper, I might as well plow it and plant spuds.

At least God takes better care of me than I take care of my house. His love is constant, steadfast, and ever-abounding—kind of like that stack of dishes! I could learn a few things from that ant in Proverbs, as long as she prepareth her food, gathereth her sustenance, *and* keepeth the house clean too!

Dear Lord, help me to deal with it now, not later—
especially since the colander needs washing too.
—Erika Bentsen

Digging Deeper: Prv 19:15, 31:27

THE TRUE GIFTS OF CHRISTMAS

Sun 28

For I live in eager expectation and hope. . . .
—PHILIPPIANS 1:20 (TLB)

LIVING IN EXPECTATION

Picking up a few last-minute Christmas things in a discount store, I noticed a rack of dog toys. Our dog has a lot of toys and such items don't usually tempt me, but the huge, plastic stockings were filled with sturdy, durable toys. Caught up in the Christmas spirit, I tossed one into my cart. Sure enough, our dog loved the toys.

I began to think about dogs waiting to be adopted and how much they'd enjoy the treats. There was a new animal shelter just minutes from us. Still, twelve dollars for each stocking was a lot. I'd need to buy quite a few stockings.

During Christmas, the idea remained lodged stubbornly in my mind. I imagined the lonely dogs playing with the toys, tails wagging. A couple of days after Christmas, I began to think, *What if those stockings have been drastically reduced, since they are holiday items?* I played a game with myself each time I drove by the store. *How much would they need to be reduced for me to get them?* I answered myself: *Um, down to two dollars each.*

Three days after Christmas, my car seemed to have a mind of its own. It took a right, and I found a parking place near the front door of the discount store. However, my heart fell when I couldn't locate the doggie stockings. They were large, too, about two feet tall. I asked a clerk if they were sold out. "No, the manager just marked them down a few minutes ago."

I literally ran through the store to where she'd directed me. There they were. Twelve of them. Marked down to two dollars each! I bought every one and hurried to the shelter.

Father, help me to live in a spirit of hope each day of the year.
—MARION BOND WEST

Digging Deeper: Ps 39:7

Mon 29

So teach us to number our days, That we may present to You a heart of wisdom. —PSALM 90:12 (NAS)

One day, I looked at my life as though it were a clock face. Imagining myself living to ninety-six years, beginning at twelve, and going once around with eight years between numbers, I placed myself smack between seven and eight. I was on the waning edge of time.

This imagery awakened in me a rich awareness of the gift of years already lived and the yet-to-be-explored opportunity in the ones left. I was reminded of a favorite Bible verse: "Abraham breathed his last and died in a ripe old age, an old man and satisfied with life" (Genesis 25:8, NAS).

It's the "satisfied with life" part—not how long I live—that speaks to me in this passage. How did he come to this fullness of feeling? Abraham endured some hard years. He was asked to leave all that was familiar and trek to an unknown land. He experienced family strife. Yet he kept trust with the God Who first spoke to him saying, "And I will bless you, and make your name great" (Genesis 12:2, NAS).

Moses wrote in Psalm 90 (NAS) about "numbering our days"—paying attention to them, growing and learning from them, making them meaningful for ourselves and others—in order to *present* (literally bring in) to God a "heart of wisdom."

Both Abraham and Moses were able to meet God at the end of their days, knowing they had lived well the gift of their years—trusting Him, becoming wise in Him, fulfilling His purpose for them. Only one phrase describes how that must feel: satisfied with life.

Lord, I so want to "bring in" satisfying years,
lived gratefully in Your name.
—CAROL KNAPP

Digging Deeper: PS 51:6; PRV 16:3, 28:26

Tue 30

I go to prepare a place for you. —JOHN 14:2 (KJV)

I'm heading home," David, my husband, says into the phone, before I even have a chance to say hello.

Home. He's worked hard all day, and the class he teaches didn't end until 9:00 PM, so when he says the word, it sounds precious.

Even as a child, I sensed the value of home and knew I was lucky because I lived in a happy one. All of my life, I've anguished for those who weren't so fortunate: Those who, by the luck of the draw, have never had a home or have, through a reversal of fortunes, lost the one they had.

Our family has always had a passion for working to secure homes for those people. We've provided homes for refugees and for those in our city with marginal incomes. In Zimbabwe, with the help of many others, we've managed to provide homes for a fair number of AIDS orphans. Yet anything we can hope to do is like a grain of sand on a vast beach. There are so many people who will never have a home like we do.

But then I remember a larger truth. In a way, we are all headed home, to a spot beyond anything we know now. Over and over, the Bible promises that such a place exists! So, surely, God has already planned a permanent home for each of His children, and most especially for those who, in this life, have done without.

Father, I pray that You will allow me to build for others
as I head toward my one true home with You.
—PAM KIDD

Digging Deeper: 1 COR 2:7–9; 2 COR 5:8; PHIL 3:20–21

Wed 31

"For the revelation awaits an appointed time; it speaks of the end and will not prove false. Though it linger, wait for it; it will certainly come and will not delay."
—Habakkuk 2:3 (NIV)

As my husband and I counted down to midnight, we looked at each other and laughed. *How did we get here?*

"Here" was on vacation, in a hotel in Orlando, Florida, with my mom snoozing next to us. On TV, a dozen pop stars helped us count down to the New Year. Brian and I did a quick inventory: married three years, completed law school, paid off student loans, bought a house, adopted a dog. With each new decision, we'd depended on God and tried to seek His will.

Brian looked at me. "Kids?" he asked. "Is it time?"

Looking into his eyes, I saw the faith and trust that had led us through seven years of dating and three years of marriage; the same eyes that had protected, encouraged, and challenged me. One thing we've certainly learned in our short marriage is that God's will isn't spelled out on a billboard. As much as I beg for God to invest in magazine ads, He won't. And now here we were asking what might be the biggest question of all. I looked at the ceiling in case the watermarks spelled out Yes or No. No such luck. I simply needed to remember to seek and follow God's will, and trust that the direction I'm moving in is His.

I turned to Brian as the ball dropped. "I'm ready if you are." I'm okay with that.

God, You've heard our prayers for the blessing of children.
We trust that You will grant us the desires of our heart in Your time.
—Ashley Kappel

Digging Deeper: Ps 37:3–6; Prv 16:9; Rom 8:28

DAILY MERCIES

1 ______________________________

2 ______________________________

3 ______________________________

4 ______________________________

5 ______________________________

6 ______________________________

7 ______________________________

8 ______________________________

9 ______________________________

10 ______________________________

11 ______________________________

12 ______________________________

13 ______________________________

14 ______________________________

15 ______________________________

16 ________________

17 ________________

18 ________________

19 ________________

20 ________________

21 ________________

22 ________________

23 ________________

24 ________________

25 ________________

26 ________________

27 ________________

28 ________________

29 ________________

30 ________________

31 ________________

SAM ADRIANCE of New Haven, Connecticut, had a year full of milestones. He watched his fiancée, Emily, graduate from college, began his first year of law school, and started planning his wedding. "I was very sad to leave my job teaching high school students," Sam says, "but I've been loving the next chapter of my life." He participated in the Temporary Restraining Order Project, helping battered women and men get restraining orders against their attackers, and has now joined the Education Adequacy Project, where he will help in an enormous litigation effort to reform Connecticut's public schools.

MARCI ALBORGHETTI and her husband, Charlie, of New London, Connecticut, have had an interesting year. They have been reminded frequently of the various forms of an adage: Man plans and God laughs. Or even more appropriate: Man proposes; God disposes! "I am not the one who has the final say in my life," says Marci, "and that's probably for the best. But I'm still not great at adjusting my routine and expectations, so I'm praying for God's help with that." Marci has two new books out: *The American Prayer Book: In God We Trust* and *Being the Body of Christ.*

"This past year has seen more changes in the household," writes ANDREW ATTAWAY of New York City. "Our children are growing in body, mind, and, we trust, spirit. Elizabeth, 18, finished her junior year at MIT; John, 16, completed his junior year of high school; Mary, 14, blossomed as a dancer, performing with confidence and, most important, with joy; Maggie, 11, amazed me with her singing at our local children's theater; and Stephen, 9, our only remaining homeschooler, has enjoyed architecture and robotics classes, and has become an enthusiastic Cub Scout."

"It's been a year of adaptation for the Attaways," writes JULIA ATTAWAY of New York City. "Mary and Maggie started school after many years of homeschooling, and that's a big change for us all." Between PTA meetings and freelance writing, Julia finds time to blog for Guideposts (Guideposts.org/blogs/Seeds-Devotion), run a preschool nature class in the park, and pray. "An active life requires active prayer, and I've been working on developing the habit of praying wherever I go." As the mom of three teens, a tween, and a 9-year-old, she also practices praying before she opens her mouth to respond to anyone!

"This past year has seen our family embarking on new phases of life: the first year of marriage for our son Chris and his wife, Grayson; the first full-time job for our son John after his college graduation; and the first year of retirement for my husband, Gordon," says KAREN BARBER of Alpharetta, Georgia. "One way that I continue to be renewed daily, even when big changes like these come in my day-to-day life, is through prayer. And one way I keep my prayer life refreshed is through trying out new prayer ideas I learn from the people who share on Prayerideas.org, which I edit."

EVELYN BENCE of Arlington, Virginia, says, "In the past several years God has expanded my heart to the needs of my neighborhood: a fragile older woman with few supports; a family with no car; a child with special needs who knocks on the door every day, asking me to read to her. Challenges, inconveniences, interruptions? Yes. But then I hear a heartfelt thank-you or see a grammar-school breakthrough, and I thank God for mercies raining on us all. I had a good business year, providing editorial services, and in August enjoyed a family reunion of my siblings at a niece's wedding in Indiana."

This year has certainly thrown extra challenges her way, ERIKA BENTSEN of Sprague River, Oregon, tells us. "I ruptured a disc in my spine, fighting a wildfire on the ranch. Suddenly thrust into an intense battle with crippling pain, I faced surgery, powerful medications, physical therapy, and months of nearly healing. Then regression, further regression, and finally, as I write this, the tiniest hope of recovery once again. This injury has changed the course of my life, much to my chagrin, but I know God has a plan for me. Every day I pray for acceptance, as I try to discover His new aim. Can I continue the life I thought He wanted me to lead? Do I yield to a different path? And the questions I fear most: Is there life after ranching? Must I lose everything I love? Can joy and peace be found elsewhere? Please pray for me as I struggle to find answers."

"This has been a very challenging year," says RHODA BLECKER of Bellingham, Washington. "In May, my husband, Keith, had a cerebellar stroke, which landed him in the hospital for three days. But we were truly blessed. He recovered quickly and well enough so that the only prescription was to return to tai chi for balance improvement. Then in July he had a COPD episode, which also meant he needed to be hospitalized, and now he's on oxygen all the time, except when he's sitting still. I've had to adjust to living with stress, which was never really a part of our lives before, and for a stubborn woman like me, it hasn't been easy. But I am getting support from our neighbors, and that reminds me every day that their generosity is God's generosity made visible."

JEFF CHU's past year was one of milestones and new beginnings. He joined his church, got married, and moved into a new home, though still in Brooklyn, New York. His work as a journalist continues to send him to and fro—he added two countries, Brazil and Colombia, to his lifetime list, and racked up more than 120,000 miles on airplanes. If anything, his peripatetic schedule has reminded him of the anchoring, unchanging presence of God. "As I visited my aging grandmother in Hong Kong, spent time with my young nephews and goddaughter, and witnessed the resurrection of my beloved San Francisco 49ers, I've been reassured of divine mercies, big and small, throughout all of life's unpredictable seasons."

SABRA CIANCANELLI of Tivoli, New York, says, "My favorite part of the day is early morning while the rest of the house sleeps. I sit by the window in my home office and look out over the field as one of our cats snuggles on my lap. In the winter, as the sun rises, I notice the deer tracks that have appeared in the snow beside Henry's and Solomon's snow angels, and our trails from sleigh riding. From above, the imprints of our lives reassure me of God's new mercies that protect and guide us as we journey life's path." Sabra lives in an almost fully restored farmhouse with her husband, two sons, four cats, and three Dumbo rats.

"When I was young, my prayers were selfish," admits MARK COLLINS of Pittsburgh, Pennsylvania. "Some were formulaic: 'Oh, God, I am heartily sorry'—which I changed to 'hardly sorry.' But mostly I prayed because I wanted things for myself." Nowadays, his prayers are both very simple and very complicated. "I have been so blessed in so many ways that it seems stupid to pray for myself. I end up praying for mercy, with only a vague idea of what that means—except that we all need it." Among Mark's blessings are recent college graduate Faith, 22, college junior Hope, 21, and high schooler Grace, 17. Mark's wife, Sandee, is the author of a new book, *Weapons upon Her Body,* which features stories of strong women from the Hebrew Bible. "Wonder what it's like to live with strong women?" Mark asks, tongue firmly planted in cheek.

"This past year I was blessed to be part of the John Maxwell Group as an independent certified coach, teacher, and speaker," says PABLO DIAZ of Carmel, New York. "I not only help others with their leadership growth, but it also keeps me focused on learning. Maxwell says, 'Most people overestimate what they can do in a day and underestimate what they can do in a lifetime.' I fret now less about the setbacks of one day and keep the lifetime contribution topmost in my mind. I am happy to share that Elba, my wife, is never short of great stories or funny moments from her work with seniors. Our son, Paul, is healthy and fully recovered from the car accident. Our daughter, Christine, is always finding a way to travel for business or pleasure."

BRIAN DOYLE of Portland, Oregon, is the editor of *Portland Magazine* at the University of Portland and the author of many books, most recently the essay collection *Grace Notes.* "Tender mercies, O my heavens," he says. "I have been inundated by them since I was a child with my mother's sweet, loving, gracious, warm hand as gentle as honey on my brow. And now my children laughing, and my lovely bride grinning at me from the corner of the kitchen, and the steady rain as clean and profligate as moist music, and the grace of friends, and the mercy of work I love, and an ever-growing awareness that awareness is prayer, attentiveness is prayer, witness is prayer. It's all sacrament—every bit of it—tender even in the bruising parts."

"I am praying for favor and breakthroughs, for all of you, for my children, and even for myself," says SHARON FOSTER of Durham, North Carolina. "The year started out rocky—faithful friends passed away, prayers seemed to go unanswered. But in November I was stunned to find myself standing before a welcoming audience in Gettysburg, Pennsylvania, where I was honored with the Shaara Prize for Fiction for my novel *The Resurrection of Nat Turner*. My son, Chase, and my daughter, Lanea, were in the audience along with a few members of the Guideposts family. (You always seem to show up wherever I am!)"

KATIE GANSHERT of Bettendorf, Iowa, graduated from the University of Wisconsin in Madison with a degree in education and worked as a fifth-grade teacher for several years before staying home to write full time. When she's not busy plotting her next novel, she enjoys spending time with her husband, playing make-believe with her "wild child," talking books and faith with good friends over coffee, and serving in the junior high ministry at her church.

"My one-word theme for this year is *surrender*," says JULIE GARMON of Monroe, Georgia. "Making the decision to totally let go brought new adventures. After blogging for Guideposts with my mother, Marion Bond West, I began blogging weekly from my own Web site at JulieGarmon.com. At first, it felt like walking into a party and not knowing a soul, but my readers have become some of my dearest friends. My daughter Katie and I began volunteering at a pregnancy resource center. Each time I reach out to others, God's mercy boomerangs back to me. Amazingly, as I daily surrender, His love covers all my fear."

"I'm constantly amazed at God's blessings in my life," says BILL GIOVANNETTI, senior pastor of the Neighborhood Church of Redding in Northern California. "Our church is growing by leaps and bounds, I continue to teach at A. W. Tozer Theological Seminary, and I'm still able to write books and articles." When he's not preaching, teaching, or writing, Bill drags his kids bass-fishing at their new secret fishing hole and squeezes in occasional spasms of fitness training. "I am thankful beyond words for God's grace in my life," he says. "Especially for my wife, Margi, and our kids, Josie, 12, and J.D., 11. Visit Bill at BillGiovannetti.com.

EDWARD GRINNAN of New York City has been spending much of his time working on Guideposts' newest venture, *Mysterious Ways* magazine. "Years before I wandered into *Guideposts* magazine, Van Varner had launched the *Mysterious Ways* column and it was always the readers' favorite. People tell us they can't get enough of these miracle stories that send a shiver down your spine and put a tear in your eye. It has been a spiritually amazing journey for me to hear from people who have had these incredible experiences of how the hidden hand of the Almighty can reach into our lives at any time and touch us in the most unexpected, inexplicable, and awesome ways."

RICK HAMLIN and his wife, Carol, celebrated their younger son Tim's graduation from college and then happily welcomed him back to his old bedroom in New York City. So they've gone from empty nesters to half-empty nesters. "Tim has acquired some cooking skills in the last four years and even remembers to clean up after himself. He's working on his music and babysits to support himself. His older brother William still lives in San Francisco and works for the networking site LinkedIn," Rick says. Rick has been talking to groups about his latest book, *10 Prayers You Can't Live Without.* He recently celebrated two thirtieth anniversaries—one in his marriage and one as a *Daily Guideposts* author. "I'm continually grateful for this spiritual community of readers and writers," he says.

"It's been a year of milestones," says JIM HINCH of San Jose, California. "Frances, 6, lost two teeth, started kindergarten, and learned to read. Benjamin, 3, dispensed with the last vestiges of babyhood. Good-bye crib, diapers, and stroller! We only (sort of) miss having a very little one in the house. Mostly we're excited to move into the big-kid phase of family life. This past year Kate and I took the kids backpacking in the Sierra Nevada, on a road trip to Seattle, and on multiple trips to

Los Angeles and San Francisco. They're game for everything. We do our best to be faithful, knowing God always is."

While JEFF JAPINGA's title may be a head-scratcher—associate dean for doctor of ministry and continuing education programs at McCormick Theological Seminary in Chicago—his work is straightforward. "I'm simply equipping people to do better what God has already called and gifted them to do," he says. Improving what already is has been a theme for the year, from his wife Lynn's sabbatical from her ongoing teaching responsibilities to a number of major home-remodeling projects to Jeff's own continuing study in leadership. (But, alas, not Jeff's golf game—nothing he tries seems to make that any better.) But Jeff says he's found one thing that just cannot be improved on: sunsets on the beach near their home in Holland, Michigan.

After years of moving, thanks to school and job transitions, ASHLEY KAPPEL and her husband, Brian, are finally settled in Birmingham, Alabama, where they are enjoying their first home. This year they added a family member to the mix: Colby, a rescued golden retriever who fills their days with walks, snuggles, and playtime. Ashley works for a national food Web site and freelances her social media skills to various outlets. "Every day brings a new chance to rejoice in what God has given us," she says. "My goal for 2014 is to make the most of God's promises."

"My wife, Corinne, and I marvel over how God continues to fill our lives with joy," says BROCK KIDD of Nashville, Tennessee. "My son, Harrison, has entered his teens and is excelling in his new school, where he has discovered a talent for writing, especially poetry. He is a phenomenal big brother to little Mary Katherine, who keeps us all entertained with her funny antics and precious giggling. With a second little girl on the way, it seems one major blessing just follows another. Corinne enjoys being a mom and still does a little real estate work on the side. And for me, the investment business is as satisfying as ever and allows time for my dad and me to take time out for our annual fishing getaways."

"Flying to Zimbabwe with most of our family in tow, we had an overnight in Dubai," PAM KIDD of Nashville, Tennessee, says. "It was surreal to stand in the street of a city where everything is taller, bigger, and more opulent than any other place on the planet. A day later it was red mud, rocky paths, and women smiling from ear to ear as they paraded their goats before us. Earlier, in the 'largest mall in the world,' the warmth of the Arab people surprised us as men in flowing white robes bowed and smiled their welcomes. We had been caught in time between the richest and poorest people on earth and, strange as it sounds, I don't think any of us would be interested in changing places."

This past year PATTY KIRK from Westville, Oklahoma, and her husband, Kris, lost first his mother to Alzheimer's disease and then her father to lung cancer. With their two daughters far away at college and all four of their parents now no longer living, Patty found herself lonesome for all these beloved ones' company and newly conscious of her own fast-approaching decline and eventual death. Paradoxically, however, the year's losses also nurtured wonderful new relationships with her siblings, who assembled in their father's last months and enhanced her awareness of our heavenly Father's ever-dependable company and love.

CAROL KNAPP of Lakeville, Minnesota, says, "God's tender mercies have been everywhere in my life this past year. From embarking on a trip to Alaska to assist our daughter in her last days of pregnancy to our son and his wife and their daughter making a home with us—and adding a baby boy to our household three months ago. Terry and I are at seventeen grandchildren! I also experienced God's tender mercies in the celebration with family and friends of my mother's 90th birthday in north Idaho. Son-in-law Joe was hit with a heart attack Christmas Day and underwent quadruple bypass surgery. Our daughter Brenda never left his side during his days on a ventilator. The mercies are yet flowing—he is home recovering. Looking back on all of God's goodness over the years, I am excited to enter the 'tent of meeting' with God—that place of His future tender mercies."

"My favorite news," CAROL KUYKENDALL of Boulder, Colorado, writes, "is that my youngest daughter, Kendall, has a heartbeat in her tummy. We look forward to celebrating new life with a tenth grandchild in August. Some of my favorite old news is how long Lynn and I have been married—forty-five years! We celebrated our anniversary this summer in the mountains with our children, grandchildren, and two dogs. A chaotic combination of sounds and activities far different from our quiet empty nest. At seven years out from my Stage 4 ovarian cancer diagnosis, I finally got up the courage to have my port for chemo and cancer tests surgically removed. 'Seven' in the Bible stands for 'completion.' I claim and celebrate that number."

"When I married Jack in 2012 after twenty-seven years of being single, we decided to keep and live in *both* our condos, which are just fifty-seven steps apart," says PATRICIA LORENZ of Largo, Florida. "We sleep and eat breakfast in his condo, eat dinner at mine. I write and work on my speaking career in my condo, and he works on his volunteer activities and watches TV sports in his condo. My condo is the official guest room. Our creative lifestyle is delightful, and we've learned that we're never too old to walk fifty-seven steps to be with the one we love. I still share the fun and laughter of our lives by speaking to various groups around the country. My favorite topic is 'Humor for the Health of It,' and I'm always hoping to get asked to speak in the states where my children live: California, Ohio, and Wisconsin."

ERIN MACPHERSON knows what it's like to live in a world where kids and life and work collide in a big, messy, and sometimes frantic way. She lives with her husband, Cameron, an assistant principal, and their three children, Josiah, 7, Kate, 5, and Will, 1, in Austin, Texas, where she spends her time writing, running, cooking, and even (sometimes) crafting. Her Christian Mama's Guide series of books walks women through the ups and downs of pregnancy and parenting in a way that always directs them to seek Jesus. Find her online at ChristianMamasGuide.com.

The Lord's mercies are indeed new every morning for ROBERTA MESSNER of Huntington, West Virginia. A survivor of thirty-two major surgeries related to neurofibromatosis, she has not had to undergo any operations to remove tumors since 2003. "This is by far the longest I have gone since my diagnosis in 1969," says Roberta, who attributes much of this positive outcome to the prayers of beloved *Daily Guideposts* readers. "Every morning I thank God for continuing to answer prayers, both my own and those offered in my behalf. I am so very grateful for this extended period of tumor remission."

LINDA NEUKRUG lives in Walnut Creek, California, with her two cats, Prince and Junior. She is thinking about getting a third cat but does not want to upset the delicate balance that exists. Linda enjoys her work at the bookstore and her knitting and sewing hobbies. She has decided to do one thing a day next year that scares her (mostly tiny things, like making that dreaded phone call—not big things, like bungee-jumping). Linda took an introductory harp lesson and enjoyed it, so after not playing a musical instrument (the flute) since high school, she may continue with the harp. "This year, I'm going to be reflecting on Philippians: 'Forgetting what lies behind and straining forward to what comes ahead.'"

REBECCA ONDOV of Hamilton, Montana, smiles as she reflects on the tenderhearted mercies God has poured out on her by leading her down an unexpected path—writing books that capture her Wild West adventures with horses during the years she worked from the saddle in the Bob Marshall Wilderness of Montana. She's excited to announce that in February 2014 her latest book, *Great Horse Stories*, will be released. Rebecca says, "My biggest blessing has been the new family God's created for me, made up of the readers of my books and articles. I invite you to connect with me through my Web site RebeccaOndov.com."

NATALIE PERKINS currently resides in New York City and is pursuing a master of divinity at Union Theological Seminary. She received her bachelor of music education from Indiana University's School of Music, where she co-founded and directed IU's first women's a cappella group. After spending a couple of years teaching in the classroom, she left for the stage. She was in *Aida* as Aida, *Ragtime* as Sarah, and completed tours with *Hairspray* and *Rent.* Recently, Natalie played Crystal in *Little Shop of Horrors,* Trix the Aviatrix in *The Drowsy Chaperone,* and Gary Coleman in *Avenue Q.* She can also be heard on the Stage Star Records recording of *Little Shop of Horrors* as one of the Street Urchins. She writes, "Praise God from Whom all blessings flow!"

The big event in the life of DANIEL SCHANTZ of Moberly, Missouri, was the celebration of fifty years together with Sharon. "It was snowing when we got married in 1963," Dan recalls, "even though it was May 10." They were both poor college students in Lansing, Michigan, at the time. Their fathers, both ministers, married them, and then they honeymooned in Holland, Michigan, where they toured the wooden shoe factory and later enjoyed a dinner of rainbow trout. "We climbed the sand dunes at Saugatuck, then drove on to the beautiful harbor town of South Haven, where Sharon waded in Lake Michigan and I fished. She threw rocks in where I was fishing because she wasn't getting enough attention. It takes a lot of mercy to make a marriage last. Mercy from God and mercy to each other."

New mercies abounded for GAIL THORELL SCHILLING of Northwood, New Hampshire, who spent two months in Istanbul, Turkey, where she finished her travel memoir. "I also visited ancient Cappadocia, the site of early Christian cave churches, with my congenial Muslim traveling companions, who shared much about their faith and culture. My hosts, Ercan and Aytül (parents of my future daughter-in-law Canay), showered me with treats ranging from visits to the Blue Mosque and Grand Bazaar to homemade *börek* (cheese pastry) and pistachio baklava. Before my former husband died of cancer in October, my four children and I joined him in Los Angeles for good-byes rich in grace and reconciliation. Next October should be much happier: Tom and Canay will marry!"

"One of God's new mercies to me is sight," writes PENNEY SCHWAB of Copeland, Kansas. "Thanks to a skillful doctor and cataract surgery, I have good vision for the first time since I was eight years old. It is pure joy to wake up each morning and see without fumbling for my glasses. It's also by God's continuing mercy that my husband, Don, and I are still living in our farmhouse eight miles from town . . . and fifteen miles from the nearest grocery store. I am grateful for the technology that allows me to keep in close touch with family and friends, even when it means regularly upgrading my smartphone. The greatest mercy of all, however, has been God's sustaining, guiding presence during a time of family upheaval. I am learning to pray the Psalms, especially 94:18: 'Thy mercy, O Lord, held me up.'"

ELIZABETH SHERRILL and her husband, John, of Hingham, Massachusetts, celebrated her 85th birthday and his 90th with three months in Europe, where they met and married sixty-six years ago. The big family news was granddaughter Kerlin's ordination to the Episcopal priesthood. "If you'd asked me when they were teenagers," Elizabeth says, "which of our eight grandchildren was least likely even to step into a church, let alone become a minister, it would have been Kerlin." Of her call to the ministry, Kerlin says, "I was the most surprised of all!" Her "amazing" husband and son left their home in Portland, Oregon, for her seminary years in New York City. Find Kerlin's sermons at RichterFamilyAdventure.com.

"I'm pleased to report that I am still dating the same girl, who is my first-ever girlfriend," says JOSHUA SUNDQUIST of Arlington, Virginia. "So that's really cool. Also still giving speeches, traveling around, and talking to pretty much anyone who will listen. I'm working on my second memoir, which will be published sometime during 2014. And I make a lot of videos for YouTube. My parents finally got text messaging on their phones, so that helps us all keep in touch. My grandfather, whom we called Papa, passed away this year, and he is greatly missed, though his legacy lives on in the memories of his family. And his bodybuilding photos from early in life and success at the Senior Olympics later in life continue to inspire me."

"It is with such sadness that I share with the *Daily Guideposts* family that my wonderful husband, John, passed away after a brief and unexpected illness," writes MELODY BONNETTE SWANG of Mandeville, Louisiana. "He was a brilliant man who loved peace, a green environment, beautiful music, and the perfect sunset. I am heartbroken over the loss of this magnificent man who added so immensely to the world but am comforted by good friends, a loving family, and the promise of our Lord in Psalm 147:3: 'He heals the brokenhearted and binds up their wounds.'"

JON SWEENEY is the grateful father of three children, ages 20, 18, and 2. He is married to a marvelous woman and they live in Evanston, Illinois. Jon is the editor-in-chief of Paraclete Press and the author of many books, including *The Pope Who Quit,* which was optioned last year by HBO. "I certainly keep busy!" Jon says. "But I wouldn't trade it for anything."

KAREN VALENTIN of New York City says, "As we prepared for kindergarten in the fall, my oldest son, Brandon, took a test to qualify for a special program. He'd never taken a test before, and for the first time his future sat in his little hands. The order seemed too tall for my baby boy. This was the first step in a lifetime of testing and trials, hard work, expectations, and experiences of suffering and joy. Tears full of love and fear, hope and ache just poured out of me. 'Lord,' I prayed, 'let it be in Your hands, not his. Keep my son's life forever in Your hands.'"

"This year has been a blending of the generations," says SCOTT WALKER of Macon, Georgia. "My mother is 91 and now lives with Beth and me. She is ever youthful while adjusting to inevitable physical change. She is teaching me to grow old with grace and beauty. All of our children were home for Christmas. Drew practices law in Columbia, South Carolina, and his wife, Katie Alice, is truly our new daughter. Luke and Jodi both live in Washington, DC, and enjoy young adulthood. And as for our three golden retrievers—Muffy, Bear, and Buddy—they keep me laughing and sane. They never have a bad day."

"I continue with my life in retirement—it feels somewhat like sewing a patchwork quilt. I have to fit all the pieces together, including five grandchildren, and not get exhausted!" says BRIGITTE WEEKS of New York City. "I continue to work in a hospice, learning new things with every visit. I'm having fun with audiobooks, a new experience for me. I can knit and listen at the same time, giving both my fingers and my brain a workout. I am more involved with my church, including parish visiting and editing a literary quarterly of spiritual writing entitled *Spirit of St. Barts.* Sometimes I hear from *Daily Guideposts* readers, who always have new thoughts to share. I feel all of you are my friends."

"I thank God that despite Gene's severe concussion from a fall and his remaining unresponsive in the ICU for two days he recognized me early on the third morning," says MARION BOND WEST of Watkinsville, Georgia. "'You're my wife,' he said, grinning assuredly. 'Which one?' I asked. A doctor and two nurses looked at me questioningly. Overwhelmed with joy, I nodded to them. 'Welcome back, Gene!' the physician said, beaming. God's mercy had once again found us. Gene and I celebrated twenty-five years of marriage. We reminisced about how without my writing for *Guideposts* and his having subscribed to it for decades, we'd never have met after we both lost our spouses—and found each other."

"This year," writes ASHLEY WIERSMA of Monument, Colorado, "I finally found my sweet spot in terms of the number of freelance projects I can say yes to, while still prizing motherhood as my primary role. And it's a gratifying place to be!" In the past twelve months, she completed three book projects—*Sons and Daughters,* a collaboration with Pastor Brady Boyd of New Life Church in Colorado Springs; *Unseen,* a collaboration with Pastor Jack Graham of Prestonwood in the Dallas area; and *Empowered to Serve,* a youth-advocacy curriculum for World Vision—and a new four-week video curriculum with Pastor Bill Hybels, based on his best-selling classic *Too Busy Not to Pray.* She and her husband, Perry, enjoy working from home and including daughter Prisca, 2, in the cooking-cleaning-chatting-reading-hiking-loving-serving flow of their daily life.

"God's mercies are indeed new every morning," says TIM WILLIAMS of Durango, Colorado. "Years ago, my wife and I were parents when most of our married friends were not. We envied their freedom but consoled ourselves with thoughts of someday becoming young, energetic grandparents. That didn't happen. New every morning are the blessings of children in our church, the children of our nieces and nephews, our neighbors' children who have been a part of our lives since their birth, and the blessings that come from having two sons who are unique among men. How could God's mercies be new every morning if each one fit a timetable designed by us?"

SCRIPTURE REFERENCE INDEX

AUTHORS, TITLES, AND SUBJECTS INDEX

CONNECT WITH OURPRAYER MINISTRY

OurPrayer, Guideposts' prayer network, prays daily for each of the requests we receive by name and need. We also invite you to join us when we observe our annual:

- Good Friday Day of Prayer (April 18, OurPrayerGoodFriday.org)
- Thanksgiving Day of Prayer (November 24, OurPrayerThanksgiving.org)

To request prayer:

- Visit OurPrayer.org
- Call the prayer line (203) 778-8063 from 7:00 AM to 10:00 PM (Eastern time zone), Monday through Friday
- Write to OurPrayer, PO Box 5813, Harlan, Iowa 51593-1313
- Fax prayer requests to (203) 749-0266

To learn how you can request prayer, volunteer to pray for others, or contribute to support our ministry:

- Visit OurPrayerVolunteer.org

A NOTE FROM THE EDITORS

Daily Guideposts is created each year by the Books and Inspirational Media Division of Guideposts, a nonprofit organization that touches millions of lives every day through products and services that inspire, encourage, help you grow in your faith, and celebrate God's love.

Your purchase of *Daily Guideposts* makes a difference. When you buy Guideposts products, you're helping fund our many outreach programs to military personnel, prisons, hospitals, nursing homes, and educational institutions. If you'd like to be part of Guideposts' ministries by making a contribution, please visit GuidepostsFoundation.org to find out more about ways you can help.

To order your favorite Guideposts publications, including books, greeting cards, and music, visit ShopGuideposts.org, call (800) 932-2145 or write Guideposts, PO Box 5815, Harlan, Iowa 51593.